BRISTOL
LIBRARY OF COMMERCE

COLLEGE GREEN

WORKSHOP MANUAL

for

FIAT 125
FIAT 125 S

intereurope

PUBLISHED BY
INTEREUROPE LIMITED
AUTODATA DIVISION
2 – 4 QUEENS DRIVE
LONDON W.3
ENGLAND

INDEX

Introduction

This Workshop Manual was compiled and written with the intention of providing the Fiat 125 owner and the non-franchised garage with details of the repair and maintenance operations that they are likely to encounter. Information from the manufacturer's original service and repair instructions has been condensed and incorporated in the manual in such a form that the reader will quickly become familiar with the idiosynchrasies and the technical pecularities of the Fiat 125 range of cars.

In certain operations it will be necessary for the repairer to make use of special tools; the appropriate tool number and the use of the tool is described either in the text or can be seen in the illustration relevant to the particular operation.

Special mention should be made of the fact that a fault finding section is annexed to most of the major sections, thus simplifying the sometimes difficult task of diagnosis. The items listed cover only the most likely causes of trouble, as it is impossible to list every aspect of malfunctioning. This list, however, has been carefully compiled and is used in all our Workshop Manual Publications. The measurement conversions given in inches have been converted as closely as possible from the original millimetre sizes, however, it is preferable to adhere to the metric dimensions whenever possible. A conversion table is included in the manual.

We have tried to make this Workshop Manual as brief as possible, illustrating rather than detailing the operations, and concentrating not so much on regular maintenance work but more on repair and overhauling operations. This will save valuable time and will also show the reader immediately whether he will be able to carry out the work or not. Experience in producing hundreds of technical publications for the motor car manufacturers has proven that this is the best way for a publication of this nature.

Happy motoring — and the fewer times you have to refer to this book the better for you.

Engine

ENGINE — Removal

In the absence of an inspection pit it is necessary to place the front and rear of the vehicle on suitably positioned stands to remove the engine together with the transmission. Drain the coolant from the radiator; If the coolant contains anti-freeze mixture it should be collected in a suitable clean container of adequate capacity (drain tap at bottom rear of radiator) and from the cylinder block. Disconnect battery cables to prevent short circuits when removing the power unit. Slacken hose clamps and remove the coolant hoses and the hose leading to the expansion tank. Unscrew the radiator securing nuts and

remove the spring washers, washers, rubber washers and spacers. Release the radiator from the lower rubber mounting and lift out the radiator. Remove the air intake hose from the air cleaner housing. Slacken hose clamps and remove the exhaust gas residues breather hose and the thick hose connecting the air cleaner housing and breather valve: remove the air cleaner. Disconnect electrical cables at the generator and starter motor, and at the oil pressure warning light transmitter located at full-flow oil filter carrier. Disconnect the telethermometer transmitter located on top of the cylinder head between spark plugs Nos. 2 and 3. Disconnect the choke cable from the carburettor, the throttle linkage at the ball joint and the plastic fuel hose

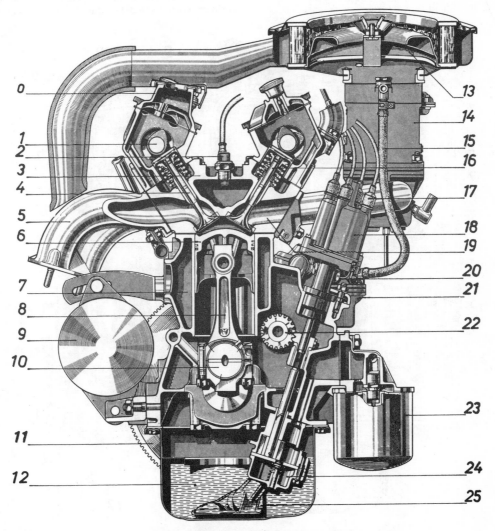

Fig.1 Cross section for the engine, through one cylinder and its valves

0. Cylinder head cover	9 Alternator	18 Distributor
1 Camshaft	10 Piston pin	19 Inlet manifold
2 Water temperature sensor	11 Flywheel with starter ring gear	20 Condenser
3 Cylinder head	12 Engine oil sump	21 Fuel pump
4 Exhaust valve with spring	13 Carburettor-air cleaner	22 Worm drive for distributor and oil pump drive
5 Exhaust pipe	14 Carburettor	23 Oil filter
6 Piston	15 Fuel pipe	24 Oil pump
7 Cylinder block	16 Inlet valve with springs	25 Gauze filter for oil pump
8 Connecting rod	17 Spark plug cable	

between fuel pump and carburettor. At the inlet manifold disconnect the brake servo unit vacuum hose. Disconnect the dual downpipe from exhaust manifold and remove spring washers and gasket. Unscrew and remove the exhaust pipe retaining bracket from the support at the gearbox.

Support the engine by means of a trolley jack and unscrew and remove the engine cover plate. Disconnect propeller shaft at the drive flange. Unscrew the gear lever connection and then remove the engine mounting bolts located at the right and left sides of the crank case. Remove the transmission cross-member at chassis and frame. Put a rope sling through the right manifold and one through the left manifold. When suspending the ropes from a lifting hook, ensure that the front rope sling is slightly shorter than the rear. Recheck that all connections have been disconnected and lift the engine together with the transmission a few inches from its mounting. Check that adequate clearance is available and then lift the engine to clear the body. Lower the engine onto an assembly stand.

The engine can also be removed separately without the necessity of removing the transmission.

The existing components, including the transmission cross-member should be disconnected as described previously. The four M12 bolts locating the clutch housing to the cylinder block can now be unscrewed. Unscrew the three starter motor fastening bolts and the exhaust pipe at the manifold and move the exhaust pipe to one side. Pull the engine forward carefully, until the lug of the main drive shaft has cleared the crankshaft spigot bearing and the driven clutch plate hub. The engine can now be lifted from its mountings.

The following chapters describe the dismantling and repair of the power unit. Repairs of individual assemblies essential for the complete overhaul, as well as repairs to be carried out with an installed engine, are detailed within the respective groups.

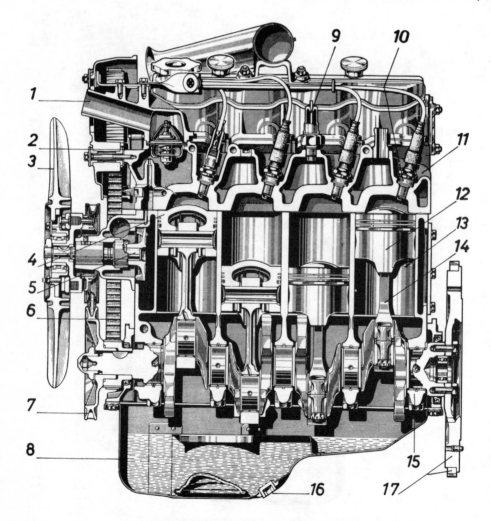

Fig.2 Longitudinal section of the engine through the cylinder

1 Upper water hose
2 Thermostat
3 Fan
4 Piston with cut connecting rod (1st cylinder)
5 Water pump
6 Toothed timing belt for camshaft drive
7 Lower belt pulley
8 Sump
9 Water temperature sensor

10 Spark plug with cable
11 Cylinder head
12 Piston (4th cylinder)
13 Cylinder block
14 Connecting rod (4th cylinder)
15 Rear crankshaft bearing
16 Oil drain plug
17 Flywheel with starter ring gear

ENGINE – Dismantling

Mount the engine into an assembly stand Arr 222 204. Drain the engine oil into a suitable container and unscrew the six bolts securing the clutch to the flywheel. Disconnect ignition cables from the spark plugs and remove the spark plugs. Remove the distributor after unscrewing the clamping plate from the distributor mounting stud by unscrewing the clamping plate stud as necessary. Unscrew oil pressure warning light transmitter from full-flow oil filter carrier. Remove the fan vee-belt, fan, water pump and alternator (see ''Cooling system'' for water pump removal). Unscrew the timing gear cover and remove the timing gear belt wheels; do not remove timing belt jockey pulley unless it is absolutely necessary.

Mark the position of the flywheel in relation to the crankshaft, unscrew the bolts and withdraw the flywheel base plate. Use a suitable puller to withdraw the crankshaft drive wheel, then remove the woodruff key. Unscrew and remove the camshaft housing covers and remove them together with their gaskets. Unscrew the nuts securing the camshaft housings and lift each housing complete with camshafts off the studs. Remove the cylinder head securing studs and lift off the cylinder head and then remove the cylinder head gasket. Note: it may be necessary to slacken the head using several blows with a plastic hammer.

Invert the engine in its stand so that the oil sump faces upwards. Remove the 18 sump cover fastening screws and washers, lift off the sump cover and discard the gasket. Unscrew the full-flow oil filter and the oil filter carrier. Remove the oil pump by unscrewing the bolts and withdrawing the pump. Unscrew the fuel pump from the cylinder block. Remove the inlet and exhaust manifolds. Unscrew the connecting rod bearing cap nuts, remove the bearing cap and push the connecting rod and piston out in the direction of the cylinder head. Attach the bearing cap to the connecting rod as each is removed and deposit in the correct sequence to facilitate correct reassembly. Unscrew the front and rear crankshaft bearing covers (the seal-rings must be repiaced before reassembly). Unscrew the five main bearing caps; the split thrust rings absorbing the axial pressure of the crankshaft can be removed together with the rear bearing cap, then lift out the crankshaft. Remove bearing shells from the crankcase and deposit with the opposing part in the correct sequence to facilitate correct reassembly. Unscrew the U-shaped retaining plate securing the auxiliary drive shaft and withdraw the auxiliary drive actuating fuel pump and oil pump towards the front of the engine. Unscrew the fastening bolts securing the alloy breather neck. Pull off the breather hoses and withdraw the breather neck.

Cylinder Block Testing

A caustic soda solution with a temperature of approximately 80ºC should be used to clean the cylinder block thoroughly from sludge, carbon and scale. All lubricating galleries should be cleaned by blowing them through with compressed air. After cleaning the cylinder block check the casting for wear and cracks. Any cracks seen during the examination will necessitate replacement of the cylinder block. Slight grooves in the cylinder bores can however be polished away with very fine emery cloth. The cylinder bores should then be measured using a good inside

Fig.3 Exploded view of dismantled crankcase and cylinder head

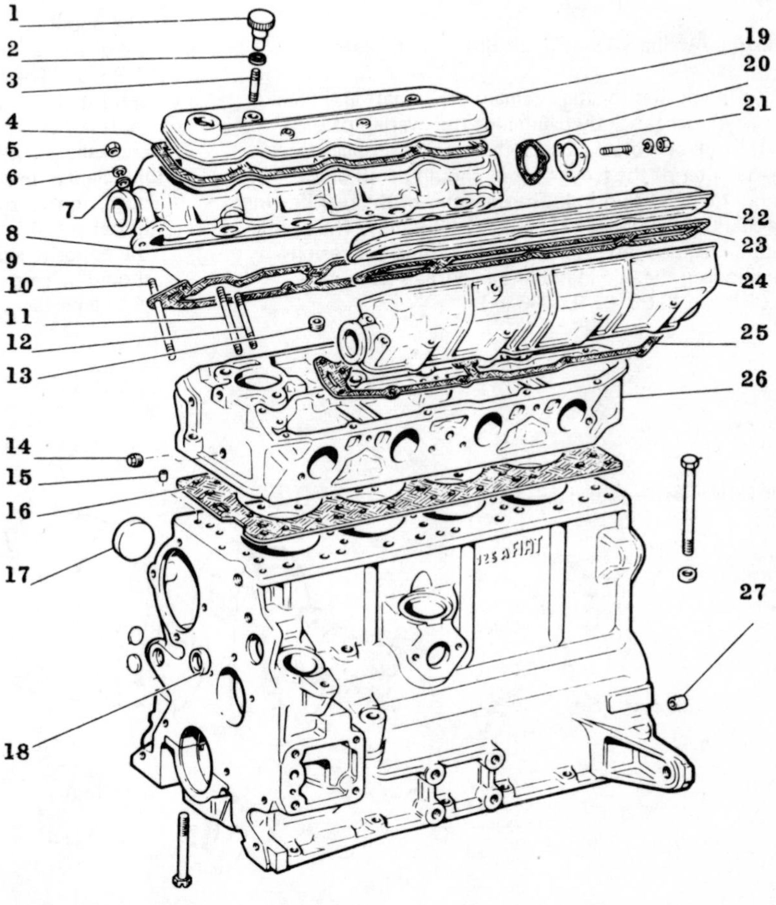

1 Clamping handle
2 Ring seal
3 Stud
4 Gasket
5 Nut
6 Circlip
7 Washer
8 Cylinder head
9 Gasket
10 Stud
11 Stud
12 Stud
13 Core plug
14 Screw plug
15 Locating pin
16 Gasket
17 Core plug
18 Core plug
19 Cover
20 Gasket
21 Cover plate
22 Cover
23 Gasket
24 Cylinder head cover
25 Gasket
26 Cylinder head
27 Locating pin

micrometer (Mercer gauge) and a dial gauge. Measurements should be carried out at the top, at the centre and at the bottom of the bore, first parallel and then at right angles to the crankshaft. If the measuring shows that ovality is apparent then reboring and new pistons may be necessary. The measurements obtained should be recorded on a schematic sketch of a cylinder bore. This will serve as a record of the extent and type of wear and facilitate selection of the correct oversize replacement pistons. The cylinder bores of new engines are graduated into the classes A, C and E according to the internal diameters and marked accordingly at the crankcase flange. The measurements of each class are as follows:

Engine 125 A.00	1,6 litre
Class A	80.00 - 80.01 mm
Class C	80.02 - 80.03 mm
Class E	80.04 - 80.05 mm

Wear, taper or ovality determined by the measurement and not exceeding 0.15 mm (0.006 in.) can be restored by honing. Any wear exceeding 0.15 mm (0.006 in.) necessitates boring and honing which should only be carried out by specialist repairers. At the present time there is no provision for the installation of cylinder liners to compensate for excessive wear.

Testing Cylinder Block Surfaces

The upper and lower separating surfaces should be examined for unevenness in the longitudinal and cross direction by means of a straight edge and a feeler gauge. A surface plate coated with engineers (Prussian) blue can also be used to locate uneven spots. High spots can then be machined by means of a surface grinder or removed manually by means of a triangular scraper. Removal should be kept to the minimum required to obtain a level surface.

Testing Auxiliary Drive Shaft Bushes and Seats

Test the bearing bushes for the auxiliary drive shaft and their seats in the cylinder block by examining the overlap of the bushes in the cylinder block. Check the bearing surfaces for wear, the diameter of the front bearing should be 48.084 - 48,104 mm (1,893 - 1,894 in.) The diameter of the rear bearing should be 39.00 - 39.020 mm (1.5354 - 1.5362 in.). The bearings should be reamed out after renewal to these dimensions. Clearance between the bearings and the journals should be 0.046 - 0.091 mm (0.0018 - 0.0036 in.)

Checking the Crankshaft

The crankshaft should be checked visually for cracks at journals, crank pins and webs. Slight scoring on the surfaces of the journals can be polished out using a fine-grained oil stone. The crankshaft should be reground in a specialist workshop to correspond to the available main- and connecting rod bearing repair sizes (0.254, 0.508, 0.762 and 1.016 mm) (0.01, 0.02, 0.02 and 0.04 in.), if the micrometer measurement has revealed excessive wear or ovality. Fillet radii must be reground as shown in the illustration.

Diameter of Main Bearing Journals:

Standard size in inches	Repair sizes in inches			
	0.01	0.02	0.03	0.04
from 1.9990	1.9890	1.9790	1.9690	1.9590
to 1.9998	1.9898	1.9798	1.9698	1.9598

Diameter of Big Eng Journals:

Standard size in inches	Repair sizes in inches			
	0.01	0.02	0.03	0.04
from 1.9980	1.9880	1.9780	1.9680	1.9580
to 1.9988	1.9888	1.9788	1.9688	1.9588

The internal lubricating oil passages should be cleaned under pressure with petrol or paraffin after completion of all machining work required. If excessive residues are present a repeat of the pressure cleaning process described above is recommended, but only after removal of the core plugs sealing the drillings. Correct the core plug seats as necessary and after successful cleaning insert the new core plugs and chamfer them over using the special drift A 86010.

The imbalance of the crankshaft should be checked with the aid of a level, true surface plate and the parallel supports A 95732. The flywheel and the clutch should be bolted to the crankshaft before balancing. Correct balancing of the crankshaft is indicated by its ability to stop in any position. If the crankshaft always stops in one position it is an indication of imbalance. Imbalance can be compensated for by attaching putty to the top side of the crankshaft. The weight of the putty (letter scale) is the weight of the imbalance to be drilled off on the opposite side at the flywheel. This removal of material should be carried out carefully and the test repeated frequently until a perfect balance is achieved. The deviation from alignment

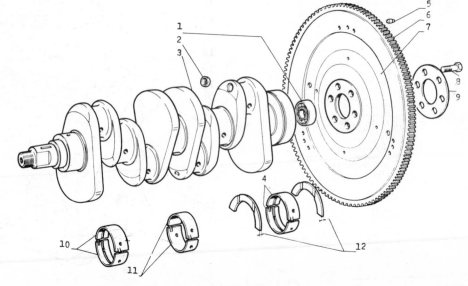

Fig.4 Exploded view of dismantled Crankshaft and flywheel

1 Spigot bearing	7 Flywheel
2 Aligning pin	8 Bolt
3 Crankshaft	9 Disc ring
4 Bearing shell half	10 Bearing shell half
5 Aligning pin	11 Bearing shell half
6 Starter gear	12 Thrust washers

between the crankpins and main bearing journals should be checked after grinding and balancing of the crankshaft. The out-of-true measure can be checked by placing the crankshaft between the centres of a lathe or by means of the parallel supports A 95732 and a dial gauge. Values exceeding the permissible figures given in the attached table necessitates straightening of the crankshaft by means of a hydraulic press or the replacement of the crankshaft.

Permissible deviation from alignment at main bearing journals: ± 0.025 mm (0.000984 in.)
Permissible deviation from alignment between crankpins and main bearing journals: ± 0.25 mm (0.01 in.)
Permissible out-of-round of main bearing journals and crankpins after grinding: ± 0.005 mm (0.0002 in.)
Permissible taper of main bearing journals and crankpins: 0.005 mm (0.0002 in.)
Permissible lateral out-of-true of flywheel flange: 0.025 mm (0.001 in.), (measured 34 mm (1.34 in.) from the centre of the flywheel flange).

Examining Bearing Shells and Clearances
(See also Examining the Connecting Rod')

The bearing shells should be examined for damage, marks and wear of the bearing metal lining. Damaged or worn bearing shells must be replaced. The bearing running clearance should be 0.050 to 0.095 mm (0.002 to 0.0037 in.) Previously to calculate the running clearance it was necessary to measure the basic bore, the thickness of the bearing shells and the diameter of the bearing journal. The bearing running clearance can now be checked by means of a plastic measuring wire gauge manufactured by "Perfect Circle", Hagerston, Indiana, U.S.A. The supplier of this plastic gauge is the Spare Parts Division of Fiat. The plastic measuring wire can also be ordered from Messrs. Ern, Kraftfahrzeugteile K.G., Düsseldorf, Cornelius Street 65 - 67. A length of calibrated plastic wire "Plastigage" PS-1, covering the range of the required 0.050 to 0.095 mm (0.002 to 0.0037 in.) clearance should be placed, according to the width of the bearing, across the whole width of the main bearing journals. Ensure the plastic wire does not enter the bore provided for the lubricating oil. The bearing cap should be fitted and the fastening bolts tightened to a torque of 60 ft.lbs. This will flatten the plastic wire into a rectangular shape, the flatter the wire is compressed, the smaller is the bearing clearance. The running clearances of all three main bearings can be checked by means of this procedure in one simple operation. The flattened wire should be measured by means of the gauge on the 'Plastigage' box after removal of the bearing cap. The resulting measurement will permit correct determination of the bearing running clearance up to 0.01 mm (0.0004 in.). Lack of measurable wire compression indicates a running clearance exceeding the measuring range of the wire and necessitates a second measurement with the next larger thickness of wire, i.e.'Plastigage' PR-1. Clearance exceeding 0.1 mm (0.004 in.) ascertained by this measurement, necessitates the installation of undersize bearing shells and a corresponding regrinding of the crankshaft. This measurement should also be carried out after the intallation of new bearing shells. The axial clearance between the thrust rings in the rear crankshaft bearing and the lapped thrust surfaces at the main bearing journal should be checked after measuring the clearance between the bearing journals and the bearing shells, 0.050 to 0.095 mm (0.002 to 0.0037 in.). An axial clearance of 0.055 to 0.265 mm (0.00216 to 0.0104 in.) is prescribed for new or reconditioned engines. An axial clearance exceeding 0.35 mm (0.014 in.) necessitates the installation of oversize thrust rings (thickness between 2.437 to 2.476 mm) (0.0959 to 0.0979 in.).

Thickness of Main Bearing Shells

Standard size in mm (in.)	Undersize in mm (in.)			
	0.254 (0.01)	0.508 (0.02)	0.762 (0.02)	1.016 (0.04)
from 1.825 (0.0718)	1.925 (0.0758)	2.079 (0.0818)	2.206 (0.0868)	2.335 (0.0918)
to 1.831 (0.0721)	1.958 (0.0771)	2.085 (0.0821)	2.212 (0.0871)	2.339 (0.0921)

Checking and Replacing Flywheel with Starter Ring Gear

Check the surfaces of the teeth on the starter ring and remove visible slight burrs by filing. If the ring is damaged and needs replacing the starter ring gear should be drilled between two teeth with an 0.2 in. drill and split by a sharp blow with a chisel. Check friction surface of driven clutch plate and the contact surface of the flywheel and the crankshaft flange for grooves. Check the flywheel flange of the crankshaft for lateral out-of-true using dial gauge. Prior to fitting a new ring gear heat the starter ring gear by immersing it into hot oil and heating the ring to 80ºC (176ºF). Fit the ring with the aid of a hydraulic press, until it is in its correct position.

Removal of Piston from Connecting Rod

The piston pin has a floating fit in the piston and a press fit in the connecting rod. Failure to dismantle the piston by the method detailed in the following text will inevitably cause deformation of the piston pin, the piston and/or the connecting rod and make replacement of the assembly necessary. The piston must be inserted together with the connecting rod into the clamping device of the special tool A 95605 and the piston pin removed using the special drift A 60308. The individual parts should now be checked for damage caused by the dismantling. Undamaged components should now be marked with paint to identify them and so ensure a correct reassembly sequence. The parts can now be deposited temporarily into a suitable receptacle to await individual inspection and reassembly as described in the following chapters.

Checking the Connecting Rods

The thin-walled connecting rod bearing shells must be replaced if they show grooves or other signs of wear. The corresponding crankpin should now be examined and reground as necessary. If regrinding is necessary then undersize bearing shells will need to be fitted(undersizes 0.254, 0.508, 0.762 and 1.016 mm) (0.01, 0.02, 0.03 and 0.04 in.)

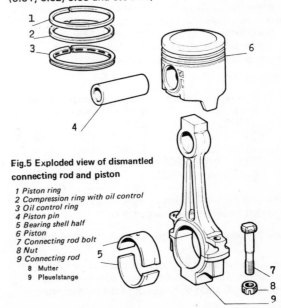

Fig.5 Exploded view of dismantled connecting rod and piston

1 Piston ring
2 Compression ring with oil control
3 Oil control ring
4 Piston pin
5 Bearing shell half
6 Piston
7 Connecting rod bolt
8 Nut
9 Connecting rod
　8 Mutter
　9 Pleuelstange

Diameter of Big End Journals:

Standard size in mm (in.)	Repair sizes in mm (in.)				
	0.254 (0.01)	0.508 (0.02)	0.762 (0.02)	1.016 (0.04)	
from 48.208 (1.9980)	47.954 (1.9880)	47.700 (1.9780)	47.446 (1.9680)	47.192 (1.9580)	
to 48.228 (1.9988)	47.974 (1.9888)	47.720 (1.9788)	47.466 (1.9688)	47.212 (1.9588)	

Checking Bearing Shell Clearances

The bearing shells should be examined for damage, marks and wear of the bearing metal lining. Damaged bearing shells must be replaced. The running clearance must be 0.036 to 0.086 mm (0.00138 to 0.00339 in.) and should be determined as follows: clean the crankpins and the bearing shells thoroughly and remove any traces of oil film. A length of calibrated plastic wire 'Plastigage' PC-1, covering the range of the required clearance should be placed according to the width of the bearing across the whole width of the oil-free crankpin and across the connecting rod bearing cap. The bearing cap should be installed and the fastening bolts tightened to a torque of 37 ft.lb. Ensure the plastic wire does not enter the bore provided for the lubricating oil. The wire will be flattened into a rectangular shape and should be measured using the gauge on the 'Plastigage' box after removal of the bearing cap. The resulting measurement will permit correct determination of the bearing running clearance up to 0.01 mm (0.0004 in.). Lack of measurable wire compression indicates a running clearance exceeding the measuring range of the wire and necessitates a second measurement with the next larger thickness of wire, i.e. 'Plastigage' R-1. Clearance exceeding 0.1 mm (0.004 in.) ascertained by this measurement, necessitate the installation of undersize bearing shells and a corresponding regrinding of the crankpin.

Thickness of Connecting Rod Bearing Shells

Standard size in mm (in.)	Undersize in mm (in.)				
	0.354 (0.01)	0.508 (0.02)	0.762 (0.03)	1.016 (0.04)	
from 0.0601 (0.0601)	1.653 (0.0651)	1.780 (0.0701)	1.907 (0.0751)	2.034 (0.0801)	
to 1.533 (0.0603)	1.660 (0.0653)	1.787 (0.0703)	1.914 (0.0753)	2.041 (0.0853)	

Checking Basic Bore Diameters for Small End

The connecting rod must be replaced if the basic bore of the small end has been damaged during the pressing out of the piston pin. The overlap of the press fit should be between 0.010 - 0.042 mm (0.0004 - 0.0016 in.) and can perhaps be achieved by using replacement size piston pins.

Fitting Dimension of Piston Pins

Piston Pin Class	Diameter of piston pin in mm	Internal diameter of basic small end bore in mm
1	21.970 - 21.974	21.982 - 21.986
2	21.974 - 21.978	21.986 - 21.990
3	21.978 - 21.982	21.990 - 21.994
Note:	21.970 mm = 0.855089 in.	
	0.004 mm = 0.000016 in.	

Only one size of 0.2 mm (0.008 in.) without graduation into classes is provided for replacement piston pins.

Permissible Deviation from Parallel of Connecting Rod Bores

The bores should be checked by means of a special tool A 5051 Deviation is corrected by means of a forked lever in the vice and the amount of deviation corresponds to the light aperture

between the angle and the surface plate. More pronounced twist requires replacement of the connecting rod. The weight of the connecting rod to be replaced must be checked, so as not to exceed the permissible difference in weight of a complete connecting rod set within one engine. Material can be removed as necessary from the shank of the big end bearing cap. The number of the respective cylinder should be stamped into the new connecting rod. Note: It should not be necessary to straighten a connecting rod and piston assemblies if they are to be reused as they should be already run-in within its bore.

Examining Pistons

If the pistons have not been damaged during dismantling they must be cleaned thoroughly and all traces of carbon removed. The crown of the piston, the ring grooves and the oil drillings leading from the base of the oil ring groove into the inside of the piston must be meticulously clean before installation of the piston. The alloy pistons have a convex raised crown with recesses for the exhaust valve and for the inlet valve. The largest diameter of the tapered oval piston is at the lower edge of the skirt vertically beneath the axis of the gudgeon pin bosses. These lie 2 mm (0.079 in.) from the centre on the side opposing the expansion slot. Pistons as well as bores are graduated into the classes A, C and E. The correct clearance for installation is between 0.008 and 0.016 mm (0.0003 - 0.0006 in.).
The identifying letter of the piston which determines the fit of the piston in the bore and the identifying number of the gudgeon pin bosses which determines the fit of the piston pin are stamped into the crown of the piston beneath the gudgeon pin boss.

Piston – Diameters

Class A	79.910 - 79.920 mm (3.1460 - 3.1464 in.)
Class C	79.930 - 79.940 mm (3.1468 - 3.1472 in.)
Class E	79.950 - 79.960 mm (3.1476 - 3.1480 in.)

Fig.6 The piston should enter the piston with light thumb pressure

Fig.7 The piston pin must not drop out by its own weight from a vertically held piston

Pistons, Internal Diameters of the Gudgeon Pin Bosses in the Pistons

Class 1 = 21.982 – 21.986 mm
Class 2 = 21.986 – 21.990 mm
Class 3 = 21.990 – 21.994 mm

21.982mm=0.86538 in.
0.004mm=0.00016 in.

Piston Pins – External Diameters

Class 1 = 21.970 – 21.974 mm
Class 2 = 21.974 – 21.978 mm
Class 3 = 21.978 – 21.982 mm

21.970mm=0.855089 in.
0.004mm=0.00016 in.

Slight thumb pressure only should suffice to push the oiled piston pin into the piston. The fit between piston pin and piston pin boss is correct if the piston pin does not slide by its own weight out of the vertically held piston.

Piston to Cylinder Bore Clearance

Piston clearance should be measured at right angles to the axis of the piston pin at a point 52.25 mm (2.057 in.) beneath the crown of the piston. The running clearance should be 0.08 to 0.10 mm (0.003 to 0.004 in.); the cylinder bore should be bored and honed to permit installation of a replacement size piston if the clearance exceeds 0.15 mm (0.006 in.). The clearance should be determined by measuring the bore and the piston or by means of a feeler gauge. The following replacement size piston diameters are available:

0.2, 0.4 and 0.6 mm (0.008, 0.016 and 0.024 in.). Replacement size pistons are supplied in graduations regarding diameters and piston pin bores.

Piston Weight and Piston Ring Side Clearance

When reusing the pistons, check the side clearance between the piston rings and piston grooves. The ring should be installed, held flush with the hand and the clearance checked by inserting a feeler gauge. If the groove is worn excessively(see following table) the rings, the piston, or the piston complete with rings will have to be replaced. Check the weight of the replacement pistons when replacing. The pistons can be weighed in pairs on suitable scales. The permissible weight difference of the pistons within one engine must not exceed 2.0 grams (0.07 oz). Material can be removed from the piston at the point marked by an arrow to compensate for any difference in weight exceeding the permissible tolerance. A maximum of 4.5 mm (0.177 in.) in relation to the height of the piston may be machined off at a width of 70.5 mm (2.77 in.).

Side Clearance of the Piston Rings in the Ring Grooves

Piston ring grooves	Height of groove in mm	Thickness of ring in mm	Side clearance in mm
Groove I	1.535–1.555 (0.06042 in.) (0.06121 in.)	1.478–1.490 (0.05819 in.) (0.05866 in.)	0.045–0.077 (0.00177 in.) (0.00303 in.)
Groove II	2.015–2.035 (0.07933 in.) (0.08011 in.)	1.978–1.990 (0.07787 in.) (0.07834 in.)	0.025–0.057 (0.00098 in.) (0.0022 in.)
Groove III	3.975–3.977 (0.15649 in.) (0.15657 in.)	3.925–3.937 (0.015499 in.) (0.15452 in.)	0.020–0.035 (0.00078 in.) (0.00137 in.)

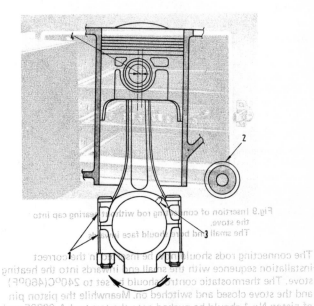

Fig.8 Correct installation of connecting rod and piston

1 Location of stamped number identifying the cylinder
2 Auxiliary drive shaft
3 Lubricating bore
4 Axial displacement of piston pin

Ring Gap

Permissible ring gaps:

Compression ring(groove I)	0.030–0.45 mm (0.0118–0.0177 in.)
Stepped compression ring with additional oil control effect(groove II)	0.20–0.35 mm (0.0079–0.0138 in.)
Oil control ring with spring expander (groove III)	0.20–0.35 mm (0.0079–0.0138 in.)

Insert the piston rings into the grooves and ensure that they can be moved freely around the periphery. Check that each ring gap is staggered at 120º and place a clamping band over the rings before inserting the piston and connecting rod assembly into the bore. The ring gap should be measured at the smallest part of the cylinder bore by means of a feeler gauge after insertion of the piston into the bore. Ring gaps should not be smaller than the values given in the above table, if they are smaller then they must be corrected as necessary using a ring gap grinder A 60188. Use a suitable ring expander tool and do not expand rings more than necessary or distortion or breakage will result. Compression rings and compression rings with additional oil control effect as well as pistons are available in standard sizes in 0.2, 0.4 and 0.6 mm (0.008, 0.016 and 0.024 in. replacement sizes. The oil control ring with spring expander is only available in the standard size and in the 0.4 mm (0.016 in.) replacement size.

Connecting Rod, Piston Pin and Piston —Assembly

Assembly must be carried out very rapidly after heating the connecting rod. It is recommended therefore, that the connecting rod and piston be prepared in their installation position on the work bench. The number identifying the cylinder should face the side of the piston pin displacement.The lubricating bore in the connecting rod should face the side opposed to the piston pin displacement (see fig.8).

Fig.9 Insertion of connecting rod without bearing cap into the stove.
The small end bore should face inwards

The connecting rods should now be inserted in the correct installation sequence with the small end inwards into the heating stove. The thermostatic control should be set to 240ºC(460ºF) and the stove closed and switched on. Meanwhile the piston pin of piston No.1 should be pushed onto the test tool A 60325 and the guide tube installed by screwing down the clamping bolt. Screw the clamping bolt down fingertight only so as to prevent seizure of the bolt upon insertion into the heated connecting rod.

Illumination of the red warning light will indicate attainment of the correct temperature of 240ºC(460ºF). Use universal pliers A81109 to remove connecting rod No.1 from the stove and insert it into the vice (use protective jaw clamps). Place piston No.1 by hand over the connecting rod. Press the piston laterally against the connecting rod so that the inside of the gudgeon pin boss contacts the small end of the connecting rod. The tool with the piston pin must be inserted very rapidly to prevent complete seizure of the piston pin in an incorrect position caused by the cooling of the connecting rod. If seizure occurs remove the piston pin by means of a drift and press as described in the relevant section. Therefore push the tool with the piston pin rapidly down to the end stop. The end stop provided on the hub of the piston ensures the correct installation position of the piston pin. Repeat the procedure and assemble the remaining connecting rods and pistons.

To ensure uniform temperatures are attained it is suggested that the connecting rods be left for 15 minutes when inserting into an already hot stove.

Checking Piston Pin Fit

The installed piston pins must be checked for correct fit. This can be accomplished by inserting the stand of tool A 95605 (already used for removal of the piston pin) into the vice. Screw the piston, complete with piston pin and connecting rod, with the aid of the threaded bolt supplied with the special tool, through the piston pin onto the stand. The threaded bolt must be screwed down until its head is flush against the piston pin. A nut should be screwed on the second side against the threaded bolt, so removing any clearance. The carrying clamp of the dial gauge should be set so that the probe of the gauge contacts the head of the threaded bolt. Zero the dial gauge and tighten the nut of the threaded bolt to 10 ft.lb. The hand of the dial gauge must return to zero when the nut is slackened again. The piston pin fit has now withstood a load of 880 lb. and can be considered satisfactory.

Displacement of the piston pin when the nut is tightened indicates an inadequate piston pin fit, this necessitates the replacement of the connecting rod. The connecting rod should now be checked using implement Ap.5051 for any deviation from parallel. Correct as necessary with the forked lever tool A 60198. Lubricate the piston pin using the bores provided in the gudgeon pin bosses.

CYLINDER HEAD – Removal and Overhaul

Removal, overhaul and installation of the complete cylinder head may become necessary due to a lack of compression, faulty valves or it may be necessary for decarbonising. The cylinder head can be removed with the engine "in situ" and is described here in detail. The cylinder head should only be removed when the engine is cold so as to prevent possible distortion of the cylinder head.

Drain the engine coolant into a suitable container. Remove the air cleaner, disconnect the breather hoses and the choke cable and throttle linkage at the carburettor. Disconnect the leads to the spark plugs and the ignition coil cables. Unscrew the upper cooling baffle at the radiator. Disconnect the water hoses leading from the cylinder head to the radiator and the hoses from the radiator to the water pump. Disconnect the fuel pipe from the carburettor. Unscrew the ten cylinder head bolts and lift off the cylinder head.

Fig.10 Exploded view of valve timing components

1 Ring seal
2 Aligning pins
3 Camshaft
4 Spacer for the adjustment of the tappet clearance
5 Tappet
6 Upper valve spring retainer
7 Inner valve spring
8 Outer valve spring
9 Lower valve spring retainer
10 Washer
11 Cotters
12 Circlip securing valve guides
13 Exhaust valve guide
14 Exhaust valve
15 Inlet valve
16 Inlet valve guide
17 Circlip securing valve guides
18 Oil trap
19 Washer
20 Lower valve spring retainer
21 Outer valve spring
22 Inner valve spring
23 Upper valve spring retainer
24 Tappet
25 Camshaft
26 Aligning pins

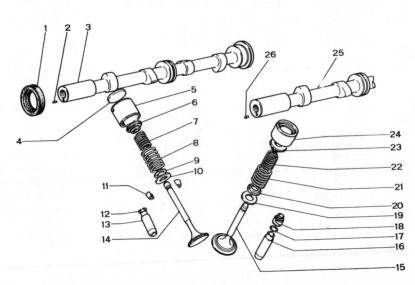

CYLINDER HEAD – Dismantling

Unscrew the two camshaft housing covers (serrated bolts with sealrings). Unscrew and remove the two camshaft housings (10 nuts each with washers and spring washers). Unscrew the two camshaft geared belt wheels then unscrew the rear camshaft cover and withdraw the camshafts from the rear of the housing. Remove the disc washers and store them in correct sequence. Remove the tappets and store them in the correct sequence. Unscrew the carburettor and the inlet and the exhaust valves. Compress the valve springs and remove the cotters, then remove the upper spring plates, the outer and inner valve springs, the inlet valve oil flingers, and the lower spring plates and washers. Remove the valves from the guides and store them in correct sequence. After complete dismantling of the head remove the carbon from the combustion chambers and from the exhaust channels. Clean the inlet channels and remove all the scale from the coolant spaces.

Cylinder Head Separating Surfaces

The cylinder head separating surface can be coated with engineers (Prussian) blue and a surface plate may be used to locate uneven spots. Bright spots can then be machined using a surface grinder or removed manually by means of a triangular scraper. The removal of the metal should be kept to the minimum required to obtain a level surface. The maximum permissible metal removal is 0.3mm(0.012in.). The depth of the combustion chamber must be examined after machining the cylinder head surface and compensated for as necessary by installing a thicker cylinder head gasket when refitting the head. The contact surfaces of the cylinder head covers should be examined for unevenness in the longitudinal direction and across the head by means of a straight edge and a feeler gauge. Unscrew the studs and remachine the two contact surfaces as described for the separating surface of the cylinder head.

Pressure Testing the Cylinder Head

The openings should be blanked off using the test implement A 60324 and the cylinder head then exposed to a leakage pressure test using compressed air at 30 - 45 lbs/sq.in.(2-3 ats.) under water which is at a temperature of 90°C(195°F). Any pressure drop during the test or a loss of water at cracks or other leaking points will necessitate the replacement of the cylinder head.

Checking Tappets and Tappet Bores

The running clearance between each tappet and its bore is extremely important for the quiet operation of the engine and the clearance must not exceed the maximum values given in the following table. Smaller unevenesses can be polished off with an oil stone. Tappets showing signs of wear or other damage must be replaced.

Dimensions of Tappets and their Bores in the Cylinder Block

Sizes	Bore Ø in the cylinder block in mm	External Ø of the tappets in mm	Running clearance in mm
Standard	37.000-37.025 (1.4567 in.) (1.4577 in.)	36.975-36.995 (1.4556 in.) (1.4566 in.)	0.005-0.050 (0.0002 in.) (0.002 in.)

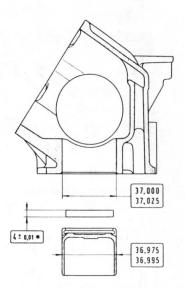

Fig. 11 Main dimensions of the tappet adjusting spacer and its seat in the cylinder head.

Nominal thickness of the adjusting spacer with basic dimension

Checking Camshaft Bearing Bores

Check the bores; the clearance between the camshaft journal diameters and the bearing bores must be within the values given in the table.

Valve Guides

Check that the valve guides are firmly seated in the cylinder head. The valve guides are pressed in with an overlap of 0.021 to 0.066 mm (0.0008 to 0.0026 in.) and are secured with a circlip. The circlip must be in first-class condition.

Valve Guides – Seat in the Cylinder Head

Diameter of bore in cylinder head in mm	Outer diameter of the valve guide in mm	Overlap in mm
14.950-14.977 (0.5886 in.) (0.5896 in.)	14.998-15.016 (0.5904 in.) (0.5911 in.)	0.021-0.066 (0.0008 in.) (0.0024 in.)

The running clearance between the valve stems and the valve guides should be measured using a dial gauge at the seat of the valve head.

Clearance – Valve Stem and Guides

Inner diameter of the valve guide
Inlet: 8.022 - 8.040 mm   (0.3158 - 0.3165 in.)
Exhaust: 8.022 - 8.040 mm
Outer diameter of valve stems
Inlet: 7.975 - 7.990 mm   (0.3140 - 0.3146 in.)
Exhaust: 7.968 - 7.983 mm   (0.3137 - 0.3143 in.)
Running clearance:
Inlet: 0.032 - 0.065 mm   (0.00126 - 0.00256 in.)
Exhaust: 0.039 - 0.072 mm   (0.00153 - 0.00283 in.)
Maximum permissible clearance: 0.1 mm (0.004 in.)

If the maximum permissible clearance of 0.1 mm (0.004 in.) is

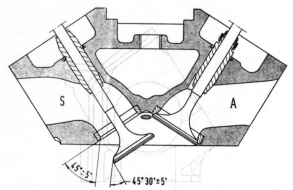

Fig.12 Valve seat angle and seat angle of valve head
S Exhaust   A Inlet

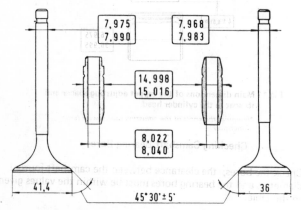

Fig.13 Main dimensions of valves and valve guides

exceeded it becomes necessary to remove the worn valve guide using the special drift A 60153 and then to install a new valve guide. The new valve guides have a finished bore and have to be reamed out (using special reamer A 90310) only in case of distortion during installation. Adherence to the correct valve guide dimensions is very important to ensure correct seating of the valve and permit exact remachining of the valve seats.

Remachining Valve Seats

The angle of the inlet and exhaust valve seats is 45° ± 5. It is recommended that a vibrocentric valve seat grinder be used together with tool Ap.5025 and carborundum grinding disc A 94097 for machining the valve seats. Metal removal should be kept to a minimum but all signs of burning, pitting or erosion must be removed from the valve seat. A drop of paraffin can be applied to the cutting tool to obtain a smooth clean valve seat surface. The following cutting tools are available to limit

and correct the width, 1.9 to 2.1 mm (0.0748 to 0.0827 in.) of the valve seats.
External: 20° corrective milling tool A 94046
Internal: 75° corrective milling tool A 94096
The valve seats should be cleaned and the valve guides cleaned using compressed air after completion of the grinding and milling. The valve seat can now be tested by means of the testing device A 60148. Insert the valve, plug the spark plug bore using the screw plug A 60018 and compress the air over the valve with the aid of a rubber ball. If the pressure gauge shows no drop in pressure the valve seat may be considered leakproof, if there is a drop in pressure then the grinding process should be repeated carefully. A line across the valve seat made with chalk or engineers blue may give an indication of leakage after a quarter rotation of the valve under slight manual pressure. The method using the test implement is to be preferred.

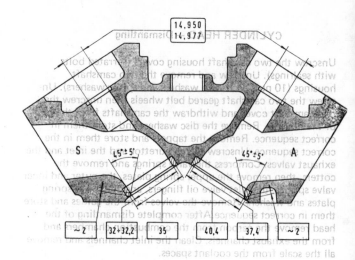

Fig.14 Main dimensions of valve seats and valve guides in the cylinder head. The width of the exhaust and inlet valve seats should be 1.9 - 2.1 mm (0.075 - 0.083 in.) and can be corrected by milling.

Examining Valves and Springs

Remove the carbon from the valve and visually check its condition. Measure the valve stem and the valve head. Valve head angles should be reground as necessary on a grinding machine using a self-centering chuck so as to obtain a smooth seat surface and a correct valve seat angle of 45° 30' ± 5'. Metal removal should be kept to a minimum. The minimum height of the valve head after regrinding must be 0.5 mm (0.02 in.).

Checking Valve Springs

Valve springs should be checked visually and also by means of the valve spring tester Ap.5049. The values indicated should be compared with the values given in the following table:

External spring

A	B	B	C	C
mm	mm	kg	mm	kg
53.9	36	38.6	26.5	59.5
(2.122 in.)	(1.417 in.)	(85 lb)	(1.04 in.)	(131 lb)

Minimum permissible load at B: 37.4 kg (83 lb).

Internal spring

A	B	B	C	C
41.8	31.0	14.9	22.0	27.4
(1.646 in.)	(1.22 in.)	(33 lb)	(0.866 in.)	(61 lb)

Minimum permissible load at B: 14.4 kg (32 lb).

A = Length untensioned
B = Length, installed
C = Minimum length during operation

Installation of Valves

Ensure that the valves are clean then lubricate valve stems with engine oil and install them in the opposite sequence of dismantling. Ensure that damaged or distorted valve guide circlips, and cracked, distorted or discoloured valve springs are discarded. Use the special drift A 60313 to install the inlet valve oil slingers.

Camshaft Bearing Journals and Bores Clearance

Internal Ø bearing journal in mm	Diameter of bearing journals in mm	Running clearance in mm
front	front	front
30.009-30.034	29.944-29.960	0.049-0.090
(1.1814-1.1824 in)	(1.1788-1.1795 in)	(0.002-0.0035 in)

Camshaft Bearing Journals and Bores Clearance (cont.)

centre	centre	centre
45.800-45.825	45.735-45.751	0.049-0.090
(1.8031-1.8041 in)	(1.8005-1.8011 in)	(0.002-0.0035 in)
rear	rear	rear
46.200-46.225	46.135-46.151	0.40-0.090
(1.819-1.820 in)	(1.8164-1.8170 in)	(0.0016-0.0035 in)

Camshaft – Checking

The camshafts should be checked between the centres of a lathe or by using V-blocks placed on a surface plate. The camshaft must be straightened on a press if the permissible radial eccentricity of 0.1 mm (0.004 in), measured at the centre bearing, is exceeded. The maximum out-of-round as measured with a dial gauge should not exceed 0.02 mm (0.0008 in). Very slight signs of grooving can be polished away using an oil stone. Otherwise the camshaft should be replaced. The height of the cam lobes should be measured by means of a dial gauge and should be 8.3 mm (0.327 in) for exhaust and for inlet valves. Should a check of the valve timing (see chapter on adjustment of tappet clearances) reveal incorrect values this could indicate excessive wear of the cam lobes necessitating replacement of the camshaft.

Camshaft – Installation

The camshafts should be lubricated with engine oil before insertion into the bearing bores in the cylinder heads. Install new front sealrings, and replace the gaskets when installing rear bearing covers. Observe the timing marks when pushing gear wheels onto the camshaft dowels. Fit the washers and tighten the fastening bolts to a torque of 35 ft.lbs. Refit the timing pointer to the front of the cylinder head.

Adjustment of Tappet Clearance

See under control and adjustment tappet clearance (engine installed).

Fitting the Cylinder Head and Timing Adjustment

See under Assembly of Engine.

ENGINE – Assembly

Engine assembly can commence after cleaning and examination of the individual components and after all parts have been re-machined as necessary or replaced by original Fiat spare parts. It is essential that new gaskets, sealrings, lockplates, splitpins, etc. should be used for engine assembly. All bolts and nuts incapable of achieving the prescribed torque without failure must be replaced. All sliding and moving parts should be subjected to an additional visual check and lubricated with engine oil before installation. The assembly is the reverse order of the dismantling procedure, observing the following points: Self-locking nuts - use of the torque spanner. The nylon ring inserted in the top of the nut prevents inadvertent slackening. Threads of bolts and studs must be free from burrs, corrosion or other damage as these faults will damage the self-locking nut and make its reuse impossible. Normally self-locking nuts can be reused several times, but only by correct use of the torque spanner and by scrupulous adherence to the prescribed tightening torques. A new nut should be used if it becomes necessary to exceed the prescribed tightening torque to tighten a nut correctly. (Exception: nuts fitted to steering components should be used once only.

Self-locking nuts with slots can be reused, as the natural elasticity provides the self-locking characteristics.

When using the torque spanner for the tightening of bolts and nuts, note that the prescribed tightening torques apply to a dry, non-lubricated condition. Threads and contact surfaces beneath nuts or bolt heads must be dry, non-lubricated and free from corrosion or other contaminations.

Attach the crank case to the assembly stand. Insert the oiled auxiliary drive shaft into the front and rear bushes which are pressed into the cylinder block. Insert the sealring, screw down the retaining plate and fit the auxiliary drive shaft wheel in its correct dowelled position. Use a new lockplate and tighten to 36 ft.lbs. and secure by bending the locking plate over one of the hexagon faces of the bolt. Insert the upper bearing shell halves into the crankcase bores; observe scrupulous cleanliness. Insert thrust ring halves at rear main bearing, lubricate the bearing shells and install the crankshaft. Install the rear main bearing cap complete with thrust ring half and then the remaining main bearing caps. Use a torque spanner to tighten the fastening bolts of the main bearing caps. (Rotate the crankshaft using a plastic hammer to tap lightly against the bearing caps and so facilitate correct seating of the bearing shells and caps). The tightening torque of the crankshaft main bearing bolts is 60 ft.lbs. Refit the rear and front crankshaft covers using a new gasket and sealring.

Checking Axial Crankshaft Clearance

Axial crankshaft clearance can be checked with a feeler gauge or by means of a dial gauge attached to the crankcase. Press the crankshaft towards the rear until the thrust surface of the rear journal contacts the thrust ring. Use a feeler gauge to check the clearance between the thrust ring and the thrust surface. If the axial clearance exceeds 0.35 mm (0.0138 in.) it is necessary to install oversize thrust rings (0.127 mm) (0.005 in.) at the rear main bearing.

Set the probe of the dial gauge against the flywheel flange when measuring with a dial gauge. Insert a large screwdriver and press the crankshaft backward and forward. The deflection of the pointer corresponds to the axial clearance. An axial clearance of 0.055 to 0.265 mm (0.0022 to 0.0104 in.) is prescribed for a new or reconditioned engine. Refit the rear crankcase cover to the crankcase, using a new gasket and sealring. Install the flywheel, observing the alignment of marks on the crankshaft flange and flywheel. Tighten the fastening bolts to a torque of 60 ft.lb.

Pistons complete with Connecting Rods – Installation

Lubricate the piston rings with engine oil. Stagger the piston ring gaps by 120°, compress the piston rings, using a piston ring clamp and insert the connecting rod/piston assembly from the top into the cylinder bore. The identifying number of the connecting rods (No. of the cylinder) should face towards the left. Refit the big end bearing caps, replace the self-locking nut and tighten it to a torque of 37 ft.lb. Note: Ensure that the correct bearing cap is installed and that the numbers on the rod and cap are identical.

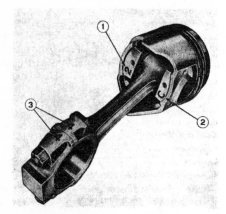

Fig. 15 Complete connecting rod with piston

1 Number identifying small end bore and its mating piston pin
2 Letter identifying the piston and its mating bore
3 Number of the respective cylinder

Fitting Auxiliary Drive Shaft

Insert the auxiliary drive shaft with its attached gear wheel into the bushes. Ensure that the eccentric cam, actuating the fuel pump, clears the connecting rod bolts of cylinder No.2.

Fitting the Oil Pump

Installation is the reverse of the removal procedure. To ensure correct alignment of the oil pump drive shaft with the distributor drive shaft it is recommended that the distributor be installed temporarily together with its drive wheel. Install the oil pump using a new gasket.

Fitting the Oil Sump

Use a new gasket. Insert the fastening bolts using lockwashers and screw down fingertight only. Tighten the sump bolts down gradually to a torque of 6 ft.lb.

Fig.16 Engine section: Lubrication

1 Oil pump housing
2 Spacer
3 Driven oil pump gear wheel
4 Screen filter
5 Coil spring of oil pressure relief valve
6 Full-flow oil filter
7 Transmitter for oil pressure warning light

Fitting the Assembled Cylinder Head

Insert two studs, diagonally opposed, into threaded holes in the front and rear of the cylinder block to serve as guides for the cylinder head. Coat the new cylinder head gasket lightly with oil and place onto the cylinder block. Rotate the crankshaft at the flywheel until pistons No.1 and 4 are in their top dead centre (T.D.C.) position; the woodruff key in the crankshaft should now be vertically upwards. The camshaft wheels should now be turned until the marks align with the pointer bolted to the cylinder head. Place the assembled cylinder head carefully onto the guide studs. Screw the cylinder head bolts down fingertight only, remove the guide studs and fit the last two cylinder

Fig.17 Exploded view of dismantled oil sump crankcase cover

1 Cylinder
2 Gasket
3 Cover plate
4 Gasket
5 Cover plate
6 Ring seal
7 Cover plate
8 Gasket
9 Ring seal
10 Cover plate
11 Gasket
12 Oil sump gasket

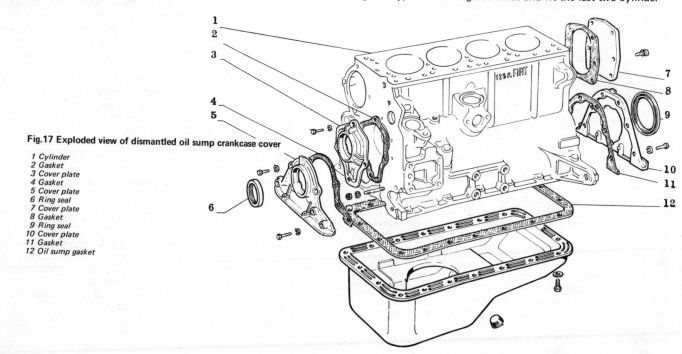

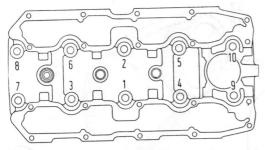

Fig.18 Tightening sequence for cylinder head bolts

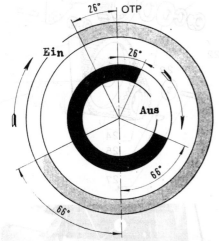

Bild 19 Diagramm der Ventilsteuerung bezogen auf ein Nennspiel
zwischen Ventilstößeln und Steuernocken von 0,50 mm

Fig.19 Valve timing relating to nominal clearance of 0.50 mm
(0.02 in.) between tappets and cams

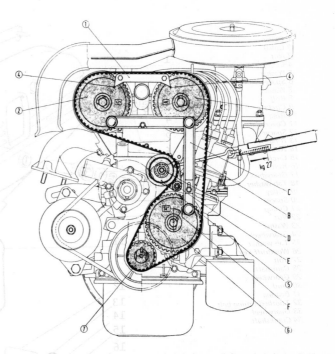

Fig.21 Diagram showing adjustment of valve timing as well
as the installation and tensioning of the toothed
timing belt

1 Fixed pointer for camshaft setting
2 Inlet valve camshaft sprocket
4 Reference marks on timing wheels
5 Tensioner pulley
6 Auxiliary drive shaft gear
7 Crankshaft gear
B Connecting rod and dynamometer A 95698 for testing and
adjustment of belt tension
C Special tool A 60319 locking the timing gears
D Tensioning locking nut
E Stud nut for swivelling mounting of tensioner
F Reference mark on timing gear and on tool for the adjustment
of the auxiliary drive shaft

Fig.20 Exploded view of dismantled valve timing

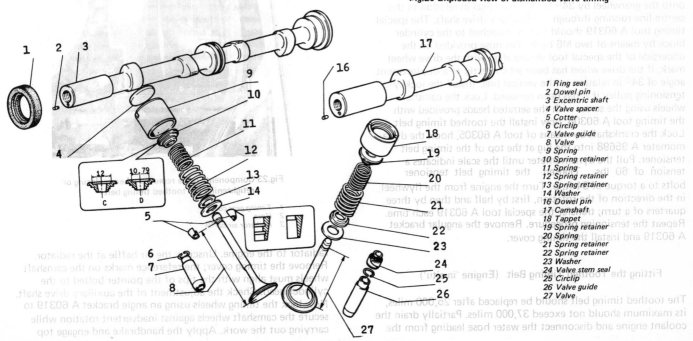

1 Ring seal
2 Dowel pin
3 Excentric shaft
4 Valve spacer
5 Cotter
6 Circlip
7 Valve guide
8 Valve
9 Spring
10 Spring retainer
11 Spring
12 Spring retainer
13 Spring retainer
14 Washer
16 Dowel pin
17 Camshaft
18 Tappet
19 Spring retainer
20 Spring
21 Spring retainer
22 Spring retainer
23 Washer
24 Valve stem seal
25 Circlip
26 Valve guide
27 Valve

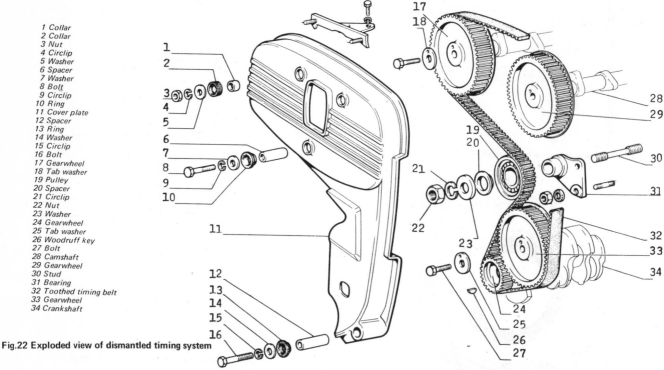

1 Collar
2 Collar
3 Nut
4 Circlip
5 Washer
6 Spacer
7 Washer
8 Bolt
9 Circlip
10 Ring
11 Cover plate
12 Spacer
13 Ring
14 Washer
15 Circlip
16 Bolt
17 Gearwheel
18 Tab washer
19 Pulley
20 Spacer
21 Circlip
22 Nut
23 Washer
24 Gearwheel
25 Tab washer
26 Woodruff key
27 Bolt
28 Camshaft
29 Gearwheel
30 Stud
31 Bearing
32 Toothed timing belt
33 Gearwheel
34 Crankshaft

Fig.22 Exploded view of dismantled timing system

head bolts. Tighten the cylinder head bolts in two stages according to the correct tightening sequence. The tightening torques are: 1st stage 30 ft.lb; 2nd stage 52 ft.lb.

ENGINE TIMING — Adjustment of Auxiliary Drive Shaft

Check that the piston of cylinder No.1 is in the top dead centre (T.D.C.) position on its compression stroke. Both valves of cylinder No.1 should be closed. The drive wheel of the auxiliary drive shaft should be set to a displacement of the line scribed onto the gearwheel by 34⁰ from the vertical in relation to the centre line running through the auxiliary drive shaft. The special timing tool A 60319 should now be attached to the cylinder block by means of two M6 bolts. The nose provided on the underside of the special tool should align with the drive wheel mark, if the drive wheel has been set correctly to a displacement angle of 34⁰ in relation to the vertical line. Install the jockey tensioning pulley if it has been removed. Lock the camshaft wheels using the screw with the serrated heads provided with the timing tool A 60305; now install the toothed timing belt. Lock the crankshaft by means of tool A 60305, hook the dynamometer A 95698 into the lug at the top of the timing belt tensioner. Pull the dynamometer until the scale indicates a tension of 60 lbs. Tighten the timing belt tensioner bolts to a torque of 34 ft.lb. Turn the engine from the flywheel in the direction of the rotation, first by half and then by three quarters of a turn; transfer the special tool A 60319 each time. Repeat the tensioning procedure. Remove the angular bracket A 60319 and install the timing cover.

Fitting the Toothed Timing Belt   (Engine 'in-situ')

The toothed timing belt should be replaced after 25,000 miles, its maximum should not exceed 37,000 miles. Partially drain the coolant engine and disconnect the water hose leading from the

Fig.23 Components to be removed when replacing or retightening the toothed timing belt

1   Timing gear cover
2   Hose
3   Radiator air baffle

radiator to the engine. Unscrew the air baffle at the radiator. Remove the timing cover; the reference marks on the camshaft wheels must align with the tips of the pointer bolted to the cylinder head. Check the adjustment of the auxiliary drive shaft. Now lock the timing wheels using an angle bracket A 60319 to secure the camshaft wheels against inadvertent rotation while carrying out the work. Apply the handbrake and engage top

Fig.24 Fitting angle bracket A 60319 to lock the timing gears

1 Toothed timing belt
2 Fixed pointer
3 Angle bracket
4 Gear arrester pins
5 Angle bracket bolts

Fig.25 Tensioning the toothed belt driving the valve timing and auxiliary drive shaft

1 Angle bracket A 60319
2 Dynamometer A 95698
3 Spanner for slackening the tensioner clamping nuts
4 Gear arrester pins

gear to prevent crankshaft rotation. Unscrew the protective plate at the bottom of the engine, slacken the alternator and remove the vee-belt driving the alternator and water pump. Slacken the nuts securing the timing belt tensioning device and remove the old timing belt. Install a new timing belt onto the gear wheels and the tensioning device. Hook the dynamometer A 95698 into the lug at the top of the timing belt tensioner. Pull the dynamometer until the scale indicates a tension of 60 lb. Tighten the timing belt tensioner bolts to a torque of 35 ft.lb. Turn the engine in the normal direction of rotation, first by half and then by three quarters of a turn, transfer the special tool A 60319 each time. Remove the angular bracket; refit the timing cover and the radiator air baffle. Reconnect the water

hose between the radiator and the cylinder head; top up engine coolant.

Tensioning the Toothed Timing Belt (Engine 'in-situ')

The procedure to be adopted is as described above, but without removing the alternator vee-belt and the lower engine plate and without removing the toothed timing belt. The tensioning devices are provided with a tensioning spring from engine No. 78216 onwards. The correct adjustment is achieved automatically by the force of the tensioning spring after slackening the nuts of the tensioning device; the nuts should then be re-tightened to 35 ft.lb. The adjustment must be repeated after approximately half and then again after approximately three quarters of a crankshaft turn. Check the timing and setting of the auxiliary drive shaft.

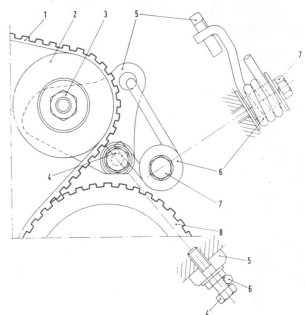

Fig.26 Arrangement of toothed belt tensioning device with tensioning spring

1 Toothed timing belt
2 Pulley with twin-race ball bearing
3 Belt tensioner securing nut
4 Threaded bolt for the swivel mounting of the tensioner and for the support of the spring arm
5 Belt tensioner
6 Tensioning spring
7 Attaching bolt of tensioning spring
8 Auxiliary gear drive shaft

Check and Adjust Tappet Clearance

Adjustment of the clearance between the camshaft cams and the valve stem ends is by a tappet and special spacers. These spacers are available in 25 different thicknesses in stages of 0.05 mm (0.002 in.) and range between 3.50 and 4.70 mm (0.138 and 0.185 in.). The thickness of each spacer is stamped into one of its faces. Using the spacers it is therefore possible to adhere always to the prescribed tappet clearance of 0.45 mm (0.018 in.) for the inlet valves and 0.50 mm (0.020 in.) for the exhaust valves, measured with a cold engine. To check the tappet clearance it is necessary to remove the cylinder head cover by unscrewing the serrated nuts. Remove the air cleaner and turn the crankshaft until the lobe of the cam faces upwards and is in a vertical position in relation to the adjusting spacer. Now

Fig.27 Tightening threaded bolt for the swivel mounting of the tensioner and for the support of the spring arm

1 Toothed timing belt
2 Belt tensioner
3 Arm spring
4 Clamping bolt of tensioning spring
5 Bolt for the swivel mounting of the tensioner
6 Clamping nut for tensioner

measure the tappet clearance between the cam and the adjusting spacer and prepare the required adjusting washer for the valve measured. All the inlet and exhaust valves should be measured in this manner. Adjustment of the tappet clearance is carried out as follows: turn the camshaft until the valve to be adjusted is completely open, then lock the tappet by means of the special slide A 60318 (the maximum mark must not be exceeded). Remove the redundant adjusting washer by directing a jet of compressed air into the slot of the tappet, then insert the selected new adjusting washer. Turn the camshaft until the cam presses against the adjusting washer, so as to permit

Fig.28 Insertion of special tool A 60318 for the adjustment of the clearance between the tappet and cam lobe

1 Special tool A 60318
2 Camshaft
3 Timing cams
4 Adjusting spacer
5 Tappet
The arrow shows one of the two slots for the removal of the adjusting spacer using compressed air

Fig.29 Locking the tappet using tool A 60318 for the removal of the tappet clearance spacer

Turn the camshaft in the direction of the arrow until the cam comes into contact with the limit stop A on the special tool in order to remove the cam from the adjusting spacer

removal of the special tool A 60318. Each tappet of both camshafts should now be measured and adjusted as described. Rotate the camshafts several times and recheck the tappet clearance by means of the feeler gauge A 95316. Refit the cylinder head covers and the air cleaner.

Alternator, Water Pump and Fan (Adjustment of Belt Tension)

The vee-belt tension is correct when it is possible to deflect the vee-belt with a slight pressure of the thumb by half an inch at a position halfway between the alternator and the water pump pulley. Inadequate vee-belt tension may cause slipping of the belt, which could result in overheating of the engine. Furthermore the battery charge would be inadequate due to the reduced alternator speed. Excessive vee-belt tension will strain

Fig.30 Checking the clearance between tappet and cam lobe

1 Timing cam
2 Adjusting spacer
3 Tappet
4 Feeler gauge

Fig.31 Exploded view of dismantled fan

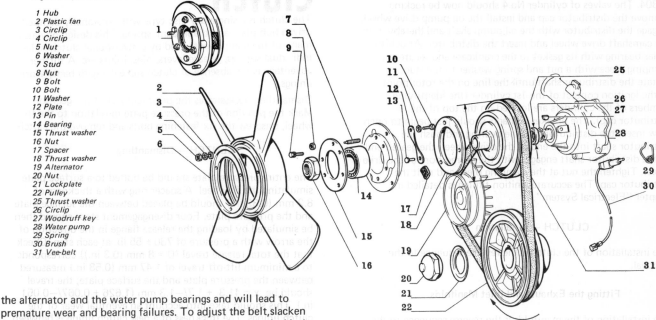

1 Hub
2 Plastic fan
3 Circlip
4 Circlip
5 Nut
6 Washer
7 Stud
8 Nut
9 Bolt
10 Bolt
11 Washer
12 Plate
13 Pin
14 Bearing
15 Thrust washer
16 Nut
17 Spacer
18 Thrust washer
19 Alternator
20 Nut
21 Lockplate
22 Pulley
25 Thrust washer
26 Circlip
27 Woodruff key
28 Water pump
29 Spring
30 Brush
31 Vee-belt

the alternator and the water pump bearings and will lead to premature wear and bearing failures. To adjust the belt, slacken the nut at the adjusting bar and the nut of the lower swivel bolt. Swivel the alternator outwards until the vee-belt can be depressed half an inch with a light pressure of the thumb and then tighten the two nuts.

CARBURETTOR – Installation

The installation of the carburettor is the reverse sequence of removal. See also chapter "Fuel System".

DISTRIBUTOR – Installation

See "Electrical System" for test and repair. Turn the engine at the flywheel until the first piston is on its compression stroke (both valves closed). Adjust the reference mark on the flywheel

Fig.32 Tensioning the alternator and fan drive belt

1 Bolt and nut for alternator fixing
2 Bolt and nut for the swivel mounting of the alternator
3 Bolts and nut for adjusting the solenoid air gap
4 Bolts securing the fan to the hub

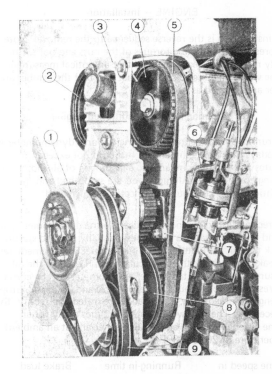

Fig.33 Engine section: Timing drive and distributor with timing cover removed

1 Fan with automatic solenoid clutch
2 Camshaft exhaust valve gear
3 Timing housing cover
4 Camshaft inlet valve gear
5 Toothed belt driving timing and auxiliary drive
6 Distributor
7 Toothed timing belt tensioner
8 Auxiliary drive shaft gear
9 Vee-belt driving fan, water pump and alternator

to 12° before T.D.C. by means of the graduated segment A
96304. The valves of cylinder No.4 should now be rocking.
Remove the distributor cap and install the oil pump drive wheel.
Engage the distributor with the oil pump shaft and thereby with
the camshaft drive wheel and insert the distributor. Attach the
collar bearing with its gasket to the crankcase and secure the
clamping piece with a nut and spring washer to the stud.
Rotate the distributor shaft until the line on the rotor points
to the ignition contact of the 1st cylinder (the identifying
numbers of the cylinders are located on the top of the
distributor cap). The breaker contacts should just begin to open.
Now insert the distributor into the bearing and push the
distributor shaft into the end of the drive wheel; the geared end
of the distributor shaft engages with the geared bore of the drive
wheel. Tighten the nut at the clamping piece and refit the
distributor cap. The accurate ignition timing is detailed in
chapter "Electrical System".

CLUTCH — Installation

The installation of the clutch is the reverse sequence to the
removal.

Fitting the Exhaust and Inlet Manifolds

The installation of the manifolds is the reverse sequence to the
removal. Replace the gaskets as necessary.

ENGINE — Installation

The installation is the reverse sequence to the removal. Note
the prescribed tightening torques of the nuts and bolts. For
safety reasons it is recommended that an optical measurement
of the wheel alignment is carried out and that the camber and
caster are adjusted as necessary.

Running-in of Reconditioned Engine

The running-in of reconditioned engines on a dynamometer is
nowadays highly recommended. It should not exceed 35
minutes and can be compared to a lapping-in of all sliding and
moving components. All high spots are smoothed and the
conditions for a continuous lubricating film created.

The reconditioned engine is attached to the dynamometer, and
should then be rotated a few times manually prior to starting.
Check the oil, the water and the fuel connections immediately
for leaks, then check the oil circulation and observe the oil
pressure gauge connected to the dynamometer for the correct
oil pressure which should be between 50 and 75 lb/in2. Stop
the engine immediately if any faults are noted and rectify them
as necessary. The following running-in times apply for an
engine fitted with a fan and an air cleaner and at an ambient
temperature of 20°C (68°F).

Engine speed in r.p.m.	Running-in time in minutes	Brake load
500	15	None
2000	15	half load
2000	5	full load

The reconditioned engine should not be run at maximum
revolutions. The running-in should be completed by the driver
giving regard to the instructions regarding maximum speeds as
detailed in the instruction manual.

Clutch

The clutch is a single dry-disc type with torsionally-damped
driven hub plate and diaphragm spring. This design obviates
many of the components used by conventional clutches, i.e.
individual springs, release levers, pins, joints etc. A further
advantage is the absence of clutch slip even with badly worn
linings.

Dismantling necessitates the prior removal of the gearbox.
Mark the position of the pressure plate in relation to the flywheel, unscrew the six fastening bolts and remove the clutch.

CLUTCH — Dismantling

The entire pressure plate should be bolted to a surface plate
simulating the flywheel. A spacer ring with a thickness of
8.2 mm (0.32 in.) should be placed between the surface plate
and the pressure plate. Four disengagement steps should then
be simulated by loading the release flange in the direction of
the arrow with a pressure of 730 ± 55 lb. at each step. Check
that the total release travel (D = 8 mm (0.3 in.)) corresponds
to a minimum lift-off travel of 1.47 mm (0.58 in.) measured
between the pressure plate and the surface plate; the travel
should be x = 41.3 + 1.7/−1.3 mm (1.626 + 0.067/−0.051
in.). This should take into account an eventual wear of the
clutch linings. The thickness of a new clutch lining is between
1.9 and 2.0 mm (0.075 and 0.079 in.). The complete pressure
plate should be replaced if it should prove impossible to
attain the above mentioned values. Replace the friction ring
of the release flange if it shows signs of scoring or other
excessive wear.

Fig.34 Cross section of installed clutch

1 Engine flywheel
2 Driven clutch disc
3 Pressure plate
4 Diaphragm spring
5 Clutch cover plate

Clutch Plate

Use only original Fiat linings and Fiat rivets when relining the driven clutch plate. If there are burnt clutch linings the torsional damper springs should be examined and replaced if distorted. After relining and when replacing a driven clutch plate it should be checked on a splined shaft between centres for out-of-true; the permissible lateral out-of-true must not exceed 0.25 mm (0.01 in.). An existing imbalance can be corrected by removing material at the heaviest point on the circumference. The clearance between the splines of the hub and the splines of the transmission drive shaft should not exceed 0.1 mm (0.004 in.) up to a wear limit of 0.3 mm (0.012 in.). The driven disc should slide freely on the splines of the transmission drive shaft as a seizing spline will prevent perfect disengagement.

CLUTCH – Installation

Initially check the spigot bearing in the crankshaft and replace

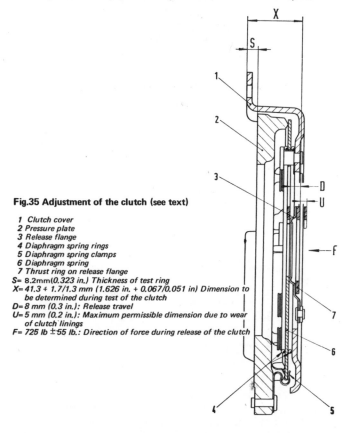

Fig.35 Adjustment of the clutch (see text)

1 Clutch cover
2 Pressure plate
3 Release flange
4 Diaphragm spring rings
5 Diaphragm spring clamps
6 Diaphragm spring
7 Thrust ring on release flange
S= 8.2mm(0.323 in.) Thickness of test ring
X= 41.3 + 1.7/1.3 mm (1.626 in. + 0.067/0.051 in) Dimension to be determined during test of the clutch
D= 8 mm (0.3 in.): Release travel
U= 5 mm (0.2 in.): Maximum permissible dimension due to wear of clutch linings
F= 725 lb ±55 lb.: Direction of force during release of the clutch

it if necessary. The blind hole in the crankshaft and the bearing itself should be packed with grease. Tap an accurately fitting drift into the bore of the spigot bearing; the grease should press the bearing out of the blind hole. Clean the blind hole thoroughly before installing the new bearing and remove all the grease. Pack the new spigot bearing with K6 15 grease and insert the clutch disc into the pressure plate; the protruding hub should face the transmission. The complete clutch should be fitted to the flywheel, so that the two dowel pins engage in the clutch cover. Realign the marks made before dismantling and attach the clutch, using 6 bolts and shakeproof washers, to the flywheel. Use a centering pin A 70081 to centre the driven disc then tighten the clutch fastening bolts to a torque of 18 ft.lb. Refit the gearbox.

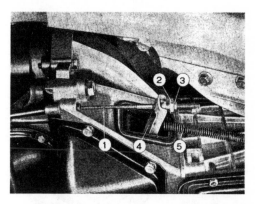

Fig.36 Operating and adjusting device of the clutch

1 Bowden cable
2 Tie rod adjusting nut
3 Locknut
4 Disengaging fork
5 Return spring of disengaging fork

Clutch Pedal Adjustment

The free travel of the clutch pedal should be adjusted whenever the clutch has been dismantled or when the clutch has a tendency to slip. Free travel before the commencement of the clutch disengagement should be 25 mm (1 in.). The clearance (free travel of the pedal) is correctly adjusted, when the gap between the sliding sleeve and the friction ring of the release flange is 2mm (0.08 in.) This measurement can be accomplished by turning the adjusting nut in front of the release fork and securing the locknut upon completion of the adjustment.

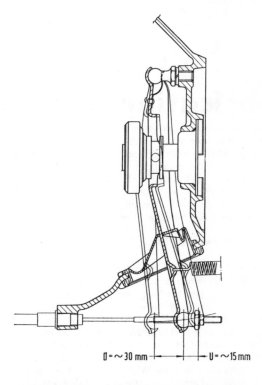

D = ∼ 30 mm   U = ∼15 mm

Fig.37 Cross section of clutch through disengaging fork and sleeve

D   Release travel
U   Maximum permissible dimension caused by wear of clutch linings

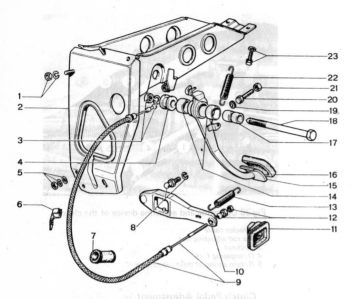

Fig.38 Exploded view of mechanical clutch operation

1 Nut and spring washer
2 Carrier bracket
3 Nut and spring washer
4 Spacer sleeve
5 Nut, spring washer and washer
6 Retainer
7 Rubber grommet
8 Ball pin with spring washer
9 Bowden cable
10 Disengaging fork
11 Dust cover
12 Adjusting nut with ball joint and nut
13 Return spring for fork
14 Bushes
15 Clutch pedal
16 Pedal cover
17 Spacer sleeve
18 Bolt
19 Buffer
20 Bolt
21 Nut
22 Clutch pedal return spring
23 Bolt and washer

Lubrication System

The lubrication system consists of:

1. Geared pump with suction trap and screen filter.
2. Full-flow oil filter with replaceable filter cartridge situated at the left side of the engine, safety valve for filter by-pass in event of blockage (inside filter).
3. Oil pressure relief valve incorporated in the pump.
4. Electric sending unit for low oil pressure indicator. Working oil pressure at rated engine speed: 50 to 71 p.s.i.

Removal, Repair and Fitting of Oil Pump with Relief Valve

In the event of repair work being necessary to the oil pump the engine should be removed and mounted onto the assembly stand Arr 22204. Drain the oil, invert the engine and unscrew oil sump (18 screws with shake-proof washers). Remove pump complete with suction trap. Unbend the tab washer at the relief valve hexagon, and unscrew the valve from the suction trap and dismantle. Unscrew the suction trap with screen filter and cover plate situated between the suction trap and pump body (4 bolts with washers). Withdraw the pump shaft together with the drive and driven gear from the pump body. Clean all components in petrol and dry them with compressed air. Check individual parts for wear and replace all damaged or worn parts. Insert the gear into the pump body and measure the clearance between the top faces of the gearwheels and the separating surface of the pump cover using a straight edge and feeler. The

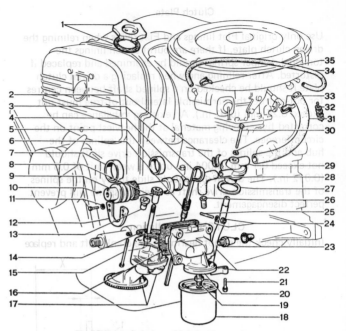

Fig.39 Exploded view of lubrication system

1 Oil filler cap and gasket
2 Clamp
3 Oil dipstick
4 Plug
5 Bush
6 Oil dipstick seal
7 Bush
8 Driven gear
9 Auxiliary drive shaft
10 Locating pin
11 Screw and lock washer
12 Bracket
13 Bush
14 Gasket
15 Screw
16 Gasket
17 Geared pump
18 Cartridge type oil filter
19 Adaptor
20 Mounting
21 Screw
22 Clamp
23 Transmitter with cap for low oil pressure indicator
24 Nut and spring washer
25 Stud
26 Adaptor
27 Ring seal
28 Hose
29 Engine breather
30 Bolt with ring seal
31 Hose
32 Flame suppressor coil
33 Clamp
34 Pipe
35 Clamp

installation clearance is 0.031 and 0.116 mm (0.0012 - 0.0045 in.) The gears and eventually the pump body must be replaced if the maximum permissible limit of clearance of 0.15 mm (0.01 in.) has been exceeded. Measure the clearance between the tip of the tooth and the pump body. The installation clearance is 0.11 and 0.18 mm (0.004 - 0.007 in.). Examine the drive wheel for tight fit on the shaft, otherwise replace. Check the fit of the driven gearwheel shaft in the pump body, replace the pump body together with the pressed-in shaft. The clearance of the driven gearwheel and its shaft is 0.017 and 0.057 mm (0.0006 to 0.002 in.), the worn part or parts should be replaced if the maximum permissible clearance of 0.1 mm (0.004 in.) has been exceeded.

Please note the following values for the relief valve: check the valve spring using the valve spring tester Ap 5049. The total spring length is 28.3 mm (1.1 in.), the length of the spring at a load of 14 lb ± 5 ounces is 20 mm (0.8 in.) If the values differ, then the spring should be compared with a new spring taken from stock.

The assembly of the oil pump is a reverse sequence to its dismantling. Prior to installing the pump the pump shaft should be checked for ease of rotation. Installation of the oil pump is the reverse sequence to its removal.

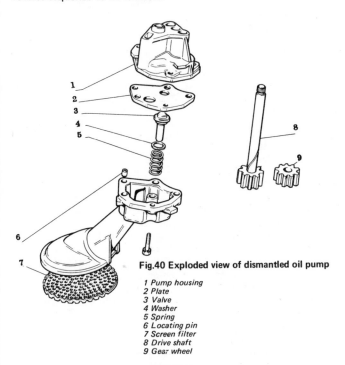

Fig.40 Exploded view of dismantled oil pump

1 Pump housing
2 Plate
3 Valve
4 Washer
5 Spring
6 Locating pin
7 Screen filter
8 Drive shaft
9 Gear wheel

OIL FILTER

The full-flow oil filter consists of a metal case and a filter cartridge, these constitute an integral unit and should be replaced as a unit. If the engine is running and the metal filter case remains cold, this is an indication that the filter is not functioning correctly and must, therefore, be replaced. The filter should be replaced every 6000 miles using the special tool A 60312 to unscrew the filter.
Coat the seat of the filter lightly with oil before installation and ensure that the sealring is seated correctly, otherwise oil leaks can result.

Fig.41 Removing full-flow oil filter

1 Tool A 60312
2 Cartridge type oil filter

OIL PRESSURE SWITCH

The sender is screwed into the oil filter support and transmits current via an electric cable to a warning light which indicates low oil pressure. The red warning light is lit when the ignition is switched on and is extinguished when the correct oil pressure (50 to 71 p.s.i.) is attained. The warning light is lit when the oil pressure drops to 6 - 12.5 p.s.i. With a hot engine idling at low revolutions the warning light may sometimes be illuminated without indicating a fault.
If necessary the oil pressure should be checked with a pressure gauge.

Cooling System

The cooling system consists of the following components: radiator, expansion tank, thermostat, water pump, fan and the electrical transmitter for indicating the coolant temperature.

RADIATOR — Maintenance

The radiator is of the tubular type with upper and lower water tanks. The total capacity of the radiator, expansion tank and engine, including the heater system is 13 pints (Imperial). The vane-type impeller pump draws the coolant from the radiator and forces it into the cylinder block and the cylinder head. Some of the coolant passes from the cylinder head to the heat exchanger or heater, and part passes into the cavities of the inlet manifold to pre-heat the fuel-air mixture. The water heated in the cylinder block rises upwards to return to the radiator, where it is cooled and sinks into the lower water tank, from where it is drawn off and re-circulated into the cylinder blocks. The thermostat fitted in the outlet opening of the cylinder head opens at a temperature of 87 ± 2°C (190° ± 3°F). The thermostat is completely open at 100°C (212°F). With the thermostat closed, the coolant is circulated from the cylinder head directly to the pump and from there to the cylinder block, without passing through the radiator. Water returning from the inlet manifold and heat exchanger flows through a pipe back into the pump. The amount of air flow through the radiator is varied by the speed of travel and is assisted by the fan.

Cleaning the Cooling System

Fill the cooling system with FIAT descaling agent or, when not obtainable, with a 5% P 3 solution and drive the vehicle for some time at normal operating temperatures. Rust and sludge removal is completed when the cooling system is drained after 24 hours. Any other deposits of scale can be removed with a 5% Soda solution. The radiator core should be flushed with clean water after draining the cleaning solution. Use compressed air from the side of the engine to clean the radiator core externally.

RADIATOR — Removal and Installation

Drain the coolant by opening the tap at the bottom of the radiator. Remove the radiator mounting bolts fastening the upper water tank. Slacken the hose clamp and remove the water hose. Unscrew the two upper and the two lower radiator mounting bolts. Lift the radiator upwards and out from the centre rubber mounting. If there has been a loss of water from the radiator then it should be checked for leaks. Seal off all outlets and then connect a compressed air line to the water inlet opening. Admit a pressure of not more than 15 p.s.i. and examine the radiator by immersing it in a water tank. Leaks can be identified by rising air bubbles. Repairs at the radiator

Fig.42 Exploded view of dismantled radiator

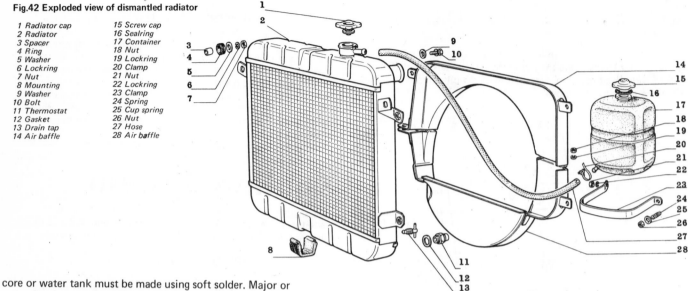

1 Radiator cap	15 Screw cap
2 Radiator	16 Sealring
3 Spacer	17 Container
4 Ring	18 Nut
5 Washer	19 Lockring
6 Lockring	20 Clamp
7 Nut	21 Nut
8 Mounting	22 Lockring
9 Washer	23 Clamp
10 Bolt	24 Spring
11 Thermostat	25 Cup spring
12 Gasket	26 Nut
13 Drain tap	27 Hose
14 Air baffle	28 Air baffle

core or water tank must be made using soft solder. Major or extensive damage should be repaired in a specialist radiator repair workshop or, if necessary, the radiator should be replaced. Fitting the radiator is a reverse sequence to its removal.

COOLING FAN

A thermostatically controlled fan is fitted as standard equipment. The fan is driven by an electric motor which is controlled by a thermostatically operated switch fitted in the water tank. The fan is operated according to the temperature of the coolant. The circuit in the thermoswitch closes at a temperature of 87 ± 2°C (190° ± 3°F), energizes the magnet and engages the fan. The thermo-switch breaks the circuit and disengages the fan when the temperature of the coolant drops to 70 ± 2°C (158° ± 3°F).

An electrical sender is connected to the indicating thermometer installed in the instrument cluster. The sender closes a circuit when the coolant reaches a temperature of 105 to 110°C (220 to 238°F); the pointer of the thermometer moves into the red section of the instrument. Engine revolutions must immediately be reduced and the driver must wait until the engine has cooled before returning to normal performance. A thermometer indication exceeding 89°C (193°F) indicates a probable defect of the switch at the radiator, revealing that the fan has not been switched on. The two switch leads can be bridged temporarily, thus causing the fan to operate permanently. The switch should be replaced as soon as possible. Failure of the fan after bridging the two leads indicates a break in the solenoid winding or in the cable leading from the solenoid to the commutator. To run the fan continuously under these conditions proceed as follows: slacken the three nuts of the adjusting bolts, then screw in the adjusting bolts until the solenoid armature just contacts the magnet body. Now re-tighten the three nuts and the fan will now run permanently. As soon as possible replace the pulley together with the coil winding and commutator. (See also Water Pump). Overheating of the engine can be caused by a loss of coolant, therefore a careful check of the radiator core, water tanks, hose clamps, water pump, cylinder head and cylinder head gasket must be made. Overheating may also be caused by excessive deposits of lime in the radiator.

The thermostat should also be checked for correct funtion if the coolant temperature is maintained above the normal values. Remove the radiator, remove the sludge (boil in a 5% P 2 solution) and place the thermostat in a container filled with water. Heat the water to 87°(190°F) the thermostat should now begin to open and should be completely open at 100°C (212°F). Normal lift of the valve is 7.5 mm (0.3 in.)., the maximum lift is 11 mm (0.43 in.). A thermostat which does not fulfill these conditions should be discarded.

Fan Belt, Water Pump and Alternator

It should be possible to depress the vee-belt in the centre between the alternator and the fan by 1.0 - 1.5 mm (½ in.) by using slight thumb pressure. Inadequate vee-belt tension results in belt slip with a resultant drop in water pump and alternator performance. Excessive vee-belt tension results in one-sided pressure on the water pump shaft and the alternator bearings causing premature wear of the bearings.
The vee-belt can be tightened by slackening the nut at the alternator adjusting rail and the bolts at the alternator pivot bracket. Swivel the alternator outwards to tighten the vee-belt. Retighten the bolts and nut and recheck the vee-belt tension using slight pressure with the thumb.

WATER PUMP — Removal and Installation

Drain the coolant and unscrew the baffle plate on the radiator. Remove the nuts retaining the radiator and lift the radiator upwards and out. Mark the ignition timing setting at the crankshaft pulley and at the protective cover of the toothed timing belt. Remove the toothed timing belt cover and slacken the toothed belt tensioning roller. Push the toothed timing belt off the camshaft wheels. Slacken the alternator and remove the vee-belt. Slacken the hose clamps and withdraw the coolant hose from the lower radiator inlet and the water pump. Unscrew the four M 8 water pump retaining bolts and remove the pump together with the fan and the pulley hub as well as the solenoid housing and the vee-belt pulley. Unscrew the nut to remove the fan blades then unscrew the three nuts with spring washers and washers from the retaining disc of the fan. Remove the disc and the fan blades and withdraw the solenoid coupling clutch. Pull the hub and pulley. Unscrew the locking bolt from the bearing and draw the shaft together with the bearing, impeller, pump seal and bearing out of the pump body. The impeller wheel must be pressed off the bearing shaft if the pump seal is to be replaced.

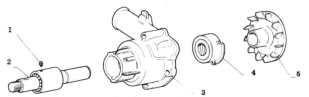

Fig.43 Exploded view of dismantled water pump

1 Grub screw
2 Bearing
3 Pump housing
4 Ring seal
5 Impeller

Repair of the water pump requires a specialist and the cost of repair includes a very large percentage of labour, we therefore, recommend that in most cases of water pump defects the entire water pump unit (exchange scheme) be replaced. If it is decided that repair is necessary it should be carried out as follows:
Clean all components with petrol and remove all residues of scale from the impeller and from the pump body. Examine all parts for wear. The pump shaft must be replaced if its axial play exceeds 0.12 mm (0.005 in.). If necessary use a surface plate to skim the separating surface of the pump sealing

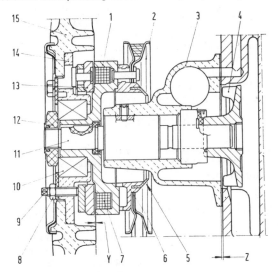

Fig.44 Cross section through water pump and electro-magnetic fan

1 Pulley hub and electro-magnet body
2 Pulley
3 Pump body
4 Impeller
5 Slip ring
6 Slip ring hub
7 Electro-magnet winding
8 Locknut of adjusting bolt
9 Screw for the adjustment of the air gap
10 Fan bearing
11 Water pump shaft
12 Nut
13 Electro-magnet armature
14 Fan hub
15 Fan

Y = 0.25 to 0.35 mm (0.0098 in. to 0.0139 in.)
Z = 1.0 mm (0.0394 in.)

against the cylinder block. Assembly is carried out as follows:
Press the new pump packing seal into the seat machined in the housing. Fit the pump shaft with bearing (lubricated for life) into the pump body; the bore of the locking bolt must align with the bore in the housing. Screw in the locking bolt and peen it over. Press the impeller onto the shaft (negative clearance - overlap 0.017 to 0.055 mm (0.00067 to 0.0022 in.)

Now use a straight edge and a feeler gauge to measure the distance between the front face of the impeller and the contact surface of the pump cover (0.20 to 0.25 mm) (0.008 to 0.01 in.). Insert a woodruff key and mount the pulley hub together with the solenoid coupling clutch. Installation is carried out in the reverse sequence to the removal procedure. The air gap between the solenoid body and the armature should be rechecked after 1000 to 1500 miles. Slacken the locknuts of the adjusting bolts if the adjustment has to be corrected, set the bolts until the above mentioned dimension has been achieved and secure the adjusting bolts with the locknuts.

Fan Drive Coupling (See Fig. 4)

The commutator should be cleaned every 13000 miles using a clean linen rag. Unhook the brush return spring and withdraw the brush holder from its seat. Check the condition of the brush and spring. The brush must move freely in its seat. Worn components must be replaced. Ensure that the spring presses correctly against the brush holder.

Fuel System
FUEL TANK

The fuel tank has a capacity of 10 gallons (Imperial) including a reserve of 1.5 gallons. The tank is attached by means of straps to the rear part of the vehicle beneath the luggage compartment floor. The filler neck with the filler cap, the fuel line leading to the fuel pump, the breather pipe and the sender for the tank unit are mounted to the top of the tank, the drain plug is fitted in the bottom part of the fuel tank. A contaminated or damaged fuel tank must be removed for cleaning or soldering. Prior to removal disconnect the positive lead from the battery terminal and drain the fuel. Remove the mats from the luggage compartment floor and then remove the spare wheel. Disconnect the earth lead and the electrical cable from the sender of the tank unit and disconnect the fuel pipe leading to the

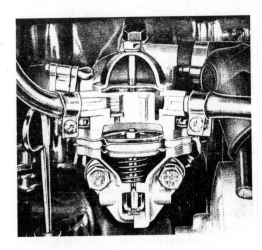

Fig.45 Fuel pump, cross section of installed unit

fuel pump. Pull off the connecting hose to the upper filler neck after slackening the hose clamps. To remove the tank unscrew one bolt with washer thereby loosening the straps and remove the fuel tank. Unscrew the tank unit. Pour in about half a pint of petrol and swill it around, then drain the petrol and dry the fuel tank using compressed air. Repeat the process as necessary until the tank is clean and dry. Any leak revealed during the examination (especially at the weld seams) should be rectified by cleaning the area and soft soldering. More extensive damage demands replacement of the fuel tank. No attempt should be made to weld the tank owing to the obvious risk of explosion. Installation is carried out in the reverse sequence to the removal procedure after careful and thorough cleaning and soldering. Ensure that the felt strip beneath the retaining straps and rubber strip protecting the fuel tank are seated correctly, replace as necessary.

A mechanical fuel pump feeds the carburettor via an 8 mm (0.3 in.) fuel pipe. The fuel pump is attached to the left side of the cylinder block and is operated by the cam of the auxiliary drive shaft acting on the pump lever. The pump itself consists of an upper part with fuel bowl, gauze filter screen, suction and pressure valve and the lower part with the operating lever and the return spring. Between the two parts is the diaphragm, which also acts as a seal, and the diaphragm spring.

Possible Fuel Pump Faults

The following should be checked if no fuel is reaching the carburettor:

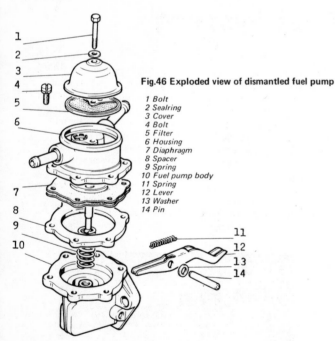

Fig.46 Exploded view of dismantled fuel pump

1 Bolt
2 Sealring
3 Cover
4 Bolt
5 Filter
6 Housing
7 Diaphragm
8 Spacer
9 Spring
10 Fuel pump body
11 Spring
12 Lever
13 Washer
14 Pin

1. Check that there is fuel in the tank.
2. Check that the pump cap and the two parts of the pump sections are screwed together.
3. Check the fuel pipes for leaks, especially at the rigid pipe to flexible hose joints.
4. Check that the nylon filter gauze in the upper pump half is not blocked by dirt particles.
5. Check for faulty valves in the top part of the pump.
6. Check the pump operating lever and pin for wear.
7. Check the diaphragm and diaphragm spring for faults.

8. Check the fuel pressure (it should be between 3 and 3.7 lb/in2. Check the pump pressure by inserting a conventional pressure gauge into the line leading from the pump outlet to the carburettor inlet. Incorrect fuel pressure can be caused by the following faults: Defective valves in the upper part - replace upper part - defective diaphragm - replace diaphragm. Incorrect distance from pump to drive cam - install thicker or thinner gasket. (Insulation spacer thickness is now 14 mm (0.55 in.) it was 6 mm (0.24 in.), therefore, the length of the pump lever and stud screws has changed).

FUEL PUMP — Removal and Overhaul

Slacken the clamping screws on the flexible fuel lines and pull off the lines, unscrew the bolts with spring washers from the pump flange and remove the insulation spacer. Mark the upper and lower halves, using a scriber, before dismantling to ensure accurate reassembly. Unscrew the top cover bolt and remove the nylon gauze filter with sealing rim. Remove the six screws with spring washers and remove the upper half. The flutter valve plates fitted in the upper part cannot be replaced independently, if they are damaged or defective the complete upper body half will need replacing. The lower half can be dismantled as follows: depress the diaphragm and rotate it to disengage the diaphragm spindle from the forked lever. Remove the diaphragm together with its spring. Use a suitable drift to remove the pivot pin locating the lever. Remove the operating lever together with the spring, forked lever and two supporting washers. Wash all components in petrol and check them for wear; replace as necessary. All the mechanical parts should be thinly coated with engine oil, all gaskets should be replaced and the pump assembled in the reverse sequence to the procedure adopted for dismantling. Depress the operating lever until the diaphragm lies flat against the pump body when installing the upper part of the pump. Align the previously made scriber marks and line up the holes of the diaphragm, and the upper and lower parts of the pump. Tighten the screws. Check the condition of the gaskets and the insulation spacer when installing the pump. Tighten the bolts gradually. Fit an exchange fuel pump if necessary.

CARBURETTOR

The fuel system is equipped either with the Solex two-stage carburettor C 34 PAIA/3 or with a Weber two stage carburettor 34 DCHE.

Adjustment Data of Solex Carburettor Type C 34 PAIA/3

Diameter	Primary stage	Secondary stage
Induction throat	34 mm (1.339 in.)	34 mm (1.339 in.)
Venturi	24 mm (0.945 in.)	24 mm (0.945 in.)
Main jet	1.20 mm (0.047 in.)	1.20 mm (0.047 in.)
Idler jet	0.40 mm (0.016 in.)	0.50 mm (0.020 in.)
Starting jet	1.20 mm (0.47 in.)	1.20 mm (0.047 in.)
Air regulator	1.60 mm (0.063 in.)	1.65 mm (0.065 in.)
Accelerator pump injection jet	0.50 mm (0.20 in.)	

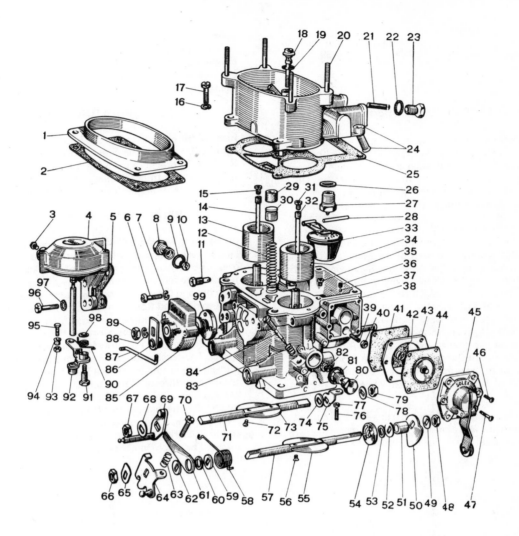

**Fig.47 Exploded view of Solex carburettor Type
C 34 PAIA/3, components**

1 Flange for air cleaner attachment
2 Gasket
3 Cable sheath retaining screw
4 Vacuum operated device
5 Gasket
6 Mounting screw and spring washer for choke cover
7 Mounting screw and spring washer for choke cover
8 Main jet carrier
9 Gasket
10 Main jet
11 Idle jet
12 Starting device spring
13 Secondary venturi
14 Mixture tube
15 Main jet air corrector
16 Mounting screw and spring washer for body and cover
17 Mounting screw and spring washer for body and cover
18 Accelerator pump valve
19 Gasket
20 Stud
21 Fuel filter screen
22 Gasket
23 Filter housing plug
24 Cover
25 Gasket
26 Needle seat gasket
27 Needle valve
28 Float pivot pin
29 Choke plunger stop bush
30 Plunger
31 Main jet air regulator
32 Emulsion tube
33 Float

34 Primary venturi
35 Starting jet
36 Pump discharge jet
37 Ball
38 Carburettor body
39 Primary venturi mounting screw and nut
40 Primary venturi mounting screw and nut
41 Gasket
42 Diaphragm spring
43 Pump support
44 Diaphragm assembly
45 Accelerator pump cover
46 Pump cover mounting screw
47 Pump mounting screw
48 Nut and washer
49 Nut and washer
50 Cam for pump control lever
51 Spacer
52 Washer
53 Spring washer
54 Blow-by gases recirculation device disc
55 Primary throttle
56 Throttle mounting screw
57 Throttle shaft
58 Throttle return spring
59 Washer
60 Bush
61 Intermediate lever for secondary throttle return
62 Washer
63 Spring
64 Primary throttle control lever
65 Washer
66 Nut

67 Nut
68 Washer
69 Secondary throttle control lever
70 Screw for throttle idle adjustment
71 Secondary throttle spindle
72 Throttle mounting screw
73 Secondary throttle
74 Washer
75 Secondary throttle stop lever
76 Adjusting screw with locknut
77 Adjusting screw with locknut
78 Washer with nut
79 Washer with nut
80 Main jet carrier
81 Gasket
82 Main jet
83 Spring
84 Idle mixture adjusting screw
85 Choke cover
86 Choke control lever
87 Link rod
88 Spring washer and nut
89 Spring washer and nut
90 Two-arm lever return spring
91 Two-arm lever pivot
92 Two-arm lever
93 Nut
94 Bush
95 Cable retaining screw
96 Screw for mounting vacuum device to carburettor body
97 Toothed washer
98 Thrust washer
99 Choke disc assembly

Needle valve seat	1.75 mm	1.75 mm
	(0.69 in.)	(0.69 in.)
Weight of float	7.2 gr.	7.2 gr.
	(0.25 oz.)	0.25 oz.)

Solex C34 PAIA/3 Carburettors

The solex two stage downdraft carburettor has an induction throat diameter of 34 mm (1.339 in.). The carburettor body incorporates two induction ports, each of them containing a throttle valve for the primary and for the secondary stage. The float chamber is situated between the two throats in the carburettor body. Each throttle valve has its own independent shaft; the throttle in the primary throat is controlled through a linkage by the accelerator pedal; the throttle in the secondary throat is controlled by a vacuum operated device and is therefore operated automatically. The shaft of the secondary throttle is connected by a linkage with the rod of the diaphragm installed in the vacuum chamber and a coil spring holds the diaphragm under pressure. The chamber in which the vacuum acts is connected through a passage with the primary throat at the point where the venturi is narrowest. In the rest position the secondary throttle is closed and it opens only when the vacuum in the primary throat has reached a value, such as is required to overcome the resistance of the diaphragm spring. A pull-back mechanism is linked to the primary throttle shaft and ensures the disengagement of the secondary system when the throttle pedal is released.

The carburettor choke ensures prompt starting and also correct idling of the cold engine and a smooth take-off. The choke should only be used until the engine has reached its normal operating temperature. The strength of the mixture (lean or rich) can be varied by the position of the choke control on the dashboard. An enriched mixture ensuring easy starting of the car even when the engine is extremely cold, will be delivered if the control knob is pulled out all the way.

CARBURETTOR – Removal

Remove the air cleaner and the intake pipe. Disconnect the throttle linkage and the choke cable from the carburettor. Remove the fuel hose from the fuel intake connection. Unscrew the carburettor from the studs and remove the carburettor together with its gasket from the inlet manifold.

CARBURETTOR – Dismantling and Overhaul

Initially unscrew the ball valve of the accelerator pump (accelerator pump valve) from the top. Turn the carburettor over carefully to permit removal of the valve ball and then remove the four screws and spring washers retaining the float chamber and detach the cover with the gasket. Remove the float spindle and float from the carburettor body then remove the gasket and withdraw the gauze filter. Remove the main jet carrier, main jet, idler jet, air regulating jets and the venturi tubes. Unscrew the mixture regulating screw complete with spring. The accelerator pump is a mechanically operated diaphragm spring connected by a lever linkage to the spindle of the primary throttle. The diaphragm spring presses the diaphragm outwards in the rest position. The movement initiated by opening the primary throttle is transferred to the pump lever, pressing the diaphragm of the accelerator pump inwards, and so delivering fuel into the mixing chambers of the primary intake. The diaphragm acts upon the suction stroke of the

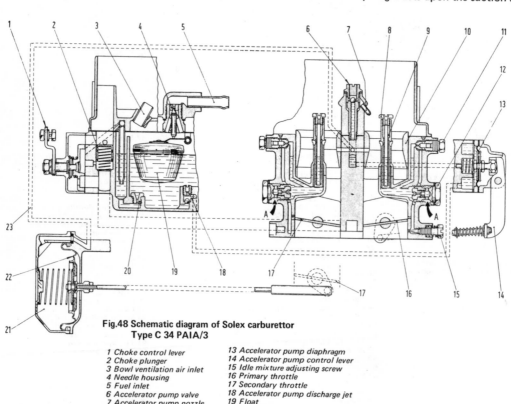

Fig.48 Schematic diagram of Solex carburettor Type C 34 PAIA/3

1 Choke control lever
2 Choke plunger
3 Bowl ventilation air inlet
4 Needle housing
5 Fuel inlet
6 Accelerator pump valve
7 Accelerator pump nozzle
8 Main air correction jet
9 Mixture tube
10 Primary venturi
11 Idle jet
12 Main jet
13 Accelerator pump diaphragm
14 Accelerator pump control lever
15 Idle mixture adjusting screw
16 Primary throttle
17 Secondary throttle
18 Accelerator pump discharge jet
19 Float
20 Starting jet
21 Vacuum chamber
22 Diaphragm
23 Vacuum passage
A Fuel inlet

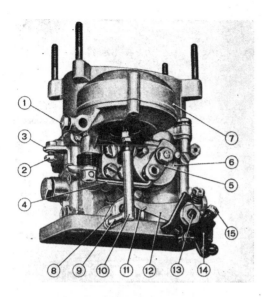

Fig.49 Solex carburettor

1 Cable sheath retaining screw
2 Choke control cable retaining nut and screw
3 4,5,6 choke control linkage and cover
7 Vacuum operated device
8 and 9 Secondary throttle control lever and pivot
10 Diaphragm rod
11 and 12 Intermediate lever and spring for secondary
   throttle return
13 Primary throttle shaft
14 Primary throttle control lever
15 Screw for idle adjustment of primary throttle

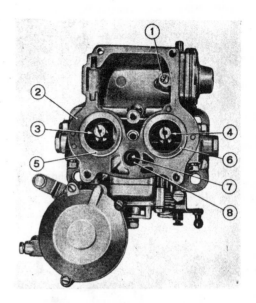

Fig.50 Solex carburettor

1 Accelerator pump drain plug
2 Carburettor body
3 Air correction jet and emulsion tube for secondary
   throttle
4 Air correction jet and emulsion tube for primary
   throttle
5 Secondary venturi
6 Primary venturi
7 Choke plunger
8 Choke plunger stop bush

pump when the primary throttle again closes and the pump chamber is refilled with fuel.

ACCELERATOR PUMP – Removal

Unscrew the accelerator pump valve from the lower half of the float chamber. Withdraw the split pin from the accelerator pump body and remove the spring and washer. Unscrew the six screws fastening the pump to the carburettor body and remove the pump together with the washer and gasket.

THE CHOKE

CHOKE – Removal

Unscrew the two screws complete with serrated washers securing the choke to the carburettor body and remove the choke together with its rotary slider assembly. Remove the choke plunger stop bush together with its spring. Remove the choke jet from the bottom of the float chamber.

Removal of Butterfly Valves

Removal should only be carried out, if an examination reveals excessive clearance in the spindle bores, necessitating replacement of the spindles and the insertion of bushes at the sides and in the centre. In such a case it is cheaper and more economical to replace the entire lower carburettor body.

Removal of Venturi Tube

Slacken the locknut securing the fastening bolt then remove the bolt and withdraw the venturi. A guide slot machined into the venturi makes incorrect installation impossible.

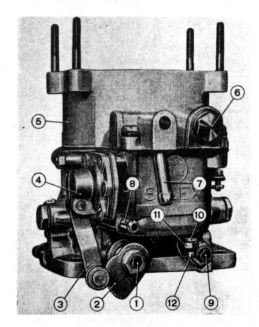

Fig.51 Solex carburettor

1 Primary throttle shaft
2 Cam for pump control lever
3 Pump control lever
4 Pump cover
5 Carburettor cover
6 Filter housing plug
7 Fuel inlet connection
8 Blow-by gases pipe connection
9 Secondary throttle shaft
10 Secondary throttle stop lever
11 Nut
12 Adjusting screw

Vacuum Chamber for Secondary Butterfly Valve

As previously described, the secondary butterfly valve is operated by a vacuum chamber. Replace the vacuum chamber if it is found to be faulty. Check the linkage between the vacuum chamber and the throttle spindle for ease of operation.

Cleaning and Checking Components

All carburettor components with the exception of the diaphragms should be thoroughly cleaned in petrol and all traces of dirt and other residues removed. Dry the components by means of compressed air. All bores and jets should be blown through with compressed air. Do not clean the carburettor components with wire or a wire brush or damage will be caused to the delicate calibration of orifices etc. Compare the

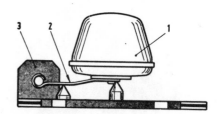

Fig.53 Setting float level on Solex carburettor

1 Float
2 Float supporting arm
3 Gauge A 95132

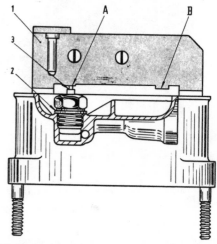

Fig.54 Checking maximum needle height in its seat on the carburettor cover

1 Gauge A 95132 for checking float level setting on Solex C 34 PAIA/3 carburettor
2 Adjusting shims
3 Needle
A Gauge reference for check of maximum needle height
B Gauge reference for check of minimum needle height

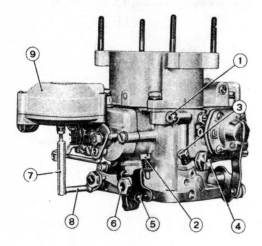

Fig.52 Solex carburettor

1 Idle jet
2 Screw for idle adjustment
3 Idle mixture adjusting screw
4 Main jet
5 Throttle control lever
6 Primary throttle shaft
7 Diaphragm rod
8 Secondary throttle control lever
9 Vacuum operated device

numbers of the jets with the numbers given in the table of carburettor jets for the appropriate model. Check the idling mixture adjusting screw for the condition of the tapered point and replace if necessary. Examine the carburettor housing components for damage. If necessary use fine emery cloth and a surface plate to refinish the contact surfaces. Check the butterfly spindles for general condition and clearances. Excessive clearance will permit the ingress of air, which will have a detrimental effect on the starting and idling properties and will make a precise adjustment impossible. Check the float, no sound should be heard when shaking the float near the ear. Alternatively the float can be immersed in hot water; if air bubbles are visible the float must be replaced. The float must also be replaced if the point on the float bearing needle valve has become impressed in the float support arm. A worn float spindle should be replaced with the float. Check the float needle valve to ensure the absence of leaks. Check accelerator pump diaphragm. All damaged components must be replaced. It is recommended that only genuine Solex spare parts are used. Solex has marketed a special repair kit for the overhaul of the carburettor and this kit contains a complete set of parts which are subject to wear and tear, including a needle valve and all gaskets and seals. All the parts included in the repair kit should

be used when assembling a dismantled carburettor. This is the reason that no special mention has been made regarding the fitting of gaskets during assembly.

CARBURETTOR — Assembly

Assembly is virtually the reverse sequence to the dismantling procedure, taking note of the following points: fitting of the venturi is facilitated by the guide slot. Screw in the mixture tubes and the main air regulating jets. Insert the ball for the accelerator pump valve and screw in the pump discharge jet followed by the choke jet. As the air regulating jets have identical threads it is important to select the correct diameter in case of replacement in accordance with the table of carburettor jets. Refit the two idle jets then fit the two main jets and the main jet carrier. Refit the vacuum chamber ensuring that the pipe between the venturi and the vacuum chamber is not blocked. Refit the choke unit (no gasket). When fitting the accelerator pump great care must be taken to ensure the holes in the diaphragm align accurately with the holes in the body, before fitting the pump cover. When fitting the diaphragm spring, ensure that the spring has its larger diameter coil facing the lever. Insert the return spring into the pump body, tighten the six screws and insert the float with the float spindle into the float chamber. Screw the needle valve and its seat into the carburettor cover (the thickness of the gasket determines the fuel level in the float chamber). The standard thickness is 1.0 mm (0.04 in.). Screw in the idler mixture regulating screw and spring and screw it down to the end. Then unscrew it one and a half turns for the preliminary adjustment. Screw the carburettor cover onto the carburettor body. Screw in the ball valve for the accelerator pump. Using a mouth suction test the ball valve should allow air to pass on one side but act as a seal on the other side.

Checking Pump Delivery

Actuate the pump lever approximately 20 times, the delivery quantity should be between 4 and 6 cc. The delivery rate can be varied by adding a washer between the lever and the split pin.

CARBURETTOR − Installation

Fitting is virtually the reverse sequence to the removal.

Checking the Float Chamber Level

The fuel level in the float chamber should be measured after overhaul of the carburettor or in the event of high fuel consumption. For this test the car should be placed on a level surface. Run the engine for approximately two minutes, then switch off the ignition. Remove the feed pipe at the carburettor. Unscrew the carburettor cover and lift out the float. Check the weight of the float (0.25 oz). The float should be placed onto the gauge A.95132 and the supporting arm allowed to rest against the two pointers of the gauge; levelling is considered to be correct when both pointers are in contact with the float assembly. If a gap can be ascertained at either pointer tip, bend the arm until the above mentioned condition is met. The gauge A 95132 should then be placed onto the needle with the reference A positioned as shown in Fig.54, in this position the gauge should be able to slide without interference from the needle and a check can be made on the maximum height of the needle. Then bring reference B, as shown in Fig.55, into line with the needle. The needle should now prevent the gauge from sliding (the needle should drag on the reference point) so permitting the minimum height of the needle in the carburettor cover to be checked. If necessary correct the height of the needle valve and thereby the fuel level by adding an adjusting washer beneath the seal ring of the float needle valve.

Idling Adjustment

Adjustment should be made with the engine operating at normal temperature. Adjustment of the idling speed involves only the primary carburettor stage and is carried out by setting both the throttle adjusting screw and the idling mixture adjusting screw. The throttle adjusting screw controls the opening of the throttle valve while the tapered idling mixture adjusting screw regulates the quantity of mixture delivered via the idle passage; this produces the mixture ratio most suitable for the engine. The idling adjustment should be made by turning the throttle adjusting screw to adjust to the minimum opening of the primary throttle to a point where the engine does not stall. Then adjust the idling mixture screw so as to achieve an air-fuel ratio that will permit the highest and steadiest engine speed at the previously selected throttle position. Now decrease the minimum opening of the throttle still further until the most suitable idling speed is obtained. At this engine speed the ignition light should be fully illuminated. The idling mixture adjusting screw must not, under any circumstances, be tightened completely. After making this audible adjustment it is recommended that an exhaust gas analizer be used to check the carbon monoxide content of the exhaust gases and thus ensure the necessary emission control in addition to maximum fuel economy.

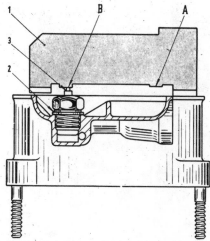

Fig.55 Checking minimum height of needle in its seat on the carburettor cover

1 Gauge A 95132 for checking float level setting on Solex
  C 34 PAIA/3 carburettor
2 Adjusting shims
3 Needle
A Gauge reference for check of maximum needle height
B Gauge reference for check of minimum needle height

Fig.56 Idle adjustment on Solex carburettor

1 Screw for idle adjustment
2 Idle mixture adjusting screw

Weber Carburettor 34 CHE 2
Adjustment Data of Weber Carburettors Types 34 DCHE 1 and 34 DCHE 2

Diameters	Primary throat	Secondary throat
Throat	34 mm (1.339 in.)	34 mm (1.339 in.)
Venturi	24 mm (0.905 in.)	24 mm (0.905 in.)
Main jet DCHE 1	1.20 mm (0.047 in.)	1.30 mm (0.051 in.)
Main jet DCHE 2	1.25 mm (0.049 in.)	1.25 mm (0.049 in.)
Idling jet DCHE 1	0.45 mm (0.018 in.)	0.70 mm (0.027 in.)
Idling jet DCHE 2	0.40 mm (0.016 in.)	0.70 mm (0.027 in.)
Starting jet	1.50 mm (0.059 in.)	1.50 mm (0.059 in.)
Main air regulator jet	2.15 mm (0.085 in.)	1.50 mm (0.059 in.)
Idle air regulator jet	1.00 mm (0.039 in.)	0.80 mm (0.031 in.)

Fig.57 Weber carburettor

1 Cable sheath retaining screw
  Cable retaining screw and nut
3 Cable retaining screw and nut
4 Lever return spring
5 Choke control lever
6 Choke cover
7 Vacuum operated device
8 Secondary throttle control lever
9 Secondary throttle shaft
10 Sector return spring
11 Sector for lever return and release
12 Primary throttle shaft
13 Throttle control lever
14 Throttle stop screw
15 Idle mixture adjusting screw

Accelerator pump jet	0.50 mm	
	(0.020 in.)	
Needle valve seat	1.75 mm	1.75 mm
	(0.069 in.)	(0.069 in.)
Weight of float	18gr.	18 gr.
	(0.63 oz.)	(0.63 oz.)

WEBER CARBURETTOR – Removal

Remove the air cleaner cover after unscrewing one wing nut or three M6 nuts. Lift out the filter cartridge. Unscrew the four self-locking nuts of the air intake connection; ensure that the spacer bushes are not lost when lifting the air intake connection clear of the carburettor. Disconnect the choke cable and then the throttle linkage at the ball joint. Slacken the clamp fastening the plastic fuel hose and pull of the fuel hose. Unscrew the carburettor retaining nuts and lift the carburettor up and out. Use a clean rag to blank off the inlet manifold opening and prevent the ingress of dirt particles.

CARBURETTOR – Dismantling, Clearning and Assembling

Unscrew the six cheese-headed screws and remove them complete with their spring washers. Lift off the carburettor cover and remove the float spindle and float. Unscrew the float needle valve complete with washer, ensuring that the needle remains in the valve. Unscrew the plug and remove its sealring and the gauze filter. Lever out the choke valve retaining ring and withdraw the choke valve together with its retainer and spring. Remove the rotary valve from the lower part of the carburettor body. Withdraw the retainer, the spring and the plunger. Unscrew and remove the main jet carrier and the two main jets from the side of the carburettor. Remove the two idling jet carriers from the side and withdraw the jets and the seal rings. Note that the main jets may be calibrated to different

values. If the venturi tubes are of identical diameter, the jets will be uniform. In this event care must be taken to ensure that the jets are not interchanged. As a rule of thumb - small venturi, small jet. Unscrew the two air regulating jets and the accelerator jet. Unscrew the choke air regulating jet; remove the circlip from the accelerator pump and remove the pump lever, spring and plunger. Unscrew the accelerator pump jet then unscrew the lentil-headed (countersunk) screws retaining the butterfly valves; the screws are peened over for safety and will prove difficult to open. Now remove the butterfly valves from the slots machined into the throttle spindles. Unscrew the outer nuts and withdraw the shafts from the carburettor body. Unscrew the vacuum chamber (diaphragm faults are extremely rare) followed by the mixture regulating screw and the idling adjustment screw.

Cleaning and Checking Components

All carburettor components should be thoroughly cleaned in petrol and all dirt particles and other residues removed; after cleaning the components should be dried with compressed air. Do not clean carburettor components with wire or a wire brush as damage can be caused to the delicate calibration of orifices etc. Compare the numbers stamped on the jets with the numbers given in the table of carburettor jets for the appropriate model. Check the carburettor body parts for damage. If necessary use fine emery cloth and a surface plate to refinish the contact surface. Examine the butterfly valve spindles and their clearance. Excessive clearance permits the ingress of air, which has a detrimental effect on the starting and the idling properties and will make accurate adjustment impossible.

Fitting an Oversize Butterly Valve Spindle

An oversize butterfly valve spindle must be fitted after reaming out the bores. Check the float for rattles when shaking it near the ear. Alternatively the float can be immersed in hot water; check that no air bubbles are visible, otherwise replace the float. If the float needle valve contact point is indented on the float arm the float will have to be replaced. If the float spindle is worn or damaged it will also have to be replaced together with the float. Check the float needle valve for

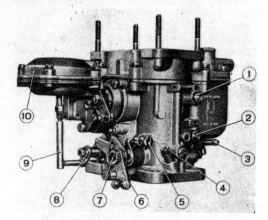

Fig.58 Weber carburettor

1 Idle jet
2 Main jet
3 Pipe connection for oil vapours and blow-by gases
4 Mixture adjusting screw
5 Idle adjusting screw
6 Throttle control lever
7 Primary throttle shaft
8 Secondary throttle control lever
9 Diaphragm rod
10 Vacuum operated device for the control of the secondary throttle

tightness and check the accelerator pump plunger; all damaged parts must be replaced. It is recommended that only genuine Weber parts be used for replacement. Messrs. Edoardo Weber of Bologna, has marketed a complete repair kit for overhauling the carburettor, including a complete set of gaskets and all material parts. If it has been necessary to dismantle the carburettor all of the parts in the kit must be fitted during replacement. No special mention has been made of replacement of gaskets and parts subject to wear and tear owing to the kit being available.

CARBURETTOR — Assembly

Assembly is virtually the reverse sequence to dismantling. When fitting the butterfly valves care must be taken to ensure that the angled edges are positioned correctly. After fitting the fastening screws, centre the flaps so that they are seated firmly against the induction port walls when closed. To check for accurate centering the carburettor must be held up to the light and, if the valve is correctly seated, no light should show between the induction port and the butterfly valve. After finally tightening down the butterfly valve screws they must be peened over, at the same time supporting the relevant spindle to prevent it being accidentally distorted.

Setting the Float Level

When adjusting the float in the carburettor the float weight (18 grammes) must first be checked. Only spindles and floats in perfect condition should be installed. Screw in the float needle valve firmly and then check to ensure that the damping ball in the valve needle can move freely. With the carburettor held vertically, and with the float tang gently touching the ball in the needle, the clearance between the float and the contact surface of the top half of the carburettor, without gasket, should be 5 mm (0.2 in.); this measurement can be adjusted by gently bending the tang as required to obtain 8.5 mm (0.33 in.). Check to ensure that the valve needle return hook allows free movement of the needle in its housing. To obtain the clearance or to adjust the float level the small flat plate and limit stop must be bent accordingly. Care must be taken to ensure that the small flat plate stands vertically in relation to the valve needle axis. After fitting the float spindle, check to ensure that the float moves freely on the spindle. Set the carburettor cover with float onto the carburettor body, taking care to prevent the float from contacting the inside rim. As a temporary idling setting, the idling mixture adjusting screw should be tightened into its seating until it is fully home and then unscrewed by 1 and 1/3 turns.

CARBURETTOR — Installation

This is carried out in a reverse sequence to the removal.

Idling Adjustment

The idling must be adjusted when the engine is running and is at its normal operating temperature.

AIR FILTER

At regular 6000 mile intervals, or more frequently in excessively dusty operating conditions, the filter cartridge will have to be replaced and the filter housing cleaned. At regular 12 000 mile intervals it is necessary to clean the hoses for drawing off oil vapours and exhaust residue and the breather valve and flame suppressor coil in the thick hose.

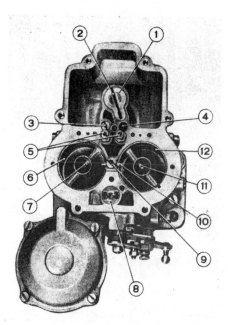

Fig.59 Weber carburettor

1 Piston spring retaining plate
2 Pump control rod
3 Choke air correction jet
4 Choke reserve supply well
5 Air correction jets
6 Secondary throat venturi
7 Secondary throat discharge nozzle
8 Choke valve spring stop
9 Pump delivery valve
10 Pump jet
11 Primary throat discharge nozzle
12 Primary throat venturi

The cause of fuel loss or excessive fuel consumption is seldom to be found in the carburettor. Leaky fuel lines, leaky connections, poor valve closure, worn valve guides, worn piston rings, dirty sparking plugs, inadequate tyre pressures, incorrect brake adjustment can all contribute to excessive fuel consumption.

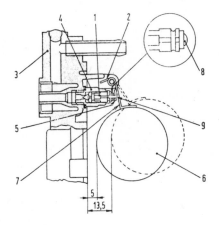

Fig.60 Diagram showing adjustment of float level on Weber carburettor

1 Needle
2 Lug
3 Carburettor cover
4 Needle valve
5 Tang
6 Float
7 Float arm
8 Moveable ball
9 Needle return hook

Fig.61 Idle adjustment on Weber carburettor

1 Screw for idle adjustment
2 Idle mixture adjusting screw

Suspension

SUSPENSION – Front

The front wheels are suspended independently. The suspension system comprises the wishbone arms, coil spring, double-acting hydraulic telescopic shock absorbers within the coil springs, transverse stabiliser and the front torsion bars.

FRONT SUSPENSION – Removal

Apply the handbrake. Ensure that the rear wheels do not move by fitting chocks. Partly loosen the front wheel nuts then jack up the front of the vehicle and position frame supports under the frame members; remove the front wheels. To remove the shock absorbers reach into the engine well, secure the threaded journal of the shock absorber and unscrew the nut and spring washer. Take off the flat top plate and upper rubber ring then unscrew the bearing flange (two nuts with spring washers) and remove the lower rubber ring. Unscrew the shock absorber from the upper wishbone member and lift out the shock absorber through the aperture in the wheel well. Insert the coil spring compressor A 74 112 through the wheel well aperture and position the top flange of this tool against the stud bolt for fastening the bearing flange of the shock absorber. The bottom flange of the tool is placed against the penultimate winding of the coil spring and the spring is then compressed completely by means of the hand crank and threaded rod. It is now possible to proceed with further dismantling and removal. Unscrew the transverse stabiliser from the bottom wishbone arm and from the floor assembly. Remove the brake calipers form their carriers right and left and withdraw the brake pads. Note: the pads must be marked carefully on removal so as to ensure correct refitting. Under no circumstances should the inner pads be fitted in place of the outside or the left hand pads be crossed

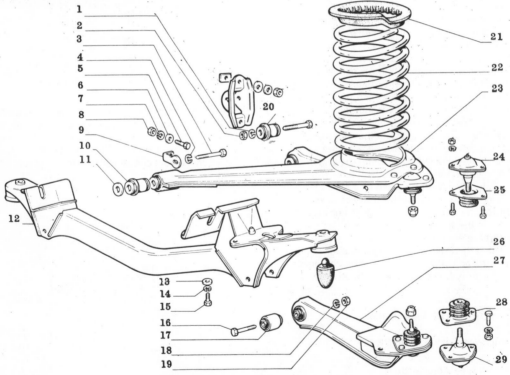

Fig.62 Exploded view of dismantled front wheel suspension system

1 Circlip	16 Bolt
2 Nut	17 Silentbloc bearing
3 Bolt	18 Circlip
4 Circlip	19 Nut
5 Bolt	20 Flexible bush
6 Washer	21 Seating ring
7 Circlip	22 Coil spring
8 Nut	23 Wishbone arm
9 Bracket	24 Swivel head
10 Flexible bush	25 Gasket
11 Shim	26 Rubber buffer
12 Cross member	27 Pivot arm
13 Spacer	28 Gasket
14 Circlip	29 Pivot head
15 Bolt	

over with their right hand counterparts. (See also "Replacing Brake Pads"). It is not necessary to disconnect the brake lines. The pads should be replaced by a piece of plywood of similar thickness to prevent the brake cylinders from sliding out of the calipers. Suspend each caliper with a piece of welding wire so that they do not hang on the brake lines. If the brake calipers are also to be removed, the feeding bore in the brake fluid reservoir must first be plugged with a pointed hardwood stick to prevent any brake fluid loss, as the brake hose will have to be separated from the rigid brake pipe. Remove the right and left track rods, using the special extractor A 47011 to extract the track rod pins. Remove the torsion bar fastening bolts on the lower wishbone arm, taking care not to mislay the spacer collars. From the floor assembly unscrew the front adjusting nuts of the torsion bars, take off each washer and rubber buffer and the spacer collar and attach the relevant parts to each torsion rod and secure it with the front adjusting nut. Prior to laying aside the torsion bars, mark them to ensure correct refitting. Press out the side track rods from the drop arm on the pivot pin. Unscrew the wishbone block from the body, removing two nuts with flat and spring washers, then unscrew the bolt and spring washer for the front mounting of the upper wishbone member to the body. Note: care must be taken of the relative position and number of shims between the wishbone and body, as these govern the track and the camber adjustments. Support the wheel suspension under the wishbones, remove the fastening pin of the lower wishbone member to the front axle member and remove the wishbone and pivot pins. Gradually release the spring tensioner A 74 112 until the coil spring is unbiased, after which the spring and spring tensioner can be taken off. To remove the front axle member the engine must be supported with a cross member A 70 506 resting on the right and left wheel mounts. Now the engine can be separated from the front axle member by taking out the rubber buffers for the front engine mounting and then unbolting and removing the front axle member from the floor assembly.

Fig.64 View of spring tensioner A 74 112 when compressing coil spring

1   Coil spring
2   Threaded bush of spring tensioner A 74 112
3   Bottom ring of spring tensioner A 74 112
4   Tierod of spring tensioner A 74 112
5   Upper wishbone arm

SUSPENSION – Dismantling

Assembly jig A 74 115 has been designed to aid in both dismantling and assembly. After removing the block from the upper wishbone the wishbones are secured with the centering arbors of the assembly jig. For the left hand group the arbor is inserted from the left and for the right hand from the right.

The unit is now dismantled. If the brake calipers have already been removed the brake lines should not be unscrewed from the brake saddle. Remove the cotter from the saddle mount, take out the holder, remove the saddle and withdraw the leaf spring, brake pads and brake pad springs. Unscrew the two bolts complete with spring washers, for fastening the

Fig.63 View of spring tensioner A 74 112

1   Hand crank of spring tensioner A 74 112
2   Roller bearing
3   Upper mounting surface, fastened to the upper shock absorber mount

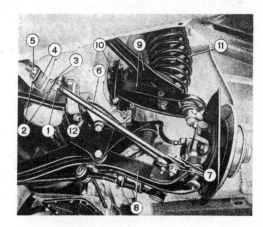

Fig.65 Front left wheel and suspension

1   Rear thrust rod adjusting nut
2   Thrust washers
3   Rear rubber buffer
4   Front rubber buffer
5   Front thrust rod adjusting nut
6   Drag link
7   Bolt and nut for bolt coupling to lower cross member
8   Lower cross member
9   Upper cross member
10 Pillow block of upper cross member
11 Coil spring
12 Transverse stabiliser

brake saddle to the carrier plate on the stub axle, and remove
the brake saddle. Remove the front wheel hub covers with
the special tool A 47 014. Release the steering pivot nut lock
by striking it with a chisel and then unscrew the steering
pivot nuts and take off the nose washer in front of the
outer ball bearing. The nuts must be discarded and replaced
for reassembly. With the aid of special tool A 40 005/1/9
withdraw the wheel hub and brake disc from the steering
pivot assembly. Unbolt the brake disc from the wheel hub
and unscrew the drop arm and plate for fastening the brake
saddle and steering pivot cover plate (four nuts with two
lock washers). Unscrew the self-locking pivot fastening nuts
from the upper and lower ball joint pins. With the aid of
extractor tool A 47 018 extract the ball joint pins and remove
the steering pivot assembly. Take the upper and lower centering pins out of the assembly jib and remove the wishbone
member.

Checking and Preparing Individual Components for Assembly

All parts must be cleaned and checked as to their suitability for
re-use. The front axle member should not be distorted. Check
the engine suspension block rubber mounting and the bores
for fastening the lower wishbone members. If any distortions at
these particular points cannot be remedied by straightening,
the complete front axle member must be replaced. If necessary,
replace the right and left rubber buffers. The upper and lower
wishbone members are checked with the aid of tool A 96 700.
The centering pins on this tool must insert easily without force
into the flexible bushes. The vertical centering pin with its
tapered seat must align with the seating of the ball joint. Minor
distortions should be remedied by cold straightening, if this is
not possible then the wishbone members involved must be
replaced. Check the flexible bushes for perfect condition - the
rubber must be resilient and undamaged. If the flexible bushes
in the upper wishbone member are damaged the wishbone
member will have to be replaced, but in the case of the lower
wishbone member the faulty bush can be extracted and replaced
with the aid of a drift pin A 74 053 and a hydraulic press. The
steering pivot is checked with the aid of tool A 95 712. Insert
the steering pivot vertically in the tool so that the side centering
pins insert easily, otherwise the pivot is distorted and will have
to be replaced. No attempt should be made to straighten the
pins. Check the torsion bars, adjusting nuts and threaded collars
for damage and replace where necessary.

Checking Front Springs

The unbiased length of the front spring should be 416 mm
(16.3 in.) and, when compressed to about 217 mm (8.5 in.), the
compression load should be 920 ± 22 lb; at 166 mm
(6.5 in.) it should be 1150 lb. Subject the springs to a visual
inspection and replace if necessary. In the centre windings the
springs are marked either yellow or green. Only springs of
identical colour marking should be fitted. The yellow marked
springs have a length in excess of 217 mm (8.5 in.) under a load
of 920 lb, whereas the green-marked springs have a length of
217 mm (8.5 in.) or less when subjected to a load of 920 lb.

Checking the Transverse Stabiliser

Any minor distortion can be remedied by straightening. Check
the centre line of both eyes, the maximum permissible deviation
should not exceed ± 1.5 mm (± 0.06 in.). If damaged, the rubber
mounts for the straps fastening the stabiliser to the floor
assembly and the mounts on the lower wishbone members must
be replaced.
Check the wheel hub play and adjust if necessary. (See under
"Suspension Assembly").

SUSPENSION – Assembly

Assembly is virtually the reverse sequence to dismantling, using
the A 74 115 assembly jig and taking due account of the
following points. Insert the upper and lower ball jointed wishbone pins in the clean and dry, upper and lower bores of the
steering pivot. Screw on the self-locking nuts and tighten to a
torque of 87 ft.lb. Fit onto the steering pivot the plate for
fastening the brake caliper, the brake disc cover plate seal and
the cover plate, but do not tighten down the two bolts as these
must be tightened subsequently when the vehicle is loaded.
Insert the two long and the two short bolts, fit the drop arm,
followed by the two locking strips, tighten the nuts with a
torque of 37 ft.lb. and bend the locking table against the nuts.
Fit the inner and the outer ball bearings in the wheel hub. The

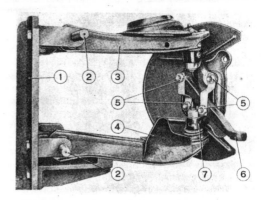

**Fig.66 Arrangement of right-hand wheel mounting on
dismantling**

1 A 74 115 assembly jig for front wheel mounting
2 Centering pins
3 Upper wishbone member
4 Lower wishbone member
5 Fastening nuts for drop arm, support plate of the
   brake caliper and cover plate of brake disc on the
   steering pivot mounting
6 Drop arm
7 Pivot pin mounts

cavity between the cage and the inner race of both ball bearings
should be packed with Fiat MR 3 grease. The hollow space in
the hub between the outer races of both ball bearings should
not be packed with grease. Only 60 grammes (2 oz.) of grease
must be packed uniformly around the circumference of the
hollow cavity. If the ring seal is not in absolutely perfect
condition it must be replaced. Bolt the hub onto the brake
plate and fit on the steering pivot. Mount the thrust plate for
the outer bearing so that the tooth is engaged in the slot in the
steering pivot pin. Discard the old hub nuts and tighten the new
nuts to a torque of 15 ft.lb. at the same time turning the hub
5 or 6 times in both directions to centre the bearings. Now
slacken off the nuts again and tighten finally with a torque of
5 ft.lb., then turn them back by 30°. Now press the nut collar
into the two slots of the steering knuckle journal, thus locking
the nut. The axial float should be 0.025 to 0.100 mm (0.001 to
0.004 in.). As soon as the axial float exceeds 0.13 mm (0.005 in.)
adjust as necessary. Knock on the wheel cap packed with 20
grammes (0.7 oz.) of grease. Fit the brake shoes and the return
springs. Fit the leaf spring and caliper on the caliper mount and
then fit the caliper mounting; insert the cotter pin. Connect
the brake line to the brake saddle. Remove the front wheel
suspension from the assembly jig. Fit the block for fastening the
upper wishbone member to the body but do not tighten the
bolts until after the unit is finally mounted.

FRONT SUSPENSION — Installation

The front wheel suspension system is fitted in the reverse sequence to its removal, particular attention should be paid to the following points: insert the rubber buffers on the front axle member. Fit the front axle member in the floor assembly with the locating pins and tighten the four fastening bolts fitted with flat washers to a torque of 65 ft.lb. Ensure that the stud bolts of the front engine mounting are seated in the appropriate front axle member bores and then tighten the engine mount nuts to a torque of 22 ft.lb. Fit the coil springs in their seating and compress them with tool A 74 112. Now fit the wheel suspension into place and bolt the lower wishbone through the flexible bush to the front axle member but do not tighten. Tighten when the vehicle is in a loaded state. Fit the upper wishbone with its block onto the two bolts on which are mounted the two adjusting bolts noted on dismantling. Screw the nuts, but do not tighten. Fit the track rod to the steering knuckle drop arm and then slowly release the coil spring by turning back the spring compressor until the bottom spring sits in the upper wishbone member. Remove the spring compressor. Fit the front shock absorbers, followed by the torsion bars. Insert the bars with adjusting nut, thrust washer, rubber buffer and spacing bush in the body mount and then fit the front rubber buffer, the thrust washer and the adjusting nut. The other end of the torsion bar is to be attached to the lower wishbone (65 ft.lb). Mount the transverse stabiliser on the body and on the lower wishbone. Bolt on the wheels and tyres (50 ft.lb) torque, noting that the wheel fastening studs have a right hand thread. The car can now be removed from the supports. As previously described, the bolts and nuts in the flexible bushes are to be tightened down only after the vehicle is loaded. For this purpose the vehicle should be driven onto a smooth horizontal surface. Check the tyre pressures and regulate as necessary - front wheels 22 lb/in.^{2}, rear wheels 25 lb/in.^{2}. With the steering wheel centered and the road wheels parallel to the longitudinal axis of the car, the four supports are positioned under the car, as illustrated, to determine the ground clearance of the loaded vehicle. (Supports A 74 144/1/7).

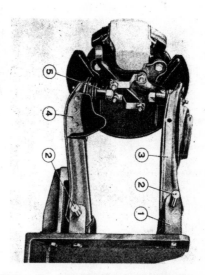

Fig.68 Complete front wheel mounting with brake caliper

1 A 74 115 assembly jig for front wheel mounting
2 Centering pins
3 Upper wishbone member
4 Lower wishbone member
5 Steering pivot mount

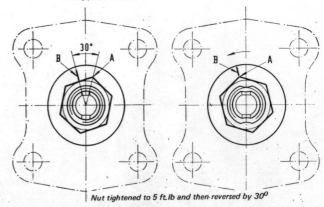

Nut tightened to 5 ft.lb and then reversed by 30°

Fig.69 Front wheel bearing adjustment

A Nut corner
B Reference mark on washer

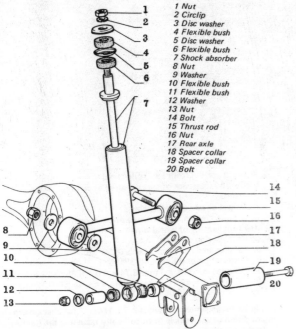

1 Nut
2 Circlip
3 Disc washer
4 Flexible bush
5 Disc washer
6 Flexible bush
7 Shock absorber
8 Nut
9 Washer
10 Flexible bush
11 Flexible bush
12 Washer
13 Nut
14 Bolt
15 Thrust rod
16 Nut
17 Rear axle
18 Spacer collar
19 Spacer collar
20 Bolt

Fig.67 Exploded view of a dismantled rear shock absorber and stabiliser

To adjust the supports insert the retaining pins in the bores marked "Ant" or "Front" in the front supports and the bores marked "Post" or "Rear" in the rear supports. Now load the vehicle until the floor of the car is level on the supports. If these special supports are not available the heights are specified at which the body comes into contact with the supports. In position A = 222 mm (8.74 in.) and position P = 255 mm (10.04 in.). The body should therefore be loaded until these values are reached, after which those nuts and bolts, which were left only hand tight when the front wheel suspension system was assembled can be finally tightened. Tighten the wishbone pivot nuts to the front axle member to a torque of 65 ft.lb. Tighten the nuts fastening the upper wishbone to the block to a torque of 25 ft.lb. Tighten the nuts fastening the upper wishbone to the body with a torque of 65 ft.lb. Tighten the threaded bolts for frontal mounting of the upper wishbone to the body with a torque of 50 ft.lb. Tighten the torsion bar fastening nuts to the body with a torque of 75 ft.lb. Remove the wooden plugs from the brake fluid reservoir and bleed the brake system.

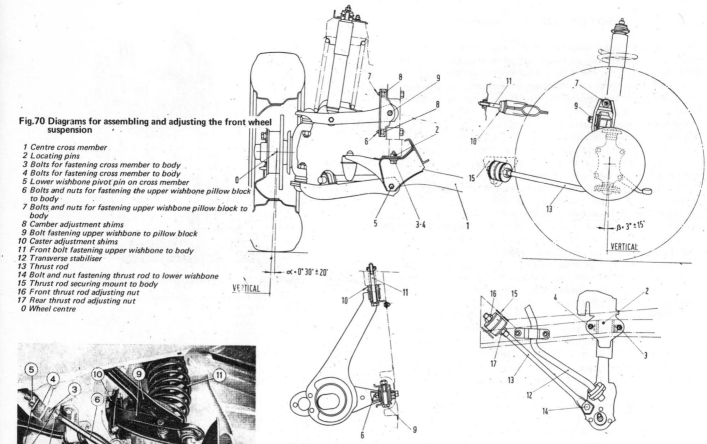

Fig.70 Diagrams for assembling and adjusting the front wheel suspension

1 Centre cross member
2 Locating pins
3 Bolts for fastening cross member to body
4 Bolts for fastening cross member to body
5 Lower wishbone pivot pin on cross member
6 Bolts and nuts for fastening the upper wishbone pillow block to body
7 Bolts and nuts for fastening upper wishbone pillow block to body
8 Camber adjustment shims
9 Bolt fastening upper wishbone to pillow block
10 Caster adjustment shims
11 Front bolt fastening upper wishbone to body
12 Transverse stabiliser
13 Thrust rod
14 Bolt and nut fastening thrust rod to lower wishbone
15 Thrust rod securing mount to body
16 Front thrust rod adjusting nut
17 Rear thrust rod adjusting nut
0 Wheel centre

$\alpha = 0°30' \pm 20'$

$\beta = 3° \pm 15'$

VERTICAL

Fig.71 Left hand front suspension system

1 Rear thrust rod adjusting nut
2 Washers
3 Rear rubber bearing
4 Front rubber bearing
5 Front thrust rod adjusting nut
6 Thrust rod
7 Bolt and nut for thrust rod fastening to lower wishbone
8 Lower wishbone
9 Upper wishbone
10 Upper wishbone mount
11 Coil spring
12 Transverse stabiliser

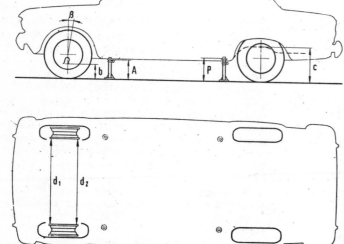

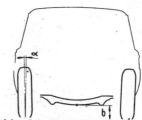

A. Height of the front adjusting stand
b. Ground clearance of car measured at centre of cross member
P. Height of rear adjusting stand
C. Ground clearance of car, measured at rear floor of car
d_1 Front spacing of wheel rims
d_2 Rear spacing of wheel rims
a = Camber angle of front wheels $0°30' \pm 20'$
β = Caster of pivot pin mount = $3° \pm 15'$
A = 222mm - b = 174 ± 3 mm(8.74in. - b = 6.85±0.12 in.)
P = 225 mm - c = 421 ± 3 mm(8.86in. - c = 16.57±0.12 in.)
$d_2 d_1$ = 2 to 4 mm (0.08 to 0.16 in.)

Fig.72 Arrangement of stands A 74 144/1/7 for checking the load condition of the vehicle prior to finally fastening the flexible bushes of the front and rear wheel suspension system and for checking and adjusting the front wheel adjustment

CONVERSION TABLE

mm	ins	mm	ins	mm	ins	mm	Ins	mm	ins
.01	.000394	.51	.020079	1	.030370	51	2.007870	105	4.133848
.02	.000787	.52	.020472	2	.078740	52	2.047240	110	4.330700
.03	.001181	.53	.020866	3	.118110	53	2.086610	115	4.527550
.04	.001575	.54	.021260	4	.157480	54	2.125980	120	4.724400
.05	.001969	.55	.021654	5	.196850	55	2.165350	125	4.921250
.06	.002362	.56	.022047	6	.236220	56	2.204720	130	5.118110
.07	.002756	.57	.022441	7	.275590	57	2.244090	135	5.314950
.08	.003150	.58	.022835	8	.314960	58	2.283460	140	5.511800
.09	.003543	.59	.023228	9	.354330	59	2.322830	145	5.708650
.10	.003937	.60	.023622	10	.393700	60	2.362200	150	5.905500
.11	.004331	.61	.024016	11	.433070	61	2.401570	155	6.102350
.12	.004724	.62	.024409	12	.472440	62	2.440940	160	6.299200
.13	.005118	.63	.024803	13	.511810	63	2.480310	165	6.496050
.14	.005512	.64	.025197	14	.551180	64	2.519680	170	6.692900
.15	.005906	.65	.025591	15	.590550	65	2.559050	175	6.889750
.16	.006299	.66	.025984	16	.629920	66	2.598420	180	7.086600
.17	.006693	.67	.026378	17	.669290	67	2.637790	185	7.283450
.18	.007087	.68	.026772	18	.708660	68	2.677160	190	7.480300
.19	.007480	.69	.027165	19	.748030	69	2.716530	195	7.677150
.20	.007874	.70	.027559	20	.787400	70	2.755900	200	7.874000
.21	.008268	.71	.027953	21	.826770	71	2.795270	210	8.267700
.22	.008661	.72	.028346	22	.866140	72	2.834640	220	8.661400
.23	.009005	.73	.028740	23	.905510	73	2.874010	230	9.055100
.24	.009449	.74	.029134	24	.944880	74	2.913380	240	9.448800
.25	.009843	.75	.029528	25	.984250	75	2.952750	250	9.842600
.26	.010236	.76	.029921	26	1.023620	76	2.992120	260	10.236200
.27	.010630	.77	.030315	27	1.062990	77	3.031490	270	10.629900
.28	.011024	.78	.030709	28	1.102360	78	3.070860	280	11.032600
.29	.011417	.79	.031103	29	1.141730	79	3.110230	290	11.417300
.30	.011811	.80	.031496	30	1.181100	80	3.149600	300	11.811000
.31	.012205	.81	.031890	31	1.220470	81	3.188970	310	12.204700
.32	.012598	.82	.032283	32	1.259840	82	3.228340	320	12.598400
.33	.012992	.83	.032677	33	1.299210	83	3.267710	330	12.992100
.34	.013386	.84	.033071	34	1.338580	84	3.307080	340	13.385800
.35	.013780	.85	.033465	35	1.377949	85	3.346450	350	13.779500
.36	.014173	.86	.033858	36	1.417319	86	3.385820	360	14.173200
.37	.014567	.87	.034252	37	1.456689	87	3.425190	370	14.566900
.38	.014961	.88	.034646	38	1.496050	88	3.464560	380	14.960600
.39	.015354	.89	.035039	39	1.535430	89	3.503930	390	15.354300
.40	.015748	.90	.035433	40	1.574800	90	3.543300	400	15.748000
.41	.016142	.91	.035827	41	1.614170	91	3.582670	500	19.685000
.42	.016535	.92	.036220	42	1.653540	92	3.622040	600	23.622000
.43	.016929	.93	.036614	43	1.692910	93	3.661410	700	27.559000
.44	.017323	.94	.037008	44	1.732280	94	3.700780	800	31.496000
.45	.017717	.95	.037402	45	1.771650	95	3.740150	900	35.433000
.46	.018110	.96	.037795	46	1.811020	96	3.779520	1000	39.370000
.47	.018504	.97	.038189	47	1.850390	97	3.818890	2000	78.740000
.48	.018898	.98	.038583	48	1.889760	98	3.858260	3000	118.110000
.49	.019291	.99	.038976	49	1.929130	99	3.897630	4000	157.380000
.50	.019685	1 mm	.039370	50	1.968500	100	3.937000	5000	196.850000

Steering

Disconnect the battery leads, remove the horn cover and unscrew the steering wheel fastening nut prior to drawing the steering wheel off while moving it back and forth. Unscrew the steering column switch cover and separate the plug coupling to remove the leads from the flasher relay on the steering column switch unit; lift off the switch unit. Unscrew the two M 6 screws on the dashboard casing; remove the parcel shelf below the dashboard. Take off the heating lever in a forward direction and unscrew the rubber gaiter at the point where the steering column tube passes through the firewall. Unscrew the pushrod on the steering linkage and disengage the ball joint. Unscrew the three retaining bolts securing the steering box to the chassis. To withdraw the detached steering assembly from below the front left spring, the shock absorber must first be removed (see under "Front Axle").

STEERING — Dismantling

Unscrew the filler plug from the cover and allow the oil to drain away. Unscrew the nut and spring washer from the drop arm spindle and remove the drop arm using the special tool. Unscrew the adjusting bolt locknut, followed by the threaded insert for the adjusting bolt. Withdraw the adjusting bolt and retaining washer from the drop arm spindle and remove the complete drop arm spindle from the steering box. Unscrew the four bolts securing the thrust bearing cover, with its shim, to the steering box on the steering worm shaft. Tap the bottom of the steering shaft so that the outer race of the bottom thrust bearing and the ball bearing race can be taken out of the case. Push the steering spindle out of the box to allow the front ball bearing race, the outer race of the rear ball bearing and the adjusting bolts to be taken out of the box. Remove the drop arm spindle from the steering box.

Inspect the tooth flanks of the steering worm and drop arm spindle. The flanks must be free of any pressure marks and must mesh centrally. If the mesh is correct the same number of shims must be fitted when assembling. If the mesh is incorrect then the degree of adjustment must be reduced or increased, depending on whether the steering height needs regulating upward or downward. Check the drop arm pin mounting and the sector in the head of the drop arm spindle for easy, smooth operation free of backlash. If there is any sign of play or backlash the drop arm spindle must be replaced. Check the ball bearing running surfaces on the steering spindle and the inner and outer ball bearing races as well as the needle bearings and mountings on the drop arm spindle and the steering box. Parts normally subject to wear and tear must be replaced. Check the drop arm spindle ring seal and replace it if necessary.

STEERING — Assembly

Assembly is virtually the reverse sequence to dismantling taking particular note of the following points: after fitting the steering column worm in the steering box, using the same number of shims under the outer race as were found when dismantling, the outer race of the front ball bearing is fitted and the thrust bearing cap is screwed on with the original number of shims. The four cover fastening bolts should be tightened with a torque of 15 ft.lb. Now use a dynamometer to check the degree of torque needed to turn the steering column with worm; the indicated torque should be 0.4 ft.lb. If the measured torque is less, it indicates that the thickness of the shims must be reduced. If the measured torque is greater, the steering worm ball bearings have excessive play and the shim thickness must be increased; 0.10 and 0.15 mm (0.004 and 0.006 in.) shims are available.

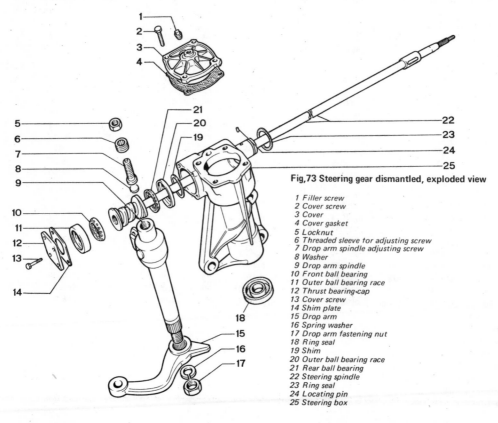

Fig.73 Steering gear dismantled, exploded view

1 Filler screw
2 Cover screw
3 Cover
4 Cover gasket
5 Locknut
6 Threaded sleeve for adjusting screw
7 Drop arm spindle adjusting screw
8 Washer
9 Drop arm spindle
10 Front ball bearing
11 Outer ball bearing race
12 Thrust bearing cap
13 Cover screw
14 Shim plate
15 Drop arm
16 Spring washer
17 Drop arm fastening nut
18 Ring seal
19 Shim
20 Outer ball bearing race
21 Rear ball bearing
22 Steering spindle
23 Ring seal
24 Locating pin
25 Steering box

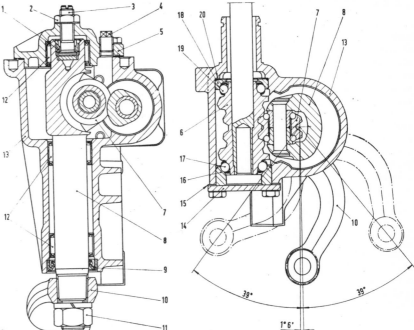

Fig.74 Steering box sections through the drop arm spindle and globoidal worm

1 Threaded sleeve for adjusting screw
2 Adjusting screw locknut
3 Drop arm spindle adjusting screw
4 Filler plug
5 Housing cover
6 Steering spindle
7 Steering sector
8 Drop arm spindle
9 Ring seal
10 Drop arm
11 Nut fastening the drop arm to the drop arm spindle
12 Drop arm spindle needle bearing
13 Steering box
14 Cover for steering worm thrust bearing
15 Shims
16 Outer thrust bearing race
17 Front ball bearing
18 Outer race of rear ball bearing
19 Rear ball bearing
20 Shims

Fig.75 Steering linkage fitted

1 Drop arm
2 Stop screw
3 Steering box
4 Centre drag link
5 Track rod
6 Track adjusting sleeve
7 Ball and socket joint

After fitting the sector and the spindle, the cover bolts should be tightened with a torque of 15 ft.lb. and the backlash adjusted between the steering worm and sector. For this purpose the temporarily fitted drop arm must be brought into the centre position; this corresponds to positioning the road wheel straight ahead. The steering spindle is turned from full lock left to full lock right and the number of turns noted. Then complete one half of the number of turns from one of the full locks. Check that the fitted drop arm, swivels by 80 to 85°. No play should be discernible in the steering spindle when it is turned 30° to right and left of centre. The existing backlash can be reduced by tightening the adjusting screw. Tighten the locknut on the adjusting shim. After backlash adjustment use a dynamometer to check the torque required to turn the steering spindle with the worm. Up to an angle of 30° right and left of centre the torque should be 0.8 to 0.95 ft.lb. and from the 30° position onward to maximum lock it should be 0.5 ft.lb.

If, during adjustment, it is found that the sector does not engage in the centre of the worm, the shims under the outer race of the rear ball bearing and those under the cover must be arranged in such a manner that the sector comes to rest exactly in the centre of the worm. The torque check must then be repeated. Secure the drop arm, fit the spring washer and tighten the nut to a torque of 175 ft.lb. The exact position of the drop arm is predetermined by a double tooth on the spindle and a corresponding tooth recess in the drop arm. Fill the steering box with just less than ½ pint (0.245 litres) of Fiat W 90/M (SAE 90 EP) oil, then screw in and tighten the adjusting screw.

Steering Linkage and Drag Link Bearing

Check the drag link thrust bearing. Distorted drag links must be replaced, as well as any worn or otherwise damaged bolts or pins. If the bushes or damping units on the thrust bearing are worn, the bearing will have to be replaced (this can be indicated by steering wheel vibrations not attributable to imbalance in the front wheels). If excessive play is found in the ball joints of the steering linkage or any other form of damage is found in the ball pins, the relevant joints will have to be replaced. The wheel lock is adjusted by limiting the swivelling range of the drop arm through appropriate adjustment of the limit stop bolt on the body side wall and on the side of the steering box.

STEERING BOX – Installation

The steering box is fitted virtually in the reverse sequence to the removal, and is followed by the checking and the adjustment of the toe-in.

Checking Camber, Caster and Track

The wheel setting is of primary importance for correct steering qualities, for the roadability of the vehicle and for tyre wear. After replacing the front axle components, or in the event of abnormal tyre wear or any steering abnormalities, the camber,

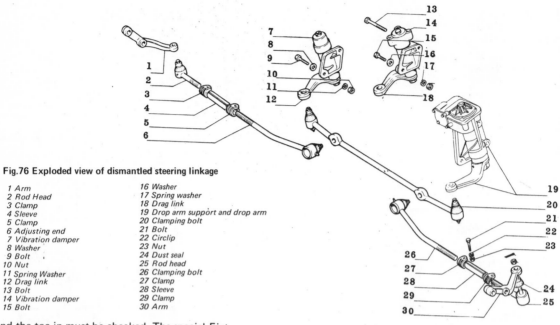

Fig.76 Exploded view of dismantled steering linkage

1 Arm	16 Washer
2 Rod Head	17 Spring washer
3 Clamp	18 Drag link
4 Sleeve	19 Drop arm support and drop arm
5 Clamp	20 Clamping bolt
6 Adjusting end	21 Bolt
7 Vibration damper	22 Circlip
8 Washer	23 Nut
9 Bolt	24 Dust seal
10 Nut	25 Rod head
11 Spring Washer	26 Clamping bolt
12 Drag link	27 Clamp
13 Bolt	28 Sleeve
14 Vibration damper	29 Clamp
15 Bolt	30 Arm

the caster and the toe-in must be checked. The special Fiat devices Ap 5106 and Ap 5107 are used to check the toe-in, camber and caster. Otherwise these measurements can be carried out very quickly and accurately with the aid of optical checking devices using projectors.

Before measuring with mechanical equipment or with optical testing devices the following work must be carried out: check to ensure that the tyre pressures are correct. The front wheels should be 22 lb/in.^{2} and the rear wheels 25 lb/in.^{2}. Check the tyres (lateral wobble and eccentricity not exceeding 3 mm (0.12 in.). Check the play in the steering worm and sector and adjust if necessary. Check the clearance between the steering knuckles and joint heads of the wishbones and replace any worn parts. Check the play between the ball pins and the track rod ends and replace the track rods ends where necessary. Check the hydraulic shock absorbers and overhaul or replace as necessary. Inspections have to be carried out with the vehicle loaded (see also under "Front Axle").

Camber

The camber is the inclination of the front wheels which are inclined outward at the top. Camber presses the wheel against the bearing and eliminates bearing play. The wheel camber angle should be 0°30' ± 20' and must be uniform on both wheels. If the measured value does not correspond to the above data the adjustment must be carried out as detailed under "Adjusting the Camber Angle".

Caster

The caster is the angle of the steering knuckle relative to a plane drawn perpendicular to the road level. The point of tyre contact follows the point of intersection with the road surface. The wheels are drawn by the caster and have the natural tendency to return automatically to the straight-ahead position in the direction of travel. With the vehicle loaded, the caster angle of the steering knuckle mount should be 3° ± 15°. If the measured value does not come up to the above figure the adjustment must be carried out as detailed under "Adjusting the Caster Angle".

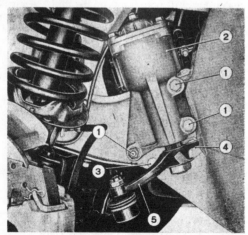

Fig.77 Steering box fitted

1 Bolt fastening steering box to body
2 Steering box
3 Stop bolt for adjusting steering lock
4 Stop bolt for adjusting steering lock
5 Drop arm

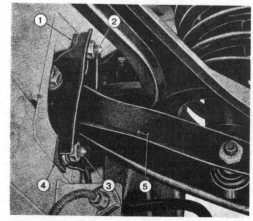

Fig.78 Fitted left-hand front wheel suspension

1 & 4 Camber adjusting shims
2 & 3 Bolt and nuts for fastening the upper wishbone to the body
5 Upper wishbone

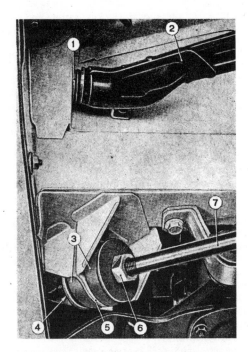

Fig.79 Detail of the left-hand fitted front wheel suspension

1 Steering knuckle mount castor shims
2 Upper wishbone
3 Rubber buffer
4 Front adjusting nut
5 Mounting to body
6 Rear adjusting nut
7 Thrust rod

Adjusting the Camber Angle

Jack up the vehicle and remove the wheel and shock absorber. Use the special spring compressor to compress the coil spring. Unscrew the nuts fastening the upper wishbone support and vary the number of shims as required. To increase the camber angle a uniform number of shims must be fitted on the bolts and to reduce the angle a uniform number of shims must be removed. Refit the block of the upper wishbone and tighten the nuts with a torque of 25 ft.lb. Release the coil spring gradually and fit the shock absorbers and wheel (see also under "Front Axle"). Re-check the camber angle.

Adjusting the Caster Angle

The caster angle is adjusted by varying the length of the front torsion bar and by varying the number of shims between the front arm of the upper wishbone and the body. If the caster angle needs only a small amount of adjustment the adjustment to the torsion bar may well prove adequate. To increase the caster angle the length of the thrust rod is reduced. To reduce the caster angle the thrust rod length is increased. If the caster angle requires considerable adjustment it will be necessary, apart from changing the torsion bar length, to vary the number of shims at the front arm of the upper wishbone. For this purpose jack up the car and remove the wheel and shock absorber. Compress the coil spring with the spring compressor. Detach the securing bolt on the leading arm of the front wishbone at the body end and vary the number of shims fitted; this avoids overloading the flexible bushes. Now tighten the securing bolt, with the vehicle loaded, to a torque of 50 ft.lb. Release the coil spring gradually and take off the compressor tool. Fit the shock absorber (see under "Front Axle"). Re-check the castor angle ; after adjusting the camber and the caster the front wheel toe-in must be checked.

Checking and Adjusting the Toe-In

Toe-in is the dimension by which the wheel rim is further apart at the rear than at the front, measured level with the wheel centre. Toe-in reduces the tendency of the wheel to flutter. Before checking the track it is necessary to check the play in the track rods, wheel bearings, wheel suspension, and the vertical and lateral wobble of the wheels, correct these as necessary. Tyre pressures should be 21 lb/in.^{2} in front and 24 lb/in.^{2} at the rear. Load the car on a horizontal, level surface until the body just comes into contact with the A 74 144/1/7 supports. When the steering wheel is centred the wheels should be parallel to the centre axis of the vehicle. The setting point of the measuring tip of the track measuring gauge Ap 5107 is marked with chalk. Lift the car slightly and rotate the wheels 180°. Lower the car and bring the measuring tips of the gauge on to the rims level with the chalk mark and read off the existing toe-in. With the vehicle loaded the toe-in should be 3$\pm$ 1 mm (0.12 ± 0.04 in.).

Adjusting the Toe-In

Slacken the four clamps on the two side track rod sleeves and turn the adjusting sleeves in opposite directions to each other by an identical amount, thus either lengthening or shortening the track rods uniformly, depending on the direction turned. It should be noted that the slots in the adjusting sleeves must coincide with the clamp apertures. When the nuts are firmly tightened down the clamps should not be closed completely; replace as necessary.

Wheels and Tyres

Disc wheels with rims	13" x 5 K
Low-pressure tyres	175S - 13
Air pressure under partial load	
front	21 lb/in.^{2}
rear	24 lb/in.^{2}
Air pressure under full load	
front	22 lb/in.^{2}
rear	25 lb/in.^{2}

If the car is to be changed over to radial tyres, the following or equivalent tyres are recommended: Pirelli 175 SR - 1B, Michelin X AS. For vehicles with serial numbers up to 48 428 this will involve replacement of the left and right drop arms.

Gearbox

The fully-synchronised four-speed gearbox consists of three separate and separable components, the clutch housing the gearbox housing and the rear cover. When the gearbox is removed the engine can be left in the car.

GEARBOX – Removal

First the selector lever on the transmission tunnel is removed by unscrewing the selector lever gaiter (four self-tapping grub screws) and the M8 bolts which connect the selector lever and the selector rod and removing the washers, rubber bush and spacer collar from the lever. Unscrew the four M6 nuts from the gear lever mounting and take out the gear lever and mounting from below. Disconnect the battery and raise the car on a hydraulic ramp. Disconnect the universal shaft at the gearbox flange. Remove the three bolts to separate the flexible three-armed flange, coupling the main shaft to the front section of the universal shaft. It is necessary to use the A 70 025 tightening strap, otherwise the bolts will be extremely difficult to move.

Unscrew the exhaust pipe at the manifold and lay it to one side. Release the two fastening bolts in the centre mounting of the universal shaft and lay the front section of the universal shaft to one side on the ramp. Unscrew the speedometer shaft collar nut and draw the shaft out of the driven speedometer gear. Unscrew the clutch cable adjusting nut and draw the cable forward and out of the clutch housing. Disengage the clutch fork return spring and unscrew the lower clutch cover. Unbolt the gearbox cross-member at the chassis ends (the cross member remains on the gearbox). Now use a ratchet, joint and extension to unscrew the three M8 starter mount bolts and the four M12 gearbox fastening bolts. Raise the engine slightly at the front and draw out the gearbox carefully to the rear, taking great care to avoid damaging the thrust ring in the clutch pressure plate through contact with the main gearbox shaft.

GEARBOX — Dismantling

Mount the gearbox on the assembly stand Arr 22 204 with the aid of the clamping jig Arr 22 206/12. Unscrew the oil filler plug on the right-hand side of the gearbox. Unbolt the rear cross-member from the drive cover and unscrew the lower cover with its gasket from the housing (ten nuts with spring washers). Remove the clutch throwout fork and the throwout sleeve and unscrew the clutch housing from the gearbox housing (seven nuts with washers). Mark the position of the spider flange on the main shaft with a painted line, as well as the relative positions of the gear wheels, in order to ensure that reassembly produces the same running conditions. Block the gear system by engaging two gears simultaneously and then release and unscrew the locknuts on the spider flange. Draw the spider flange from the main gearbox shaft. Unscrew the speedo drive from the drive cover and then unscrew the rear cover (nine nuts with spring washers) and draw the cover off the stud bolts in the gearbox housing.

Unscrew the cover plate for the locking springs and remove the gasket. Withdraw the three locking springs and the synchromesh locking balls: it is preferable to mark the spring for the reverse gear engagement with a painted line as it has a stronger spring action than the two other springs. Unscrew the drive cover and withdraw it from the stud bolts, if necessary removing the ring seal. Draw the speedometer drive pinion and ball bearing from the main gearbox shaft. Remove the reverse gear selector shaft and its selector fork and reverse gear wheel. Use a pair of circlip pliers to remove the circlip from the reverse gear driving cog then remove the cog and spring washer. Remove the circlip of the driven cog for reverse gear from the main shaft, followed by the spring washer and cog. Remove the fitting key from the main shaft. Engage two gears simultaneously to lock the gear system and then remove the socket head grub screw, and the circlip and washer from the front twin-race ball bearing on the layshaft. Remove the front ball bearing and rear roller bearing from the gearbox housing and then take out the layshaft. Draw out the selector shaft for the 3rd and 4th gears. Release the fastening screw on the selector fork for the 1st and 2nd gears. Take the selector shaft out of the gearbox housing and remove the selector forks for the 1st, 2nd, 3rd and 4th gears. Unscrew the supporting plate for the centre ball bearing and remove the central mainshaft ball bearing from the gearbox housing. Take the drive shaft with the 4th gear cog, ball bearing and synchromesh ring of the 4th gear from the mainshaft, thus releasing the 23 bearing needles and the two end plugs, which can be removed from the housing. Now remove the gearbox mainshaft with gear wheels, sliding sleeves, sleeve carriers and synchromesh rings from the gearbox housing. With the shaft clamped in a vice the 1st gear cog with its bush, the synchromesh ring for the 1st gear, the sliding sleeve with its mount, the sliding dogs and springs for the 1st and 2nd gear, the synchromesh ring and the 2nd gear cog can now be withdrawn from the rear of the mainshaft. Remove the circlip

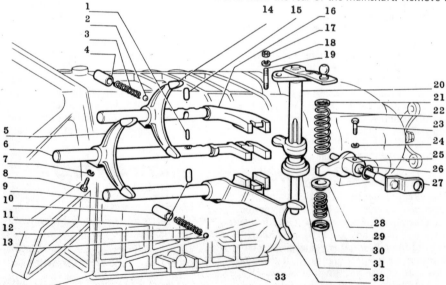

Fig.80 Exploded view of the dismantled inner gear selection system

1 Roller pin	12 Spring	23 Bolt
2 Arrestor ball	13 Ball	24 Circlip
3 Spring	14 Fork	25 Lever
4 Bush	15 Roller pin	26 Ring seal
5 Selector fork	16 Selector shaft	27 Shaft
6 Selector shaft	17 Nut	28 Disc washer
7 Circlip	18 Circlip	29 Spring
8 Bolt	19 Stud screw	30 Disc washer
9 Selector shaft	20 Shaft	31 Dog
10 Bush	21 Ring seal	32 Selector fork for reverse idler gear
11 Roller pin	22 Spring	33 Gearbox housing

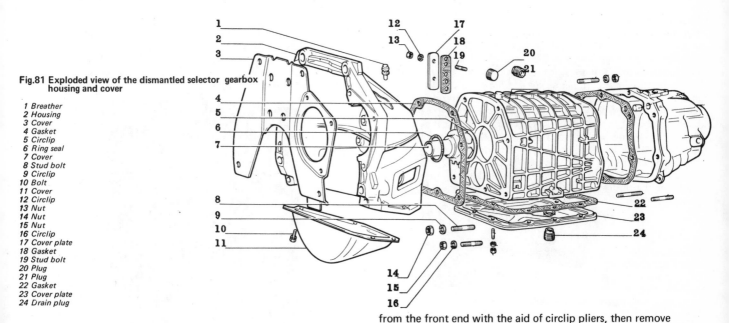

Fig.81 Exploded view of the dismantled selector gearbox housing and cover

1 Breather
2 Housing
3 Cover
4 Gasket
5 Circlip
6 Ring seal
7 Cover
8 Stud bolt
9 Circlip
10 Bolt
11 Cover
12 Circlip
13 Nut
14 Nut
15 Nut
16 Circlip
17 Cover plate
18 Gasket
19 Stud bolt
20 Plug
21 Plug
22 Gasket
23 Cover plate
24 Drain plug

from the front end with the aid of circlip pliers, then remove the spring washer, the sliding sleeve with its mount, the sliding dogs and springs for the 3rd and 4th gears, the synchromesh ring and the 3rd gear cog. Remove the circlip and take off the spring washer and ball bearing.

Checking the Dismantled Gears

Before assembling the gearbox, all of the parts must be cleaned thoroughly with washing petrol or paraffin and then blown dry with compressed air, after which they can be examined thoroughly for wear and replaced as necessary. Particular attention must be paid to all contact fitting surfaces for the clutch housing and the cover, which must be refinished with great care, using a scraper where necessary. If the amount of

Fig.82 Exploded view of dismantled gears and shafts

1 Ring
2 Roller pin
3 Ring
4 Ring seal
5 Circlip
6 Circlip
7 Bearing
8 Synchromesh gear
9 Toothed dog
10 Shim
11 Synchromesh gear
12 Spring
13 Retaining ring
14 Synchromesh hub
15 Spring
16 Bolt
17 Circlip
18 Washer
19 Bearing
20 Layshaft
21 Shaft with 4th gear
22 Circlip
23 Retaining ring
24 3rd gear cog
25 Lock washer
26 Plate
27 Bearing
28 Main shaft
29 Shim
30 2nd gear cog
31 Retaining ring
32 Bearing
33 Cog
34 Screw
35 Key
36 Speedometer gear
37 Bearing
38 Seal
39 Nut
40 Ring seal
41 Ring collar
42 Circlip
43 Retaining ring
44 Dog
45 Retaining ring
46 Circlip
47 Reverse gear cog
48 Bush
49 1st gear cog
50 Synchromesh gear
51 Dog
52 Spring
53 Hub
54 Spring
55 Synchromesh gear
56 Circlip
57 Reverse gear
58 Bush
59 Reverse gear pinion

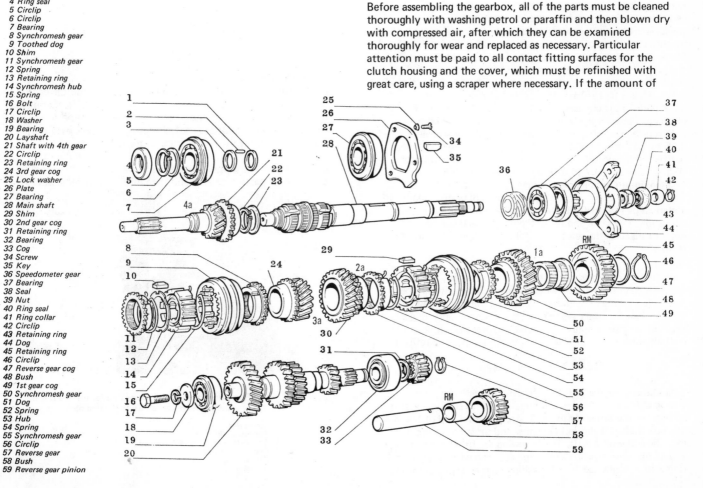

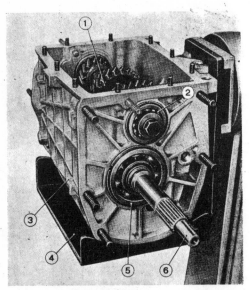

Fig.83 Selector gearbox, partly dismantled

1 Layshaft
2 Front two-row ball bearing on layshaft
3 Front gearbox housing
4 Assembly jig
5 Front ball bearing of gearbox drive shaft
6 Drive shaft of selector gearbox

Fig.84 Selector gearbox, partly dismantled

1 Drive shaft
2 Layshaft
3 Selector fork for 3rd and 4th gear
4 Selector sleeve for 3rd and 4th gear
5 Selector rod for 3rd and 4th gear
6 Selector sleeve for 1st and 2nd gear
7 Driven cog for reverse gear
8 Selector rod for reverse gear
9 Reverse gear idler
10 Driving cog for reverse gear
11 Reverse pinion
12 Selector fork of reverse gear
13 Mainshaft

wear is excessive the part concerned must be replaced. Gaskets and ring seals showing the slightest signs of damage must be replaced. Shafts, spindles and gears must be in perfect condition or they must be replaced. Check the mainshaft and the layshaft between centre points. Wobble or deflection, measured with a gauge, should not exceed 0.025 mm (0.001 in.). Particular note must be taken of the following clearances; if they are exceeded the parts concerned must be replaced. The fitting clearance between the reverse gear shaft and the layshaft gear bush is 0.05 to 0.10 mm (0.002 to 0.004 in.) the maximum permissible clearance is 0.15 mm (0.006 in.). The fitting clearance between the bush and the gear wheel for 1st gear between the mainshaft and the 2nd and 3rd gear wheels is 0.05 to 1.10 mm (0.002 to 0.043 in.). The fitting clearance between the groove flanks of the 1st, 2nd, 3rd and 4th gear sliding sleeves is 0.07 to 0.16 mm (0.0027 to 0.0063 in.) The maximum permissible clearance is 0.2 mm (0.0079 in.). Ball and roller bearings must be in absolutely perfect condition and must be replaced if there is the slightest doubt as to their condition. The same applies to sliding dogs and springs, the detent rollers on the selector shafts, the locking balls and the springs.

Only perfect circlips should be used and preferably these should always be replaced when removed. When fitting, it is advisable to use a drift and not to spread the circlips any further than necessary when using the pointed pliers. In general the following rules apply for assembly: total cleanliness and coat all parts with Fiat W 90 oil before assembly and refitting.

GEARBOX — Assembly

Slide the cog for the 3rd gear, the synchromesh ring, the sliding gear carrier (and the sliding sleeve with sliding dog and springs for the 3rd and 4th gear) onto the front end of the main gearbox shaft. Fit the spring washer and drive the spring ring into the slot with a drift. The following are fitted onto the rear end of the main gearbox shaft: 2nd gear cog with synchromesh ring, sliding sleeve carrier with sliding dogs and springs for the

1st and 2nd gear, the synchromesh ring and the bush. Insert the preassembled mainshaft in the gearbox housing; slide the central ball bearing onto the mainshaft and position it into its seating in the gearbox housing. Fit the reverse gear pinion, followed by the mounting plate for the central bearing, and lock with the slotted screws. Fit the ball bearing on the driveshaft, fit the spring washer, and use a drift to insert the spring ring in its groove. Insert the supporting washer in the driveshaft, use grease to fit the 23 bearing needles and then insert the outer support

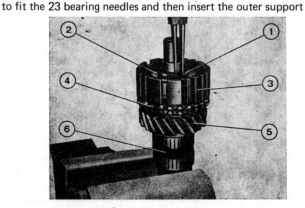

Fig.85 Removing the retaining spring ring for the 3rd & 4th gear sliding sleeve carrier, using pointed pliers

1 Spring ring
2 Flexible washer
3 3rd & 4th gear sliding sleeve carrier
4 Synchromesh ring
5 3rd gear cog
6 Mainshaft

washer. Fit the driveshaft in the gearbox housing, then fit the 4th gear synchromesh ring and insert the needle bearing in the driveshaft on the gearbox mainshaft journals. Fit the selector fork for the 1st and 2nd gear in the 1st and 2nd gear sliding sleeve and insert the selector shaft into the selector fork bore, followed by the locking pin. Fit the 3rd and 4th gear selector fork in the 3rd and 4th gear sliding sleeve. Fit the selector shaft and insert the locking pin. The selector fork is subsequently mounted on the shaft. Fit the layshaft with the 1st, 2nd, 3rd and 4th gear wheels into the gearbox housing. Install the two-sided ball bearing and the rear roller bearing on the layshaft. Engage two gears so as to lock the gearbox, then screw the hexagonal bolt with spring ring and washer onto the front of the layshaft, tightening to 70 ft.lb torque. Fit the reverse gear with fitting key on the mainshaft, fit the spring washer and insert the circlip with the aid of the drift. Ensure that the spring washer is centered accurately and that the groove for accommodating the circlip is free. Mount the reverse gear cog on the rear end of the layshaft and secure it with a circlip. Fit the reverse gear idler shaft with the reverse gear cog, then fit the speedometer drive pinion and rear ball bearing on the mainshaft. If the selector linkage has been removed, prepare the drive cover for fitting in the vice. If necessary, replace the ring seal and the inner spring and fit it with the aid of a drift.

Insert the ring seal in the double seating in the selector shaft. Insert the gear change lever in the drive cover and fit the inner lever. Secure the lever with its screw and lock washer, then fit the eccentric selector shaft for the 1st and 2nd gear together with the thrust spring, the reverse gear thrust spring, the disc springs and the selector eccentric. Mount the gear shift lever on the drive cover (stud bolt on the cover, two nuts with spring washers). Fit the drive cover gasket on the stud bolts of the gearbox housing. To engage the selector eccentric in the selector forks of the selector shafts, push the 3rd and 4th gear selector shaft outward. Screw on the drive cover, tightening the nuts to a torque of 22 ft.lb. Set the 3rd and 4th gear selector shaft to the idle position. Fit the speedometer drive bearing and screw the drive bearing with the nut and spring washer into place on the drive cover (grub screw). Fit the spider flange for the flexible disc on the main gearbox shaft. Engage two gears so as to lock the gear system, and tighten down the fastening nut to a torque reading of 57 ft.lb., after which it can be locked into position. Fit the dust protector cap, fit the centering ring of the flexible disc using a drift and lock it with a circlip. Fit the centre cover with its soil sel on the clutch housing.

Using new gaskets and spring washers bolt the clutch housing to the gearbox housing. With the exception of the smaller ones (18 ft.lb), tighten the nuts to a torque reading of 37 ft.lb. Screw on the 3rd and 4th gear selector fork and secure the bolt by fitting the washer. Fit the detent balls with springs. Note: the reverse gear detent spring was marked on dismantling. Screw the spring support plate with its gasket onto the gearbox housing. Tighten the lower cover with a torque of 8 ft.lb (ten nuts with spring washers). Screw in the oil drain plug. Fit the rear cross-member onto the drive cover, tightening the nuts to a torque of 24 ft.lb. Fit the clutch throwout sleeve and the thrust bearing on the driveshaft centre cover, followed by the clutch throwout fork. Remove the gearbox from the assembly jig and fill it with Fiat W 90 M SAE 90 EP oil, up to the edge of the filler hole (approx. 1 quart). Screw in the filler plug.

GEARBOX — Installation

The gearbox is fitted in the reverse sequence to the removal, taking due note of the following points. Centre the clutch plate

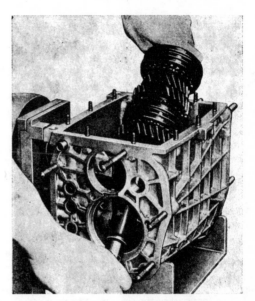

Fig.86 Fitting the complete mainshaft in the gearbox housing

with centering bolts. When inserting the gearbox shaft into the hub of the clutch plate and the ball bearing in the crankshaft, the gearbox, seated on the vehicle jack, is pushed slightly back and tilted slightly to one side. Now push it in very carefully and tighten the cross member together with its rubber liner, spacer collars, flat washers, spring washers and nuts, to the floor using a torque of 19 ft.lb. Tighten the three self-locking nuts on the flexible disc to a torque of 73 ft.lb. Adjust the clutch pedal to a free travel of 25 mm (1 inch) by regulating the clutch throwout fork, leaving a clearance of 2mm (0.08 in.) between the contact surfaces of the clutch throwout fork and the thrust bearing. To tighten the bearing strap of the centre bearing on the universal

Fig.87 Fitting the complete layshaft in the gearbox housing

Fig.88 Using a torque wrench to tighten the front ball bearing bolt on the layshaft (to 70 ft.lb)

GEARBOX — Overhaul and Refitting
(See also 'ENGINE — Removal')

Position the vehicle over a workshop pit or onto a hoist ramp. The following procedure is adopted to remove the complete universal shaft: remove the four bolts and self-locking nuts from the sleeve on the drive pinion, then unscrew the three self-locking nuts from the bolts connecting the spider flange on the front tubular shaft with the rubber coupling. Fit the clamping strap A 70 025 around the rubber coupling and remove the three bolts. Unbolt the thrust bearing from the floor assembly. Prior to removing the thrust bearing and separating the two shafts, a check must be made of the marking on the sliding sleeves of the rubber coupling and on the front shaft section and the marking on the front shaft section and on the universal joint driver on the rear shaft section. If a universal joint has to be dismantled, the relative positions of the joint ends and the trunnion must be marked. Check the bearing, circlips and trunnion journals for wear. Both shafts must be clamped in place individually on the Ap 5052/1 with flange Ap 5052/3 and checked for concentricity and balance. The individual shafts can be straightened using a hydraulic press. If any out-of-balance is found, then that part of the shaft must be replaced. Check the centre ball bearing for firm seating on the shaft, and also see that the axial float has not become excessive. Replace as necessary. Check the clearance in the splined shafts and the grooves in the flange and, if the clearance or play is excessive (wear limit 0.30 mm (0.012 in.)), the worn parts must be replaced. Check the grease port in the spider flange (sealed with plugs) to ensure that it is not clogged. If necessary replace the seal, the sleeve and the bush in the spider flange (driver). Check the rubber coupling for suitability for re-use. In the event of wear or damage to individual coupling parts, the part must be replaced.

Assembly of the universal shaft is the reverse sequence to the dismantling. The keyways of the front shaft and the trunnions of the universal joints on the rear shaft, should be fitted with Fiat Jota 1 grease. Refitting of the two-section universal shaft is virtually the reverse sequence to the dismantling. The following points must however be taken into account: before assembly, the splined shaft ends and the universal joints of the shaft should be greased with Fiat MF 2 grease. The marking on the front shaft must coincide with the marking on the sliding sleeve of the driving flange. The self-locking nuts should be tightened to a torque of 70 ft.lb. Bolt the cross member to the thrust bearing. The fastening bolts of the centre thrust bearing are to be tightened provisionally only finger-tight. Now fit the rear shaft. Slide the drive of the universal joint onto the splines of the rear shaft end of the front shaft, ensuring that the reference mark on the shaft end and on the universal joint driver are opposite the rear shaft. Now fit the driver flange on the universal joint of the rear shaft, to the drive flange of the axle drive bevel pinion. The four self-locking nuts must be on the side of the rear axle (tighten to 90—160 ft.lb). The two fastening bolts of the cross member of the centre thrust bearing can now be finally tightened down to 18 ft.lb. At regular 25,000 mile intervals the plug must be unscrewed from the sliding sleeve on the gearbox end and greased with Fiat MF2 grease. Screw the plug back in. Grease the needle bearing of the universal joints with Fiat MF2 grease.

Rear Axle

The rigid rear axle is suspended from the floor assembly by two leaf springs, two longitudinal struts and two double-acting hydraulic, telescopic shock absorbers.

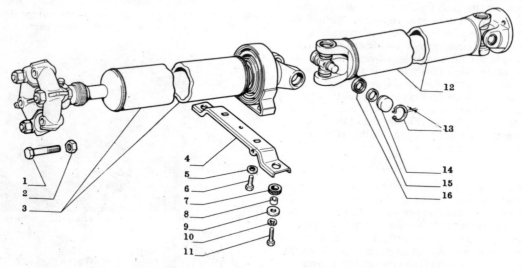

Fig. 92 Exploded view of dismantled transmission shaft

1 Bolt
2 Nut
3 Shaft
4 Mount
5 Spring washer
6 Screw
7 Isolating washer
8 Spacer collar
9 Washer
10 Circlip
11 Bolt
12 Shaft
13 Circlip
14 Mount
15 Ring seal
16 Disc washer

Fig. 89   Fitting the retaining circlip for the reverse gear
           driven cog

1 Rear roller bearing for the layshaft
2 Layshaft
3 Reverse gear pinion
4 Spring washer
5 Circlip
6 Drift
7 3rd and 4th gear selector shaft
8 1st and 2nd gear selector shaft
9 Locking ball springs
10 Support plate for centre manshaft ball bearing

shaft the four bolts are screwed down to a torque reading of
19 ft.lb. The selector lever is assembled in the reverse sequence
to the removal. After the gearbox has been fitted, the gearshift
must be actuated to check the complete system for functional
efficiency.

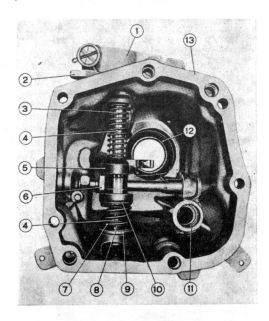

Fig. 90   Selector linkage in rear gearbox cover

1 Connecting linkage for gearbox selector system
2 Outer selector lever
3 Thrust spring, imparting perceptible thrust force when 1st and
   2nd gears are engaged
4 Selector shaft
5 Inner selector lever
6 Shaft with intermediate lever
7 & 8   Thrust springs imparting perceptible thrust force when
         reverse gear is engaged
9 Lower spring washer
10 Locknut
11 Tierod
12 Gear selector lever
13 Gear selector lever

Cone Clutch Synchromesh

Since July 1968 a different type of synchromesh ring has been
used alternately in the gearbox.
The new synchromesh arrangement of the four forward gears
consists of one each selector sleeve, a guide sleeve, a tapered
synchromesh ring and a thrust spring. When fitting the thrust
spring care must be taken to ensure that the bent corners of the
spring are engaged correctly in the selector wheel. Under no
circumstances should any change be made in the diameter or
length of the thrust spring.
As both gearboxes are still being fitted alternately the previous
spares are still available for repair purposes.

Fig. 91   Internal view of gearbox housing

1 1st gear cog
2 1st and 2nd gear selector fork
3 2nd gear cog
4 3rd gear cog

5 3rd and 4th gear selector fork
6 Constant mesh gear
7 1st gear layshaft cog
8 1st and 2nd gear sliding sleeve
9 2nd gear layshaft cog
10 3rd gear layshaft cog
11 3rd and 4th gear sliding sleeve
12 Constant mesh gear

Gear Selection

The gears are selected by actuating the gear shift lever on the
central transmission tunnel. Assembly is a reverse sequence to
the removal. If adjustment is necessary after assembly, the
protective gaiter must be removed and the nuts securing the
thrust bearing released to allow the thrust bearing to be dis-
placed. If engagement of the 1st and 3rd gears is faulty the
thrust bearing is pushed forward; if the 2nd and 4th gear
engagement is faulty the thrust bearing is moved back. If
necessary the tierod locknut should be released and the length
of the tierod adjusted accordingly.

UNIVERSAL SHAFT

The universal shaft consists of two section, the front and the
rear tubular shaft. The front tubular shaft runs in a ball bearing
embedded in rubber. This thrust bearing is bolted to the floor
assembly. The front tubular shaft is connected by a rubber
coupling on the spider flange with the main gearbox shaft. The
rear end carries a universal shaft to which the rear tubular shaft
is hinged. The rear end of the rear tubular shaft is connected
with the rear axle by a universal joint with the sleeve on the
journal of the drive pinion.

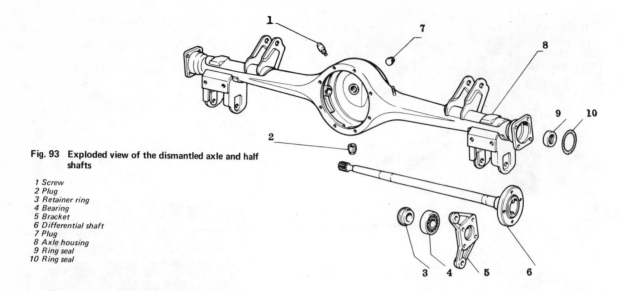

Fig. 93 Exploded view of the dismantled axle and half shafts

1 Screw
2 Plug
3 Retainer ring
4 Bearing
5 Bracket
6 Differential shaft
7 Plug
8 Axle housing
9 Ring seal
10 Ring seal

REAR AXLE – Removal

Remove the rear wheel hub caps and loosen the wheel fastening nuts. Jack up the car and place supports in position. Remove the rear wheels and insert a sharpened hardwood plug into the outlet bore in the hydraulic fluid reservoir to prevent any loss of fluid. Unscrew the brake hoses from the rigid brake line. Take out the universal shaft and then disengage the handbrake return spring. Unscrew the nut from the brake compensator and remove the compensator from the lever. Remove the cable sheath from its holder and unscrew the cable sheath retaining clips on the right and the left of the floor assembly. Place a jack under the differential housing. Remove the thrust rods on the rear axle housing and fastening on the floor assembly. Unscrew the hydraulic shock absorbers on the clamping plates on the rear axle housing over the leaf springs and remove them together with the flexible bushes and washers.

If the rear wheel suspension springs have to be removed, the shock absorbers will also have to be unscrewed at the top in the boot. Remove the front leaf spring fastening pins at the rear shackle. Lower the jack and run out the rear axle and the springs to the rear of the vehicle.

REAR AXLE – Dismantling

A description is given of the dismantling and overhaul of the complete rear axle. If necessary, the rear axle half shafts and/or differential can be removed individually without removing the entire rear axle assembly.

HALF SHAFTS – Removal

Drain the oil from the rear axle housing. The following tasks must now be carried out at both the left and right shafts. Take off the rear brake saddles and remove the brake hose. Unscrew the fastening bolts of the brake saddle mount from the thrust plate and withdraw the brake saddle with its mount from the brake disc. Unscrew the two centering bolts for securing the brake disc to the half shaft flange and for centering the wheel. Take off the brake disc and its spacer. Now unscrew the four fastening nuts in the thrust plate for the brake saddle mount on the axle tube flange: the rear half shaft with thrust plate, ball bearing and mounting can now be removed with the aid of the A 47 017 extractor tool.

REAR SPRINGS – Removal

Remove the bolts and nuts for fastening the right and left

Fig. 94 Exploded view of the final drive and differential gear gear

1 Gear
2 Bolt
3 Circlip
5 Axle bearing box
6 Spacer collar
7 Bearing
8 Washer
9 Ring seal
10 Sleeve
11 Nut
12 Washer
13 Bevel gear
14 Wheel axle
15 Pinion gear
16 Differential housing
17 Threaded ring
18 Retainer clip
19 Bearing
20 Bevel gear drive
21 Bearing
22 Thrust washer

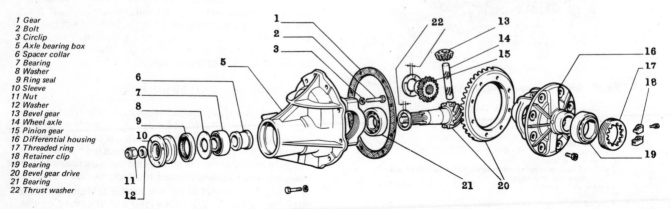

spring mounting support to the rear axle. Release the spring shackle nuts and unscrew them. Take out the spring shackles, and the spring mount with its flexible bush from below. Lift out the isolating plate and spring from above.

DIFFERENTIAL GEAR — Dismantling

Bolt the differential gearbox onto the Arr 22 206/4 assembly stand (mark with a painted line the position of the bevel pinion relative to the crown wheel). Block the differential and unscrew the self-locking nut from the bevel pinion flange and remove the flange and washer. Invert the differential, mark the bearing cover and unscrew. Remove the adjusting nut lock washers and then remove the adjusting nuts and outer races of the roller bearing. Lift out the differential gear. With the aid of the extractor, take off the inner roller bearing races from the

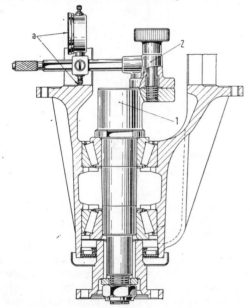

Fig. 95 Assembling the dummy bevel gear A 70 167 and gauge A 95 690 to determine the shim thickness required for the rear bevel gear bearing

1 Dummy bevel gear A 70 167
2 Gauge A 95 690 (with 1/100th graduation)
a Value indicated by the gauge and from which the correction value stamped on the gear by the maker is to be deducted

axle journals of the differential housing. If necessary, unbolt the crown wheel from the housing. Knock out the differential pinion with a drift and then rotate the halfshaft pinions so that the differential bevel gears can be extracted through the housing aperture. Now take the halfshaft gears and shims out of the housing, followed by the bevel pinion and shim, the inner race of the rear roller bearing and the spacer collar. Remove the ring seal and the inner race of the front roller bearing followed by the outer races of the two roller bearings. Extract the spacer bush from the bevel pinion and use the extractor tool A 40 005/1/8 and jig A 45 009 to draw off the inner race of the rear roller bearing from the bevel pinion and to take off the shim behind the bearing.

DIFFERENTIAL GEAR — Assembly

After all parts have been cleaned thoroughly in washing petrol or paraffin and blown dry with compressed air they must be inspected carefully for wear. It may be possible to remedy slight imperfection (for example on the differential pinion,

on the inner running faces of the differential bevel gears, on the inner faces of the halfshaft bevel gears or their seating in the differential housing and the surfaces of the shims) by polishing with finest emery cloth, but otherwise all worn parts must be replaced. As the crown wheel and pinion bevel gears are mated from the outset they can be replaced only in pairs. If the slightest double exists as to the condition or serviceability of the roller bearings they must be replaced.

Fit the halfshaft bevel gears and shims. The following thicknesses of shim are available: 1,95 mm, 2,0 mm, 2,05 mm and 2,10 mm (0.0767, 0.0787, 0.0806 and 0.0826 in.) Insert the differential bevel gears and pinion. The axial float of the differential bevel gears must be between 0 and 0,10 mm (0.004 in.) if this figure is exceeded the shims must be replaced by the next higher thickness. Now re-check the play. If it is still not within the range of 0 to 0,10 mm (0.004 in.) this can only indicate cog wear and the cogs will have to be replaced. Check the differential housing and remove any burring which may be present on the crown wheel seating or around the bolt apertures. Fit the crown wheel and screw on the bolts and spring washers, tightening down in a cross-over pattern to a torque of 75 ft.lb. Fit the inner races of the roller bearings on the differential housing journals with the aid of the drift A 70 173. The differential housing assembled to this stage is now laid aside, as the bevel pinion must first be fitted.

Fitting and Adjusting the Bevel Pinion

It is first necessary to ascertain the thickness of the shim between the bevel pinion and the rear roller bearing. The dummy bevel pinion A 70 167 and the gauge A 95 690 should be used for this purpose. The outer races of the front and rear roller bearings of the bevel pinion are fitted with the aid of a suitable drift. The inner race of the rear roller bearing is fitted on the dummy bevel pinion A 70 167, after which the dummy is pushed into the seating in the drive housing. Fit the inner race of the front roller bearing and mount the flange for fastening the universal joint. Tighten the fastening nuts with the flange plate of the dummy pinion. Rotate it several times to allow the roller bearing races to seat, then set the gauge to zero

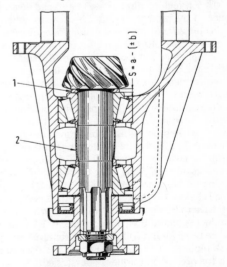

Fig. 96 Bevel pinion adjustment

S Required thickness of the rear roller bearing shim
a Value indicated by the gauge
b Correction value shown by the maker on the gear
1 Rear pinion bearing shim
2 Spacer bush

and fit it to the dummy pinion with the probe tip resting on the seat of a roller bearing. Move the gauge bracket to right and to left, stopping in each case at the point where the lowest reading is shown. The means of the two indicated values corresponds to "a", which must be subtracted from the value stamped on the bevel gear. Note whether the value on the bevel pinion is preceded by a plus or minus symbol. As the bevel pinion and crown wheel are mated and run-in in pairs to within the closest tolerances during manufacture, the ideal fitting value is stamped on the bevel pinion and crown wheel down to the nearest hundredth of a millimetre (inch).

The following formula applies for calculating shim thicknesses:

$$S = a - (+b) = a - b \text{ or}$$
$$S = a - (-b) = a + b$$

or

a = the value read off from the gauge
b = the value stamped into the bevel pinion and
S = the thickness of the shim required
1. If a plus symbol is stamped on the bevel pinion this denotes that the value stamped on the pinion is to be deducted from the gauge value.
2. If a minus symbol is stamped on the bevel pinion the gauge value is to be added to the value stamped on the pinion in order to arrive at the thickness of the required shim.

e.g. value indicated on the gauge a = 2,90 mm
value stamped into the pinion b = 5 (in 1/100 mm)
according to the formula S = a − (−b) we derive:

$$S = 2,90 - (-0,05)$$
$$S = 2,90 - 0,05$$
$$S = 2,95 \text{ mm}$$

Therefore a 2,95 mm thick shim is to be fitted.

The following thicknesses are available: 2,40, 2,45, 2,50, 2,55, 2,60, 2,65, 2,70, 2,75, 2,80, 2,85, 2,90, 2,95, 3,00, 3,05, 3,10, 3,15, 3,20, 3,25 and 3,30 mm. After calculating the shim thickness the appropriate shim is fitted on the bevel pinion, and tool A 70 152 is used to fit the inner race of the roller bearing followed by the spacer bush. The spacer bush is a flexible clamping bush which allows the bevel pinion to run free of backlash after the self-locking nut has been tightened down on the driver flange. If the prescribed torque is exceeded when setting the clamping pressure of the bevel pinion roller bearing, the spacer sleeve will be distorted and must be replaced, together with the overtightened self locking nut. For differential gear repairs where the bevel gear, roller bearing and drive housing do not need replacement, the spacer bush does not have to be replaced. After removing the bevel pinion, the preassembled bevel pinion assembly with shim, inner roller bearing race and spacer bush is fitted in the drive housing. The bevel pinion drive flange is secured on the assembly stand with the aid of the retainer Arr 22 206/4. The self-locking nut is tightened with a torque wrench to between 90 - 160 ft.lb, meanwhile frequent checks must be made using the A 85 697 dynamometer on the rolling torque of the bevel pinion (1 to 1.1 ft.lb.). If the reading is below 1.0 ft.lb., the nut on the bevel pinion flange will have to be tightened down further without exceeding the maximum tightening torque. If 1.1 ft.lb. is exceeded the bevel pinion will have to be removed and the spacer bush replaced. The spacer bush will also have to be replaced if the prescribed torque is not reached.

Fitting the Differential Gear in the Drive Housing

The preassembled differential gear is set into the drive housing together with the outer races of the roller bearing. Note the painted marks applied to indicate the bevel pinion position

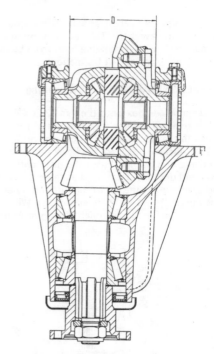

Fig. 97 Setting and checking the differential bearing bias

D Clearance between both differential bearing covers: the adjusting nuts must be tightened so that the clearance "D" is enlarged by a spread dimension of 0.08 to 0.10 mm (0.003 to 0.004 in.)

relative to the crown wheel when dismantling. Fit the right and left bearing adjusting nuts and tighten the bearing cover to 75 ft.lb. The A 95 688 tool is used to regulate the roller bearing bias in the differential housing and to adjust the clearance between the bevel pinion and the crown wheel. Initially there is a provisional adjustment of the pinion and crown wheel to approx. 0.08 to 0.12 mm (0.003 to 0.005 in.) with the aid of the adjusting nuts, but this must be so that the bearings are not subjected to any bias, i.e. the adjusting nuts may only just contact the bearings. Now tighten the adjusting nuts uniformly and alternately with the A 55 043 spanner. This results in a spread between the bearing caps which is indicated by the arm of the front gauge. This spread should be between 0.08 and 0.10 mm (0.003 and 0.004 in.). Now measure the clearance between the crown wheel and pinion, locking the pinion with the holder Arr 22 206/4. Bring the crown wheel into contact with the pinion on one side then set the other gauge needle to zero, resting the probe tip on the flank of a tooth on the crown wheel. Move the crown wheel in the opposite direction and read off the displacement on the gauge the value or backlash between the crown wheel and pinion should be between 0.10 and 0.15 mm (0.004 and 0.06 in.). If the backlash is above or below this level, the crown wheel to pinion clearance will have to be increased or reduced accordingly. This is achieved by slackening one adjusting nut and tightening its counterpart. As the cover spread increases above 0.10 mm (0.004 in.) after tightening an adjusting nut, the other adjusting nut must be slackened by the same amount in the opposite direction. The cover spread is checked on the front gauge over the toggle lever. As soon as the bearing cap spread and the clearance between the crown wheel and pinion are correct, the A 96 688 tool should be removed and the lockwashers fitted for the adjusting ring nuts with hexagonal bolt and spring ring. Depending on the setting of the adjusting nuts a lock plate with one or two teeth should be used.

LEFT   RIGHT

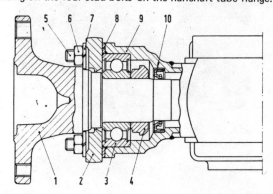

Fig. 98 Contact reflection check

a) Correct
The picture shows even contact distribution over the whole tooth contact
surface of the crown wheel, on the face and flank sides.

b) Incorrect
Left column: contact on the point and towards the middle of the teeth.
Right column: contact on the heel and towards the middle of the teeth.
Increase clearance between crown wheel and pinion by fitting a thinner shim.

c) Incorrect
Left column: contact on the tooth point restricted to the lower tooth flank.
Right column: contact on the tooth heel, restricted to the lower tooth flank.

d) Incorrect
Left column: contact on heel and towards the middle of the tooth.
Right column: contact on the point and towards the middle of the tooth.
Decrease clearance between crown wheel and pinion by fitting a thicker shim.

e) Incorrect
Left column: contact on the tooth heel, restricted to the tooth edge.
Right column: contact on the tooth point, restricted to the tooth edge.
Decrease clearance between crown wheel and pinion by fitting a thicker shim.

Checking the Tooth Mesh

After coating several teeth on the crown wheel with red lead or engineers blue, the differential should be rotated and then braked several times. The differential should then be rotated in the opposite direction and the differential gear again braked. If the contact surfaces are distributed uniformly over the entire tooth surfaces on face and flank sides this will indicate that the contact, and thus the adjustment, is correct. If the contact is inaccurate or only partial it may be necessary to increase the clearance between the crown wheel and pinion. If this is so then a thinner shim should be fitted behind the bevel pinion head, or the bevel pinion head must be brought up to a closer proximity with the crown wheel. For this purpose a thicker shim must be fitted behind the bevel pinion head. If the shim needs changing it will be necessary to dismantle once again and repeat all operations involving preloading the roller bearings and adjusting the crown wheel and pinion. This can be avoided by carefully calculating the shim requirement.

REAR AXLE — Installation and Assembly

Prior to assembling, the cleaned rear axle housing must be checked for serviceability (particularly in vehicles which have suffered accident damage). The housing must be measured in both horizontal and vertical planes and, if necessary, straightened under heat treatment or replaced completely. The rear axle is assembled on the assembly stand Arr 22 210, and is virtually the reverse sequence to the dismantling, particular attention must be paid to the following points: the gasket between the differential housing and rear axle housing must always be replaced. Tighten the bolts fastening the differential gearbox housing and the rear axle to a torque of 22 ft.lb. Fit the oil ring seals, for the rear axle halfshafts, in the seating in the axle housing. Fit the rear halfshafts after checking them for serviceability. Any damage to individual components on the rear halfshafts must be entrusted to a workshop having the correct testing and handling equipment: this is due to the assembly of the ball bearing with its pressed-on seating ring. Shafts with this type of defect must be replaced complete with the rear axle halfshaft replacement unit. The halfshaft is inserted into the halfshaft tube, after fitting the thrust plate of the brake saddle mounting on the four stud bolts on the halfshaft tube flange.

Fig. 99 Partial cross-section through the left hand halfshaft

1 Shaft
2 Brake caliper support
3 Ball bearing
4 Ball bearing retainer ring
5 Stud bolts
6 Support fastening nuts
7 Spring washer
8 Tube mounting
9 Rear axle tube
10 Ring seal

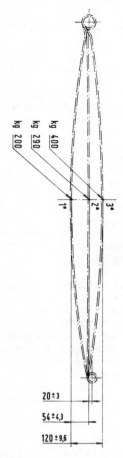

Fig. 100 Camber of main leaf in rear wheel suspension spring

kg 400
kg 290
kg 200

1° 2° 3°

20 ± 3
54 ± 4,3
120 ± 9,6

Tighten the thrust plate nuts and spring washers with a torque of 18 ft.lb. Fit the brake saddle and mount it onto the thrust plate. Tighten the two bolts on the mount to a torque of 25 ft. lb. Before attaching the rigid brake line, check the three-way connection and the flexible brake hoses, brake piping, other connections and all the hoses.

Fig. 101 Suspension system on left rear wheel

1 Spring shackle
2 Spring mount on the body
3 Thrust rod mount on rear axle housing
4 Thrust rod
5 Thrust rod fastening on body
6 Front leaf spring body fastening bolt
7 Shackle fastening bolt on leaf spring
8 Rear axle housing
9 Leaf spring
10 Self-locking shock absorber nut
11 Spring rest with flexible bush

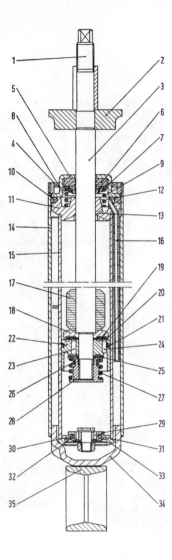

Fig. 102 Section through a rear suspension hydraulic shock absorber

1 Threaded journal for top fastening
2 Upper stop ring
3 Piston rod
4 Top locking ring on cylinder
5 Seal holder
6 Piston rod seal
7 Table spring
8 Disc spring
9 Seal thrust spring
10 Bottom seal
11 Piston rod guide bush
12 Chamber for bleeding gas bubbles
13 Capillary bore for bleeding gas bubbles
14 Outer cylinder of fluid chamber
15 Inner cylinder
16 Capillary tube for bleeding gas bubbles
17 Buffer
18 Suction valve stroke limiting plate
19 Star spring for valve
20 Suction valve
21 Piston ring
22 Piston
23 Recoil valve piston bores
24 Suction valve piston bores
25 Recoil valve
26 Spring sleeve
27 Recoil valve spring
28 Piston fastening lock
29 Compensating valve
30 Annular cavity for compensating valve
31 Pressure valve bores
32 Cumulative action pressure valve
33 Cover with compensating and pressure valve
34 Bottom cap
35 Eyelet for lower shock absorber mounting

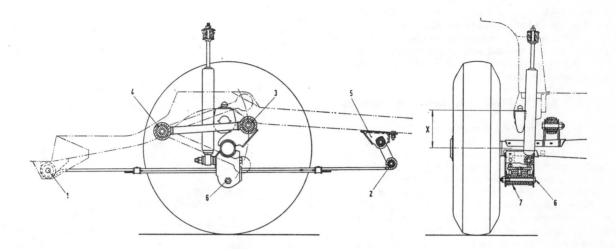

Fig. 103 Diagram for assembling and adjusting the rear wheel suspension

1 Bolt for frontal fastening of the leaf spring to the body
2 Bolt fastening leaf spring to shackle
3 Fastening point for thrust rod to rear axle
4 Fastening point for thrust rod to body
5 Spring bracket on body
6 Fastening bolt of spring rest with flexible bush on rear axle
7 Spring rest with flexible bush
X - approx. 138 mm (5.4 in.): setting measurement before clamping
     the flexible bushes (position under static load)

Before fitting the leaf springs to the rear axle housing, a careful inspection must be made of the springs with flexible bushes, the bearing with flexible bush for the spring shackles and the shims. If necessary, press new flexible bushes into the spring eyelets. If a spring leaf is broken the complete spring unit must be replaced, all damaged parts must also be replaced. Fasten the leaf spring assembly, including the mounts with the flexible bushes in the spring shackles and shim, to the rear axle housing. Tighten the spring shackle nuts to a torque of 21 ft.lb. and secure by bending up the locking tabs. Now fit the spring shackles and the rear spring mount. Push the pin through the spring mount and tighten the spring rest hand tight to the rear axle. After lifting the complete rear axle fit the leaf spring to the front spring mounts and attach it to the body through the rear spring mounts, tighten temporarily the rear spring mount nuts to a torque of 13 ft.lb. The nuts on the front spring mounts should be tightened only when the vehicle is loaded. Fit the shock absorbers, with rubber buffers fitted to the top and bottom. The lower shock absorber fastening nuts are tightened to a torque of 23 ft.lb. Attach the two thrust rods to the rear mountings on the rear axle housing and to the front mountings on the body; these bolts are also tightened only temporarily. Connect the bevel pinion flange to the rear universal shaft flange (four bolts with self-locking nuts) and tighten the wheel fastening nuts to 50 ft.lb. After connecting the brake lines, remove the wooden plugs from the brake fluid reservoir. Fill the reservoir with Fiat W 90/M (SAE 90 EP) hydraulic fluid to the edge of the filler hole - approximately 1 quart. As the temporarily finger tight nuts are to be tightened down to the prescribed torque ratings only when the vehicle is in loaded state, in order to avoid distortion and abnormal stresses, the vehicle must now be run onto a flat and lever surface. Check the tyre pressures and adjust where necessary - front 22 lb/in.², rear 25 lb/in.². As shown in the illustration for fastening the front wheel suspension system, the four supports for determining the ground clearance of the loaded vehicle (A 74 144/1/7) should now be placed in position. The two front supports with

the pin set to "A", and the rear supports with the pin set to "P", are positioned as shown in the drawing and the vehicle is then loaded until the body floor panel just rests on the supports. If these prescribed supports are not available, the heights of the supports are specified at which the body floor panel comes into contact with them. At position A - 222 mm (7.85 in.), ground clearance b = 174 ± 3 mm (6.85 ± 0.12 in.), at position P - 225 mm (8.07 in.), ground clearance C = 421 ± 3 mm (16.57 ± 0.12 in.). The body is thus loaded until these figures are reached after which the finger tight nuts can finally be tightened down to the following torque ratings: Leaf spring and shackle nuts on the spring mounts 65 ft.lb, thrust rod nuts on the body and on the rear axle 65 ft.lb. Remove the supports, bleed the brake system and adjust the handbrake.

Brakes

The system consists of disc brakes on all four wheels with servo assistance and a mechanical handbrake acting on the rear wheels.

BRAKE SYSTEM — Maintenance

In general the brake fluid should be checked and topped up at regular 6,000 mile intervals. However, the entire system must be checked thoroughly at regular intervals, with particular attention to the condition of the brake lines. Tighten all joints as necessary. Any damaged pipes and brake hoses must be replaced. Brake hoses which distend when the brake pedal is depressed must be replaced. The standard rule of thumb for brake hoses dictates that owing to natural wear and tear they must be replaced throughout at regular 5-year or 60,000 mile intervals. In addition to washing the brake system with hot water and Fiat LDC detergent, followed by a thorough blowing through with compressed air, check the thickness of brake pads and change where necessary. Bleed the brake system and adjust the handbrake cable. Otherwise no direct maintenance work is required. Adjustment between the brake pads and the discs is automatic, on the front wheels through the ring seal and on the rear wheels by the ring seal and automatic compensator device. Any further repair work which may be necessary is described in detail in the following text.

MASTER BRAKE CYLINDER — Removal and Dismantling

The master brake cylinder is secured by two M8 nuts to the brake servo unit in the engine compartment on the left spur gear side. First remove the brake fluid reservoir cover and seal off the outlet aperture with a sharpened wooden plug. Unscrew the three-way valve to the front and rear wheel brakes. Slacken the hose clamp and remove the brake fluid reservoir to brake master cylinder hose. Unscrew the brake cylinder fastening nuts and spring washers and take off the master cylinder. The brake pedal, thrust rod and servo unit remain in the vehicle. Remove the protective cap and withdraw the circlip on the piston with the aid of pointed pliers. Extract the piston, ring seal, valve carrier, valve ring and piston return spring from the brake cylinder housing. Clean all parts in brake fluid and check for wear. Smooth any scoring or corrosion on the inside surface of the brake master cylinder and the outside surface of the piston or replace if necessary; always replace the rubber valve rings. Coat the individual parts with brake fluid and assemble. Assembly is the reverse sequence to the dismantling, as is the installation. Before fitting the brake master cylinder on the servo unit the intermediate lever must be adjusted to bring the thrust rod into a position where it protrudes to 1.25 mm (0.041 to 0.049 in.) out of the contact face on the brake servo unit. After assembly the brake fluid must be topped up and the brake system bled.

BRAKE CALIPER — Removal

Clean the disc brakes with hot water and Fiat LDC detergent and then blow dry with compressed air. The brake pad thickness can now be checked by laying the arc-shaped gauge against the brake disc and pads. The brake shoes must be replaced if the

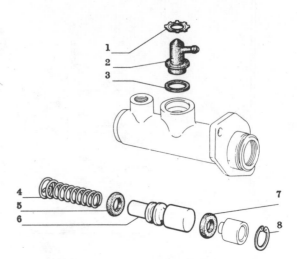

Fig. 105 Exploded view of the dismantled brake master cylinder

1 Serrated washer
2 Union
3 Ring seal
4 Spring
5 Ring seal
6 Valve mount
7 Ring seal
8 Circlip

pads have worn down to a thickness of no more than 1.5 mm (0.06 in.). To replace the brake shoes the brake caliper assembly (including saddle) must be removed, for which the spring clamp cotter on the sliding dog holder is extracted and the holder is removed. Take out the brake caliper and the leaf spring and brake shoes. If the shoes are to be refitted they must be marked before removal in order to eliminate any possibility of confusion between left and right and between front and rear. Unscrew the brake hose from the brake saddle and protect it against penetration of dirt and dust.

Fig. 104 Brake servo unit fitted

1 Brake fluid reservoir
2 Brake servo mount
3 Thrust rod actuating the brake servo
4 Intermediate lever
5 Brake servo unit
6 Vacuum line connection from carburettor
7 Hydraulic master brake cylinder
8 Fluid line connection from reservoir
9 Three-way union for brake lines
10 Brake line to rear wheel brakes
11 Brake fluid line to left hand front brake
12 Brake fluid line to right hand front brake

Fig. 106 Removing a front brake caliper

1 Brake caliper
2 Protector and air baffle plate
3 Brake shoe spring
4 Brake disc
5 Brake caliper carrier

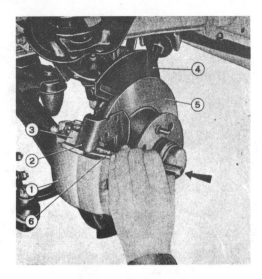

Fig. 107 Removing a front brake caliper

1 Brake caliper
2 Brake caliper carrier
3 Brake caliper holder
4 Protection and air baffle plate
5 Brake disc
6 Drift

BRAKE DISCS — Checking

The brake discs should be checked for side wobble. If necessary, before measuring the wobble, the wheel bearing play may have to be adjusted. It may prove necessary to displace the brake disc by 180° before again measuring as described. The brake disc seating must be marked before removal. Fit the gauge with its magnetic base so that the probe tip of the dial comes into contact about 10 mm (0.4 in.) from the top edge of the disc. Then turn the disc and measure the amount of deflection; the deflection should not exceed 0.15 mm (0.006 in.). If the deflection is greater, the disc must be replaced. Any scoring, damage or traces of wear must be smoothed away without using metal cutting methods. If this reduces the disc to a thickness of less than 9.5 mm (0.37 in.) it will have to be replaced.

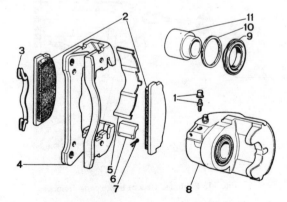

Fig. 108 Exploded view of front brake caliper and carrier, removed

1 Bleed screw with cap
2 Brake shoe
3 Brake shoe spring
4 Brake caliper carrier
5 Radial-acting leaf spring for tightening the caliper
6 Brake caliper holder
7 Cotter
8 Caliper
9 Brake piston gaiter
10 Ring seal
11 Brake piston

Replacing Brake Pistons and Ring Seals

The front wheel brake piston can be ejected from the caliper with the aid of compressed air. Set the compressed air hose on the brake fluid hose bore. On the rear wheel brakes, the piston is unscrewed with a screwdriver, using the slot provided for that purpose in the piston end. When removing and refitting the pistons, ring seals and collar seals (damaged or defective seals must be replaced) the sliding surfaces of the piston and cylinder should not display any trace of damage. Before fitting the brake shoes in the front brake caliper the brake piston must be pressed fully home into the cylinder.

When fitting the piston in the rear wheel brake caliper (screwing in clockwise) care must be taken to ensure that the line marking (A) over the rear brake caliper piston recess is at right angles to the bleed screw. This setting is extremely important because only with this arrangement is it possible to achieve efficient bleeding. The new brake shoes can now be fitted; it should be noted that brake shoes are available from a number of suppliers, but all brake shoes on the vehicle must originate from the same maker. After fitting the rear brake shoes, the clearance must be checked between the inner faces of both shoes, the clearance should not be less than 10.5 mm (0.41 in.). Replace as necessary.

BRAKE SYSTEM — Bleeding

To bleed the brake system efficiently is a job for two people unless a pressurised bleeding unit is available. Fill the brake fluid reservoir with Fiat brake fluid (blue label). Bleeding is commenced at the rear wheel and then progressed through all four wheels. Clean all the bleed screws of any dirt. Remove the rear wheel: to facilitate bleeding slacken the bleed screw and insert the brake fluid into the brake system through the threaded brake hose connection bore. Push a rubber hose over the bleed screw and suspend the free end of the bleed hose in a clean glass jar filled two thirds with Fiat brake fluid (blue label). Slacken the bleed screw by one half turn. The second person

Fig. 109 Complete brake on front right wheel

1 Caliper carrier
2 Cotter
3 Caliper holder
4 Caliper
5 Brake shoe
6 Brake shoe spring
7 Protection and air baffle plate
8 Brake disc

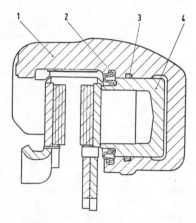

Fig. 110 Diagrammatic longitudinal section through a front
brake caliper complete with brake shoes

1 Brake caliper
2 Brake piston collar
3 Ring seal
4 Brake piston

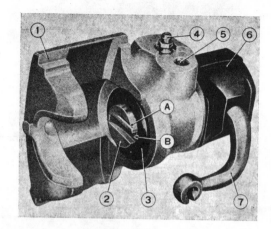

Fig. 112 Rear brake caliper, complete

1 Brake caliper
2 Brake piston
3 Collar
4 Bleed screw
5 Brake fluid feed union seating
6 Collar
7 Handbrake actuating lever
A Line marking
B Screwdriver slot

should now depress the brake pedal once strongly and then
allow it to return slowly. This procedure is repeated until no
further air bubbles appear in the glass jar. With the brake pedal
depressed tighten down the bleed screw and remove the hose;
replace the cap. The bleed screw is located on the inside of the
brake caliper. If necessary, fresh brake fluid must be used to
top up the reservoir during bleeding in order to prevent air from
getting into the system. Repeat the bleeding process on all four
wheels. The fluid pumped out of the system should not be fed
in again.

HAND BRAKE — Adjustment

Adjustment of the handbrake acting on the rear brake calipers
is fully automatic. If the handbrake does not function or if the
free travel on the hand lever is excessive this can only be
attributable to the brake cable. To remedy this, jack up the car
at the rear to allow access to the slack cable. Depress the brake
pedal two or three times sharply. Release the handbrake and
push it fully forward into its rest position and then pull it back
three clicks on the quadrant. Release the cable tensioner locknut

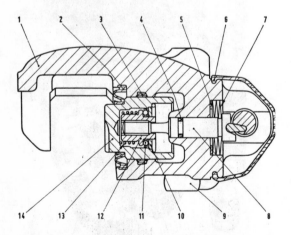

Fig. 111 Longitudinal section through a rear brake caliper

1 Brake caliper
2 Brake piston collar
3 Piston ring seal
4 Spindle ring seal
5 Disc spring washer
6 Handbrake lever collar
7 Disc spring
8 Automatic adjuster spindle
9 Handbrake actuating lever
10 Shim
11 Ball bearing
12 Automatic adjuster nut
13 Nut spring
14 Brake piston

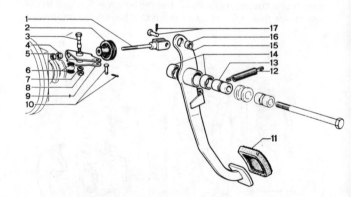

Fig. 113 Exploded view of brake pedal, removed

1 Linkage rod
2 Gaiter
3 Fulcrum pin
4 Nut & locknut for adjusting linkage rod
5 Nut & locknut for adjusting linkage rod
6 Washers
7 Washer
8 Nut
9 Intermediate lever
10 Head pin & cotter
11 Brake pedal pad
12 Return spring
13 Spacer sleeve
14 Bearing bush
15 Brake pedal
16 Bush
17 Head pin and cotter

Fig. 114 For handbrake adjustment

1 Brake cable
2 Adjusting nut & locknut
3 Adjusting balance
4 Return spring
5 Intermediate lever
6 Connecting rod

and turn the tensioner until the cable is taut and the rear wheels can no longer be turned by hand in the direction of travel then tighten the locknut. The wheels must be locked when the handbrake lever is pulled four clicks on the quadrant. If the handbrake still fails to function, after this adjustment the adjusting and lock nut on the connecting linkage must be slackened and the handbrake-actuated lever on the caliper pushed fully back. Check the mobility of the lever and remove any dirt or residue. Depress the brake pedal strongly several times until the brake pads and brake disc adopt their minimum clearance and the automatic adjuster device cancels out any play between the adjusting spindle and the actuating stud on the handbrake lever. Adjust the handbrake as detailed.

BRAKE SERVO UNIT

The Bonaldi Master Vac servo unit is mounted with a pillow block on the firewall on the left-hand side of the engine well. This unit utilises the pressure differential between the negative pressure existing in the engine intake manifold and atmospheric pressure. The unit functions in conjunction with the pressure generated in the brake master cylinder, the combined pressure then acting on the brake caliper slave cylinder. A vacuum hose leads from the engine intake manifold to the servo unit. The unit itself consists of the negative pressure cylinder, hydraulic servo cylinder and the hydraulically-controlled actuating valve.

Fig. 115 Exploded view of the hand brake actuating linkage, dismantled

1 Gaiter
2 Screw
3 Pawl rod
4 Thrust spring
5 Washer
6 Ring seal
7 Pushbutton
8 Screw & spring washer
9 Handbrake lever
10 Cotter
11 Washer
12 Gaiter
13 Connecting rod
14 Nut and washer

15 Toggle
16 Washer
17 Cotter
18 Tie rod
19 Tie plate
20 Cotter
21 Flexible bush
22 Fulcrum
23 Nut and washer
24 Return spring
25 Tie rod nuts
26 Equaliser
27 Brake cable
28 Nut and spring washer

Fig. 116 Longitudinal section through brake master cylinder & servo unit

1 Brake master cylinder housing
2 Seating of 3-way union for brake lines
3 Equalising bore
4 Brake fluid feed bore
5 Hydraulic piston spring
6 Valve ring seal
7 Valve ring carrier
8 Ring seal
9 Hydraulic piston
10 Front seal
11 Seating for connecting the negative pressure line from the carburettor
12 Hydraulic piston actuating pushrod
13 Front vacuum chamber
14 Negative pressure channel
15 Control piston
16 Seal centering ring
17 Valve
18 Valve disc
19 Thrust spring disc (23)
20 Filter
21 Valve pushrod
22 Cap
23 Valve piston return spring
24 Valve return spring
25 Disc for valve (17)
26 Rear seal
27 Seal
28 Disc
29 Rear chamber
30 Thrust washer
31 Diaphgram
32 Piston
33 Front cover
34 Return spring
35 Washer
36 Guide bush

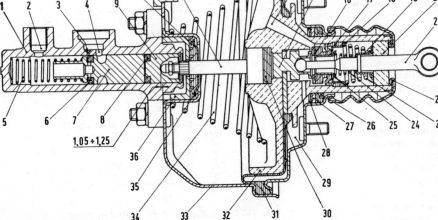

1,05 ÷ 1,25

Fig. 117 Brake servo system, fitted

1 Servo system bracket
2 Toggle arm
3 Tie rod
4 Adjusting nut
5 Brake servo
6 Hydraulic master brake cylinder

In the event of failure of the unit or if no negative pressure is available, the brakes are actuated by the normal brake system, but the required brake pedal pressure is about 1/3rd greater. The servo unit is virtually maintenance-free, merely requiring replacement of the filter insert positioned at the back of the unit at regular 30,000 mile intervals.

BRAKE SERVO UNIT — Checking

The functional efficiency of the unit can be checked without any special testing device. With the engine switched off and the gears in neutral, the brake pedal is depressed several times to eliminate the negative pressure in the servo unit. When the brake pedal is depressed atmospheric air enters through the outer air valve and the negative pressure is reduced through the negative pressure hose to the exhaust manifold. Now hold the brake pedal down and start the engine. If the brake pedal tends to sink further without added foot pressure this indicates that the negative pressure system is in order. If the pedal fails to sink further the system is not in order. It will then be necessary to check the negative pressure line, tighten the connections to the unit and the manifold and replace any defective hose where appropriate. If the brake pedal recoils upward, this indicates either that the ball valve in the hydraulic cylinder is not sealing correctly or that the diaphragm is defective. In such cases the brake servo unit must be replaced.

Electrical Equipment

ALTERNATOR

A Fiat Type A 12-M-124/12/42M alternator with rectifier is fitted as standard equipment. The rotating field in the outer, with 3-phase AC winding, generates a three-phase current which is rectified through silicon diodes in a bridge circuit. When the engine is started the excitation current is fed from the battery through the voltage regulator RC1/12B to the field. The regulator is fitted with vibrating contacts and has two regulating steps and is virtually maintenance-free. The field, which revolves in the armature, is fed with current through two sliprings and two carbon brushes. With fluctuating engine speed and load conditions the alternator voltage is regulated to just above battery voltage. Therefore, the output of the alternator increases in proportion to the load up to the rated output level consequently no current is drawn from the battery. The charge

monitoring relay indicates faults in the alternator or voltage regulator by full or flickering illumination of the lamp in the dashboard.
The alternator offers the following advantages by comparison with the conventional DC generator:

1. the alternator is much lighter than a DC generator of equivalent output and requires much less space;
2. even when the engine is idling the alternator still supplies output to the battery, thus ensuring more efficient battery charging - particularly important in dense traffic;
3. as only two carbon brushes are fitted to transmit the excitation current to the sliprings a higher standard of operating reliability is achieved, together with longer periods between servicing.

ALTERNATOR — Maintenance

The two ball bearings are permanently lubricated. The sliprings must be cleaned at 36,000 mile intervals. The brushes must be inspected and the complete brush holder replaced as necessary. The vee belt tension must be checked at 6,000 mile intervals and tightened as necessary. A new vee belt must be checked after the first 3,000 miles to ensure correct tension.

Faults in Generating System

The battery warning lamp will light up when the engine is idling if the battery is exhausted. The lamp will extinguish if the accelerator is depressed. If the lamp lights up while driving this can be attributed to one of the following faults:

Alternator not charging

Slack vee belt, open circuit in the charging or earthing circuit or the excitation current circuit. Field winding open circuit. Faulty regulator or poor earthing. Defective diode. Armature winding or diode carrier plate earthed.

Weak or irregular charging current

Slack vee belt, loose contact in charging current circuit, commutator brushes worn or not bedding correctly on the sliprings, faulty regulator, defective diode. Short circuit in the field winding, stator winding open circuit, coil shorted or earthing out.

Excessive charging current

Faulty regulator, poor connection between regulator and alternator.

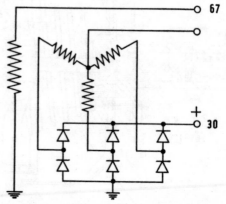

Fig. 118 Circuit diagram of the A12M-124/12/42M alternator

Warning Lamp Remains Alight, even at high revs, or flickers after extinguishing at certain alternator rev speeds or also when loads are switched on.

A positive or negative diode rectifier shorted or open circuit. Brushes worn or jammed. Charging or earthing circuit open-circuit. Excitation current open circuit. Faulty regulator (dirt or wear). Warning lamp sensor faulty.

Warning lamp failure with engine running

Warning lamp bulb burned out. Charging indicator current open circuit, faulty steering lock/ignition switch contacts, faulty warning lamp sensor.

Warning lamp lights feebly with engine at high speed

Broken lead, 8-amp fuse for the warning lamp sensor blown.

Loud noises in alternator

Severe vee belt wear, loose pulley, misalignment in pulleys, rectifier diode shorted.

Squeaks or rattles in alternator

Faulty ball bearings, loose alternator mounting bracket. To remedy faults in the alternator system any defective parts must be replaced with new parts. Apart from the amount of time and experience required, special devices, equipment and testing rigs will be needed, so that repair will frequently prove more expensive than new parts. Consequently faulty voltage regulators, battery warning lamp sensors or alternators must be replaced by new parts which must be of genuine Fiat origin. Nevertheless a few hints are provided for checking and repair and the necessary measurement values for testing equipment are shown under "Technical Data" (Table of Dimensions and Adjustments).
It is essential to note the following points when working on the alternator generating systems:

1. **Never** disconnect the regulator or battery when the alternator is running, as this will cause irreparable damage to the alternator.
2. **Never** touch the exciter coil leads of the alternator, the voltage regulator or the connecting lead to earth.
3. **Never** change the regulator lead.
4. **Never** start up the regulator without connecting with the negative lead of the alternator, as this will damage the regulator.
5. **Never** attempt to remove the alternator without disconnecting the battery.
6. When installing the battery ensure that the negative terminal is connected to earth and ensure good connection with the terminal clamps.
7. If, in exceptional instances, the battery is recharged without removal, it is essential to detach the positive and negative leads.
   The positive terminal of the charger is to be connected to the positive terminal of the battery and the negative terminal of the battery with its counterpart on the charger.
8. Any wrong connection of leads will destroy the rectifier diodes and the voltage regulator.
9. **Never** use a testing lamp connected direct to a mains supply (110 or 220 volts) Only an 0.1 amp test lamp supplied by a 12 V battery may be used.
10. Disconnect the positive and negative battery leads when carrying out assembly or welding work on the vehicle or when fast-charging the battery.

ALTERNATOR — Checking in Position

Flickering of the battery warning lamp is an indication of existing faults. To trace faults in the alternator system, which are less frequently encountered than with conventional dynamos, a mini-tester with Ohm meter and Voltmeter or a testing lamp of 0.1 amp 12 V must be used. When the alternator is still in the vehicle only the charge output can be checked. If this proves inadequate the alternator will have to be removed and a check made of the brush holders, rotor and rectifier diodes. Before proceeding to test the charge output the vee belt tension and the battery must first be checked. Ensure that all lead connections and terminals have good, secure contact.

ALTERNATOR — Output

If inadequate output from the alternator is not attributable to a slack vee belt the battery terminal voltage must be measured with a voltmeter. After starting the engine the voltage should rise to the rated 12 V level and at 950 ± 50 rev/min. the voltage at the battery should be about 13 Volts. At 1000 to 5000 rev/min the current flow to the battery should be about 42 amps. If these values are not reached the alternator must be removed and the various components checked in a dismantled state.

ALTERNATOR — Removal, Dismantling, Repair and Installation

Disconnect the battery and the alternator connecting lead. Slacken the alternator bracket and adjusting rail. Unscrew the fastening bolt. Remove the alternator and the vee belt. After unscrewing the self-locking nut from the alternator shaft, remove the washer and draw off the pulley. Take the fitting key out of the shaft. Unscrew the negative brush holder from the drive bearing and remove the brush. Unscrew the fastening bolt of the positive brush holder on the mount on the rectifier side and remove the brush. Unscrew the two connector fastening bolts for the diode and current phase ends and take the current phase ends out of the grooves. Now remove the three clamping bolts from the bearing flanges and the standing armature. Remove the bearing flange on the drive side and the bearing flange with the diode rectifiers. Remove the field with its exciter winding out of the armature. Draw off the roller bearing from the armature on the drive side (using a special extractor tool). The rectifier plate can now be unscrewed from the bearing flange on the underside of the rectifiers. The defective diode rectifiers are now pressed out of their seatings on the bearing flange or carrier plate, using the special tool supplied for that purpose. With the aid of an extractor tool draw the roller bearing out of the field.

Checking the Carbon Brushes and Brush Holder

Check the carbon brushes for good contact with the copper sliprings. Check the ease of movement of the brushes in the brush guides and, if necessary, clean the brush holder with trichlorethylene. To check current passage lay one probe tip of the tester on the insulated carbon and connect the other tip with the brush holder. In both cases the resistance must be zero, even if the brushes are moved during the test. For an insulation test each probe tip of the tester is placed on a brush and the resistance should be infinite.

Checking the Rotor

If the sliprings are dirty or greasy they must be cleaned with a cloth soaked in trichlorethylene. Any scoring of the rings should be removed with finest emery cloth. For an insulation test one probe tip is connected to the alternator earth and the other should touch against one of the sliprings. There should be no needle deflection. To check the stator winding an Ohmeter must be used. The two probe tips are touched against one slip-ring each. At normal temperature of 20° C (68°F) the Ohm-meter should show 4.5 ± 0.1 Ohms. If the resistance is zero this indicates a short in the stator winding. If the resistance is lower than the figure given, a short is present in individual stator windings. If the resistance is higher than indicated then the rotor winding is open circuit.

Checking the Winding of the Standing Armature

In the event of a short circuit, the damaged point can usually be recognised from the severe heating, which will be readily evident on visual inspection. Otherwise lay a probe tip of the tester on one phase end and the other probe tip on the armature plates. The tester should now show a reading. If a passage of current is indicated, the coil is earthed and the armature must be replaced. The windings of the other phases must be checked in the same manner.

Checking the Diodes

A precise test of the diodes covering forward current and ascertaining the reverse current is possible only with the aid of a special tester. Otherwise a standard tester will have to be used. One probe tip of the unit is laid on the connection lead of the diode and the other tip against the metal cap of the diode, then the probe tips are interchanged. In both tests a forward current in only one direction should be indicated. If the unit shows current passage in both directions this denotes a short in the diode. If there is no passage in one directon the diode is open circuit. The remaining diodes must be checked in the same manner. If a diode is found to be defective it must be pressed out with a special tool and the seating must be reamed out with a special reamer, as the replacement diode has a slight oversize on the metal cap. The replacement diode must be pressed in with the aid of the special press and drift designed for that purpose. Never strike a diode with a hammer. Ensure that the flexible wire of the diode lies correctly in the groove in the connector, so that the wire needs no bending after the diode is pressed in.

Fig. 120 Alternator fitted, partial section

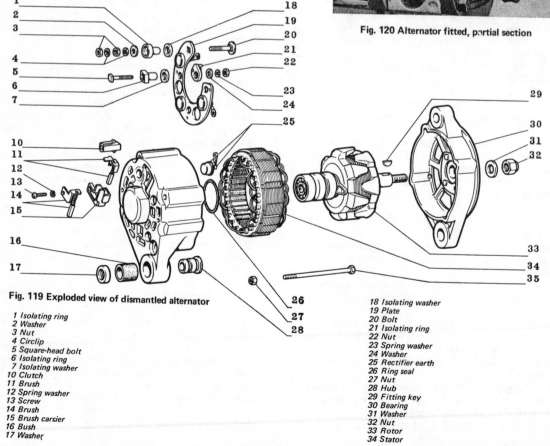

Fig. 119 Exploded view of dismantled alternator

1 Isolating ring
2 Washer
3 Nut
4 Circlip
5 Square-head bolt
6 Isolating ring
7 Isolating washer
10 Clutch
11 Brush
12 Spring washer
13 Screw
14 Brush
15 Brush carrier
16 Bush
17 Washer

18 Isolating washer
19 Plate
20 Bolt
21 Isolating ring
22 Nut
23 Spring washer
24 Washer
25 Rectifier earth
26 Ring seal
27 Nut
28 Hub
29 Fitting key
30 Bearing
31 Washer
32 Nut
33 Rotor
34 Stator

ALTERNATOR — Assembly

Assembly is virtually the reverse sequence to the dismantling. Particular attention should be paid to the following points: clean all parts with a clean, dry cloth and blow off with compressed air. Grease the front and rear roller bearings with Fiat MR 3 grease. Insert the field in the standing armature and fit the bearing flange. Slide in the three clamping bolts. Tighten the nuts with a torque of 2 ft.lb. With the machine standing vertically, the lower insulating plate is inserted in the bearing flange. Fit the current phase ends in the grooves in the insulating disc. Now lay the flexible wires of two diodes in position and fasten the spring plates by bending over the tabs. Fit the upper insulating plate and clamping plate and tighten the connector with the two crosshead screws. Tighten the self-locking nut in front of the vee belt pulley to a torque of 30ft.lb.

STARTER

The Fiat 125 is fitted with an E 100 1.2/12 mechanical gear shift starter, constructed as a right-hand rotation, main current motor. The ignition is switched on after inserting the ignition key in the ignition starter switch or in the ignition/steering column lock ("O") (optional extra) and turning the key to the right to "1". When the key is turned further to the right to

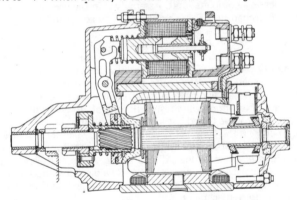

Fig. 121 Fiat E 100-1, 3/12 starter, in sectional elevation

"2" the solenoid switch on the commutator bearing is triggered and actuates the starting motor shift lever to bring the drive pinion forward to mesh with the starter ring gear. The ignition starter switch must be replaced as a unit in the event of mechanical or electrical faults. After the engine has started, the ignition key is released and returns automatically to position "1" (ignition position). If the key is not released after the engine has started the engine will revolve at a faster rate than the pinion and cause the pinion drive to freewheel. The freewheel rollers run in the pinion and the freewheel hub is provided with four angled milled recesses for the shaft splines. The pinion is entrained by the shaft when the hub revolves in a right-hand direction. The hub moves on the armature spindle in spiral grooves. At regular 20,000 mile intervals the carbon brushes must be checked for wear. Dirty or oily brushes must be cleaned and replaced if unduly worn. Clean the commutator with a dry cloth. If the commutator is out-of-round (maximum permissible amount 0.01 mm (0.0004 in.) or shows traces of scoring the starter must be taken out and overhauled by an approved Fiat agent. Clean the coarse thread of the pinion drive and lubricate it with Fiat VS 10 W oil. Lubricate the bearing bushes and pinion bush with engine oil. Grease the centre steel washer on the driver for the pinion track, using Fiat MR 3 grease.

In the event of faults in the starter system it is possible that the origin can be attributable to other parts of the general system, including the battery, leads, solenoid switch, etc. The headlamps can be used as a means of indicating and localising the fault.

1. Switch on the headlamps with the engine stationary, the headlamps must display a full normal cone of light. If they do not, the battery must be checked to ensure an adequate charge and the terminal poles on the battery must be clean and secure. If necessary trace the fault in the charging system as described above.
2. With the headlamps switched on the starter is actuated; the following should occur:
   a) the light extinguishes - indicating faulty connections between the battery and starter.
   b) the light fades, the starter turns only slowly and comes to rest. The engine is unable to turn efficiently owing to the low temperature or owing to heavy oil viscosity, or due to a large voltage drop. Battery terminals are loose or oxidised, bearings worn, armature spindle distorted, winding and earthing shorts in the starter.
   c) the light remains bright but the starter turns only slowly or remains stationary - either the solenoid switch connecting terminals are loose or the regulator switch contacts are oxidised. Ignition starter switch faulty. Brushes worn or jammed.

BATTERY

At regular 6,000 mile intervals the lug head and battery terminals must be cleaned and the battery voltage must be checked. This battery maintenance is important as starting efficiency and general operation of the vehicle depend on the condition of the battery. The battery must be kept clean and dry. Clean off the surface with a brush, examining closely for cracks through which battery fluid could escape. Tighten the battery terminals and coat them lightly with heavy petroleum jelly. In Spring and Autumn the battery must be checked for electrolyte level and density and charge level.

BATTERY — Electrolyte Level

The electrolyte level must be checked at 1,500 mile intervals,

or more frequently in Summer. As only water is lost through evaporation and natural disintegration only distilled water may be used for topping up. This must always be done when the battery is cold (20°C) (68°F). The electrolyte must be filled to the bottom rim of the lower filler hole in each cell. Only if excessive electrolyte has been lost through accidental spillage should diluted sulphuric acid of equivalent density be used for topping up.

Checking the Electolyte Density

To check the charge the acid density is measured with a hydrometer. Depending on the specific gravity the reading is shown by the height of the float.

Charged battery:	32° Bé or 1.28 sg
Half-charged battery:	27° Bé or 1.25 sg
Discharged battery:	18° Bé or 1.23 sg

BATTERY — Recharging

In normal operation the battery is recharged by the charging system in the car. In special circumstances there is no objection to rapid charging of a battery in good condition provided this

is done in accordance with the maker's instructions.
When a battery fitted in the car is being recharged with an
auxiliary charger it is essential to shut off the battery from the
charger circuit, as otherwise the diode rectifiers will be damaged
irreparably.

DISTRIBUTOR

The Marelli distributor has the following characteristics:
Initial retard: 10°
Centrifugal timing adjustment advance   24°

Contact-Breaker Maintenance

The contact points actuated by the four cam studs interrupt the
primary current fed from the battery to the ignition coil. The
capacitor coupled in series with the contacts prevents arcing. A
high-voltage current is generated in the secondary winding of
the coil and passed via the distributor to the sparking plug.
Points which are dirty or slightly scorched must be cleaned or
smoothed with a clean contact file. Emery cloth should never
be used for this purpose. The cam must be greased lightly to
reduce wear of the fibre blocks to a minimum. The tip of the
rotor arm and the brass studs in the distributor cap are subject
to a certain amount of wear (maximum wear 0.3 mm (0.012 in.)
and it may prove necessary to replace the distributor cap and
rotor arm. If the sliding member is badly worn or the point gap
exceeds 0.4 mm (0.016 in.) or the fixed contact adjusting
screw cannot be tightened further, the moving contact assembly
will have to be replaced. If the distributor shaft shows
excessive play, the shaft or the complete distributor will have
to be replaced. Check the return springs of the centrifugal
governor and, if necessary, replace the springs with genuine
Fiat spares. Clean the inside and outside of the distributor cap
and keep it dry to prevent arcing or creepage of current.
Before refitting the distributor cap check the thrust spring and
carbon brush. Smooth the carbon brush contact surface with
a fine file or replace both parts if necessary.

Adjusting the Contact-Breaker Gap

Take off the distributor cap and rotor arm. Turn the crankshaft
to revolve the distributor shaft until the cam lifts the contact
breaker arm to maximum clearance. Slacken the two screws for

Fig. 122 Distributor on engine

1 Distributor cap fastening screws

fastening the contact breaker base. Insert the screwdriver in the
plate aperture and turn the plate until the gap is 0,42 to 0,48
mm (0,016 to 0,0190 in.). After tightening down the contact
breaker base recheck the point gap with a feeler gauge. After
adjusting the points the timing will also have to be reset. Check
the distributor shaft lubrication and, if necessary, feed in a few
drops of Fiat engine oil into the shaft lubrication bore.
In addition to checking with the feeler gauge the gap setting
should also be checked with a closing angle gauge, as this gives
a more accurate adjustment. Connect up the gauge and tacho-
meter in accordance with maker's instructions. At idling speed
the closing angle should be 66% ± or 60° ± 3°. An unduly wide
point gap indicates an excessively large closing angle, while a
tight gap denotes a small closing angle. If necessary, the closing
angle must be corrected by adjusting the point gap at idling
speed.

Replacing the Points

If the points are badly scorched (faulty capacitor) beyond
smoothing with a file or beyond further adjustment, then the
points themselves will have to be replaced. Take off the distributor cap, the rotor arm, low-tension lead and disconnect the
capacitor. Unscrew the contact plate complete with points and
replace as a complete unit. Assembly is in the reverse sequence
to the dismantling. Set the point gap and adjust the timing.

Checking the Capacitor

A faulty capacitor is shown by badly scorched points or weak
ignition sparks. An efficient test for disruptive discharge,
insulation losses and adequate capacitance is possible only with
the aid of an appropriate tester. In general, however, the
capacitor can be tested with a DC testing lamp. The capacitor
is in order if the lamp lights up once briefly and them remains
out when the probe tips are applied. The capacitor has charged.
Then, after a few seconds, discharge the capacitor by connecting terminal 1 to the capacitor case. The discharge should take
place with a strong arcing spark. Only genuine Fiat spares should
be used for replacement.
After fitting the new capacitor the point gap and timing will
have to be reset.

TIMING — Setting

If the auxiliary shaft has been removed and the distributor taken
out for overhaul the timing will have to be reset.
After setting the engine timing and tightening the drive belt
adopt the following procedure:

1. Set the cylinder to compression stroke: the intake and
   exhaust valves are closed. The notches around the periphery
   of the pulley on the crankshaft must be aligned with the 1st
   rib on the timing box cover. Remove the distributor cap and
   turn the distributor shaft until the rotor arm points to the
   ignition contact of the 1st cylinder. Check that the point
   gaps are 0,42 to 0,48 mm (0,016 to 0,019 in.). In this
   position the contact points should just be opening. Now,
   without changing the setting of the distributor shaft, insert
   the distributor in the neck bearing on the engine and engage
   the shaft in the drive gear teeth. Fasten the distributor with
   the retaining plate (nut and serrated washer). Fit the
   distributor cap and attach the leads to the coil and the
   sparking plugs. The number of each plug lead is on top of
   the distributor cap. The timing setting and automatic timing
   adjustment can be checked with the aid of the Ap 5030
   stroboscope and the Ap 96 304 plate fastened to the timing
   box cover.

Fig. 123 Timing adjustment

1 10° advance
2 5° advance
3 0° advance

800 revs	10°
1700 revs	10 to 18°
3600 revs	27 to 33°
4500 revs	32°

SPARKING PLUGS

Bosch, Marelli and Champion plugs are suitable for the 125 A 000 engine. (See Table of Dimensions and Adjustments for details).

Spark Plug Maintenance and Testing

The plugs must be checked at regular 3,000 mile intervals for appearance, electrode gap and performance. Before unscrewing the plugs make sure that there is no dirt in the plug recess. Washers, screws, stones or similar items falling accidentally into the plug bore can cause serious damage to the valves, valve seatings or cylinder head when the engine is started. A visual inspection of the plug can give indications of suitability and functional efficiency, carburettor adjustment, state of mixture and the condition of the engine (piston, etc.). In general the following apply:

Fig. 124 Distributor fitted, with cap removed

1 Lubrication port for distributor shaft
2 Recess for adjusting the breaker points
3 Distributor fastening nut
4 Bracket for fastening distributor to engine
5 Plate clamp screw
6 Contact points

Insulator: medium brown
Electrodes: blank or grey

Functional state: plug, carburettor, engine in order

Insulator: black or sooty
Electrodes: black or sooty

Functional state: over-rich mixutre, over-wide gap

Insulator: light grey, white
Electrodes: grey, fine molten beads

Functional efficiency: lean mixture, plug loose or leaking, valves not closing fully

Insulator: oily
Electrodes: oily

Functional state: leaking piston, plug cutting out

When using lead-additive fuels the insulator will be burned grey in its normal state. Clean off any deposits between the porcelain insulator of the central electrode and the plug casing, preferably with the aid of a sand blaster on the plug testing stand. Check the electrode gap with a feeler gauge and bend the outer electrode to obtain the correct gap. For Bosch Marelli and Champion plugs the gap is 0,5 to 0,6 mm (0,020 to 0,023 in.). When fitting, tighten the plugs to 25 to 30 ft.lb.

HEADLAMPS

Twin headlamps are fitted as standard. On high beam all four headlamps are lit uniformly and on low beam only the two outer headlamps are lit. Consequently the high and low beam adjustments must be carried out independently. Headlamp adjustment is carried out quickest and most reliably with the aid of a commercial type of headlamp adjuster. If this is not available the following procedure must be adopted: run the empty vehicle with prescribed tyre pressures (front 20 lb/in.^{2} rear 24 lb/in.^{2}) onto a flat, level surface about 5 yards from a wall in shadow. The centre line of the car must be perpendicular in relation to the wall. Draw two pairs of vertical lines on the wall, a-a and a'-a', A being spaced at 31 inches and A' at 44 inches. These lines correspond to the centre spacing between the inner and outer headlamps and must be equidistant from the car centre. Now two horizontal lines b-b and b'-b' are drawn at the following heights:

B = C minus (0.45 in.) with new cars or cars fitted with an overhauled suspension system
B = C minus (0.35 in.) with cars fitted with run-in suspension
B' = C minus (0.2 in.) with cars fitted with both new and run-in suspension

The height C corresponds to the height of the headlamp centre from the ground.
Now switch on the low beam (outer headlamps) and adjust the headlamps vertically with screw B, and horizontally with screw A so that the horizontal light-dark limit coincides with the line b-b and the angle points of the light-dark limit(line angled approximately 15° upward) coincides with the intersecting points Pe of the vertical line a'-a' and the horizontal line b-b. Switch on the high beam and adjust the elevation and lateral setting with screws B and A so that the beam of light of each headlamp lies on the corresponding intersecting point Pi of the vertical line a-a and the horizontal line b'-b'. Increasing the

distance between A and A' by 10 inches, corresponding to an overall deviation of 3°, is permissible.

Replacing the Filament Bulbs

The filament bulbs may only be replaced by those of equivalent type and wattage. When fitting new bulbs they should not be held in the bare hand but handled with a clean cloth or tissue.

Replacing the Headlamp Units

Unscrew the headlamp fitting. Stretch the headlamp insert spring holder and disengage the insert. Disconnect the insert from its plug coupling and release the lamp holding springs. Note the position of the locating pin when inserting the bi-filament lamp in the headlamp insert.

Front Side and Flasher Lamps

Unscrew the lens plate right and left, push and twist the bulbs out of the bayonet fitting and replace.

Side Flasher Lamps

Press the lamp fitting out of the mudguard from the inside, disengage the bulb from its bayonet fitting and replace.

Tail, Brake & Rear Directional Flasher Lamp

Unscrew the screws from the bottom of the lens plate and remove the lens plates. Push and twist the tail, brake and directional flasher bulbs out of their bayonet sockets and replace as necessary.

Replacing the Registration Plate Bulb

Take off the rubber cap and withdraw the socket lamp fitting in the centre of the bumper. Push and twist the bulb out of its bayonet socket and replace.

Replacing the Reversing Bulb

Unscrew the screws on the right and left of the lens plate and take off the lens plate. Push and twist the bulb out of its socket and replace.

Replacing the Front Interior Courtesy Light Bulb

Open the flap on top of the rear view mirror and draw the lens plate downward to remove. Take the tubular bulb out of the clamp spring on the lens plate and replace.

Replacing the Side Interior Courtesy Light Bulbs

Take the rectangular lens plate with lamp fitting out of the door post, remove the socket bulb and replace.

Replacing the Dashboard Instrument Cluster Bulbs

Remove the complete instrument cluster after depressing a clamp spring on the inside of the dashboard. Take out the speedometer drive shaft and the two electrical socket leads. The bulbs can then be removed from their bayonet sockets and replaced.

FUSES

The electrical system is protected by 9 cartridge type 8-amp and one 16-amp fuses, which are positioned below the dashboard on the right-hand side. If a fuse is ruptured it is not sufficient merely to replace the fuse; it is essential to trace the cause of the short circuit. Tracing is greatly facilitated by the circuit diagram. Under no circumstances whatsoever should fuses be repaired provisionally with silver paper or wire, as this will merely result in serious damage elsewhere in the wiring system.

Protected Current Circuits

Front interior courtesy light	Fuse A
Side interior courtesy lights	16 amps
Horn	16 amps
Hand lamp socket	16 amps
Cigar lighter	16 amps
Clock	16 amps
Engine compartment lamp	Fuse B
Dashboard lighting	8 amps
Directional flasher	8 amps
Brake lamps	8 amps
Windscreen wiper	8 amps
Heater and ventilation fan motor	8 amps
Left high beam headlamp	Fuse C
High beam warning lamp	8 amps
Right high beam headlamp	Fuse D (8 amps)
Left low beam headlamp	Fuse E (8 amps)
Right low beam headlamp	Fuse F (8 amps)
Left front side lamp	Fuse G
Front & rear lamp pilot light	8 amps
Right tail lamp	8 amps
Left registration plate lamp	8 amps
Baggage boot lamp	8 amps
Reversing lamp	8 amps
Right front side lamp	Fuse H
Left tail lamp	8 amps
Right registration plate lamp	8 amps
Cigar lighter courtesy lamp	8 amps
Handbrake warning lamp	Fuse I (8 amps)
Oil pressure warning lamp	8 amps
Battery warning lamp & relay	8 amps
Water temperature gauge	8 amps
Fuel gauge	8 amps
Fan	8 amps
Glove compartment courtesy lamp	8 amps
Automatic choke warning lamp	8 amps
Voltage regulator	Fuse L
Alternator exciter coil	8 amps

The following are not protected by fuses: the ignition, starter, battery charge (except the voltage regulator and battery warning lamp) and the high beam relay.

Body

The all-steel unitary body consists primarily of the floor assembly, front panel, right and left door frames, right and left side wall with mudguards, windscreen frame, roof and internal bracing and bonnet and boot lid. These components are formed of pressed sheet steel panels joined by electrical spot welding. The grid structure of the body produces an integral and durable construction with distortion-resistant passenger compartment and impact-damping front and rear sections. Before commencing body repair work, following an accident, a thorough visual inspection must be carried out to ascertain whether the damage is of slight, medium or serious character. Slight panel damage without affecting load-bearing members can be rectified with the aid of a hydraulic jack and by hand. Beaten areas and any welds can be finished with a file and surface grinder. Any residual recesses or dents can be tinned out or finished with plastic filler compound. After finally finishing the area with the surface grinder the spray coatings can be applied. At this juncture it is worth mentioning that the accessories trade carries plastic compound and fibreglass panel kits with which it is possible to repair and patch fairly large holes and damaged areas. More serious or extensive repair work to the body should be entrusted to qualified workshop specialists. Distorted and defective panels must be detached from their main members with the aid of a chisel or cutting grinder. The fitting of a new panel is more practical and economical than repairing the damaged panel, furthermore, this method restores the original strength and rigidity to the body structure. If the body of a vehicle involved in an accident has been distorted to such an extent that the connection points between engine and chassis are no longer in line, the floor section will have to be redressed on a straightening jig with hydraulic jacks until the dimensions for the floor assembly and the mounting points for the front and rear suspension systems correspond to the floor assembly diagram. After completing body repair work all weld seams and other untight points must be packed out with filler compound under pressure.

Replacing Weatherstrip

Remove the old door weatherstripping and any traces of old adhesive with the aid of rags and washing petrol. Any rusty patches must be carefully isolated from the adhesive surfaces: do not touch the adhesive surface by hand. Clean the new weatherstrip of any traces of protective coating and clean the adhesive areas with a rag soaked in washing petrol; leave them to dry thoroughly. Use a brush to apply standard commercial adhesive to the door and coat the adhesive surface of the weatherstrip with adhesive. Allow the rubber adhesive coat to set in accordance with the maker's instructions and then apply each weatherstrip section carefully and without stretching. Before closing the door for the first time the weatherstrip must have been allowed to adhere firmly. No attempt should be made to test the bond by pulling at the weatherstrip, as the cement does not cure completely until some days have passed. If a section of weatherstripping has come away on the door or elsewhere on the body it should be pulled away a little further and then cemented down thoroughly.

WINDOWS and WINDSCREEN — Removal and Installation

Removal and refitting of the windows does not pose any particular problems provided the following procedure is observed: push the bottom centre clip to one side and press the windscreen bead carefully out of the rubber channel with the aid of a thin, flat hardwood wedge, after which the beading can be taken by hand out of the rubber frame. Using the hardwood wedge, detach the rubber frame from the body and apply flat hand pressure from inside to push the rubber frame out to the edges of the windscreen. Support the windscreen from outside by hand to prevent it from slipping out of its seating. Remove the old sealing compound from the body and the rubber frame, if the latter is suitable for re-use. Fitting is carried out as follows: draw the rubber frame onto the windscreen. Coat the beading groove lightly with petroleum jelly. As an assembly aid a curtain cord (3 to 4 mm thick) (0.12 to 0.16 in.) is laid in the outer groove in the rubber frame so that the cord ends cross at the bottom centre of the windscreen. Apply soapy water to the body channel to facilitate fitting of the rubber frame bead into the body frame. Two people are needed to fit the windscreen into place. Insert the screen and rubber frame as a unit from outside into the bottom of the windscreen aperture. Press the windscreen down hard to ensure that the rubber engages correctly on the bottom edge. Now one man stands to the right and the other to the left and each grips one end of the cord by reaching through the open door window. Pulling out the two cord ends causes the rubber bead to slip over the body channel. Now pull the cord uniformly around through to the top centre edge of the windscreen, at the same time striking the windscreen gently by hand to bring it into correct seating. Fit the chrome beading and then use the pressure pump to feed sealing compound in between the rubber frame and body and the frame and windscreen. Surplus compound can be trimmed away with a scraper and the windscreen can then be wiped carefully clean with a pad of wadding soaked in petrol.

WINDOW — Rear

Removal is carried out as described for the windscreen. When fitting, insert the cord so that the ends cross at the top of the frame. Insert the top edge of the window in its aperture in the body. When pulling out the cord take care to ensure that the rubber is correctly seated on the outside and is not damaged by the cord. Fit joint buckles in the bottom corners and then seal the window as described for the windscreen.

WINDOWS — Front and Rear Doors

Wind down the door window. Remove the clip behind the window crank cover ring and take off the crank handle. Unscrew the armrest (2 crosshead screws on the front door and 3 on the rear door). Pull off the inside door panel which is clipped to the door. Take out the window crank assembly. Unscrew the window guide rails and lift out of the frame; remove the bottom bead. Pull the window inward and lift it out of the door aperture. Take the window out of the rubber channel in the bottom window rail. When fitting the new window, coat the rubber channel with French chalk or talcum. The window is refitted in reverse sequence to removal.

Removing and Fitting the Front Door Quarterlight

Wind down the front window. Unscrew the two crosshead screws fastening the quarterlight frame to the door frame. Remove the door panel as described above. Take out the vertical guide rail, pull out the window with its frame and rubber weatherstrip to the rear; detach the window from the rubber weatherstrip. The window is framed in blank beading, which is seated in a rubber weatherstrip frame within the quarterlight aperture. Position the frame around the window and push it on by hand as far as possible. Lay the window on a soft underlay and tap the chrome frame gently onto the window with a rubber mallet: take care to avoid breakage. Possibly gentle pressure by hand will be sufficient to seat the glass firmly in place. The quarterlight is then fitted in the reverse sequence to its removal.

Removing and Fitting the Rear Fixed Quarterlight

Wind down the rear side window. Remove the clips behind the cover ring on the crank handle and take off the handle. Remove the chrome ring on the door handle by drawing it forward over the handle lever. Unscrew the armrest (three crosshead screws) and remove the inside panel which is clipped to the door. Remove the vertical guide rail and draw the window with its frame and rubber weatherstrip with the aid of an awl. The new window is fitted in reverse sequence to its removal.

Tightening Torques

The specified tightening torques are valid for threads and contact surfaces in dry state.

Engine		ft.lb
Self-locking fastening bolts on main bearing cap	M 10 x 1.25	59.3
Oil sump fastening bolts	M 6 x 1	5.8
Cylinderhead bolts	M 10 x 1.25	55.7
Nut fastening upper head to cylinderhead	M 8 x 1.25	21.0
Nut fastening intake and exhaust pipes to cylinderhead	M 8 x 1.25	18.1
Self-locking connecting rod bolt nuts	M 9 x 1	37.6
Flywheel fastening bolt	M 10 x 1.25	58.6
Camshaft gear wheel fastening bolt	M 10 x 1.25	35.4
Nut fastening bracket rail to crankcase	M 10 x 1.25	34.0
Crankshaft pulley fastening nut	M 20 x 1.5	88.0
Bolt fastening alternator rail to crankcase	M 10 x 1.25	38.3
Nut fastening alternator bracket to crankcase	M 10 x 1.25	31.8
Nut fastening alternator to lower bracket	M 12 x 1.25	50.6
Nut fastening alternator to upper rail	M 10 x 1.25	31.8

Clutch and Gearbox		
Self-locking bolts fastening clutch to flywheel	M 8 x 1.25	18.1
Clutch-actuating cable clamping nut	M 6 x 1	3.6
Bolt fastening gearbox housing to engine	M 12 x 1.25	61.5
Clutch housing fastening nut	M 10 x 1.25	36.2
Gearbox housing drive cover fastening nut	M 8 x 1.25	18.1
Layshaft front roller bearing fastening bolt	M 12 x 1.25	68.7
Dog fastening nut on main gearbox shaft	M 20 x 1	57.9
Bottom gearbox cover fastening nut	M 6 x 1	7.2
Gearbox retainer plate fastening nut	M 6 x 1	7.2
Gear selector rod detent spring cover nut	M 8 x 1.25	18.1
Speedo and trip counter drive bearing nut	M 6 x 1	7.2
Gear selector fork and intermediate lever bolt	M 6 x 1	7.2
Reversing lamp switch on gearbox	M 14 x 1.5	28.9

Universal Shaft		
Universal shaft flexible joint fastening nut	M 12 x 1.25	68.7
Nut fastening rear driver to front universal shaft section	M 16 x 1.5	68.7
Universal shaft thrust bearing bolt	M 8 x 1.25	18.1
Cross-member bolt fastening thrust bearing to body	M 8 x 1.25	18.1

Front Axle		
Front bolt for upper wishbone	M 12 x 1.25	50.6
Nut for front thrust rod to body	M 16 x 1.5	72.3
Nut for upper wishbone pillow block	M 10 x 1.25	25.3
Nut for lower wishbone to cross-member	M 12 x 1.25	65.1
Rear nut for upper wishbone	M 12 x 1.5	65.1
Nut for thrust rod to lower wishbone	M 12 x 1.25	65.1
Bolt for front wheel suspension cross-member	M 12 x 1.25	65.1
Nut for ball joints on steering knuckle mount	M 14 x 1.5	86.8
Nut for upper shock absorber socket	M 8 x 1.25	10.8
Nut for upper shock absorber fastening	M 10 x 1.25	25.3
Nut for lower shock absorber fastening	M 10 x 1.25	36.2
Mounting bolt for transverse stabiliser	M 10 x 1.25	28.9
Nut for transverse stabiliser shackle to lower wishbone	M 8 x 1.25	10.9
Nut for brake saddle mount and steering arm on steering knuckle mount	M 10 x 1.25	36.2
Bolt for brake saddle to support	M 10 x 1.25	25.3
Bolt for brake disc to wheel hub	M 8 x 1.25	10.9
Nut for wheel hub bearing at steering knuckle	M 18 x 1.5	See Page 43
Wheel fastening bolts	M 12 x 1.25	50.6

Steering		
Steering wheel fastening nut	M 16 x 1.5	36.2
Steering column tube mount fastening bolt	M 6 x 1	3.6
Steering column fastening bolt	M 6 x 1	5.8
Steering worm thrust bearing cover bolt	M 8 x 1.25	14.5
Steering box cover bolt	M 8 x 1.25	14.5

Nut fastening steering box to body	M 10 x 1.25	36.2
Nut fastening drop arm to steering box	M 20 x 1.5	173.6
Fastening nut for drag link bearing	M 10 x 1.25	36.2

Rear Axle

Fastening bolt for differential bearing cap	M 12 x 1.5	72.3
Bolt fastening bevel pinion housing to rear axle	M 8 x 1.25	21.7
Nut fastening dog to bevel pinion	M 20 x 1.5	86.8-166.4
Crown wheel bolt	M 10 x 1.25	72.3
Brake saddle bracket plate nut	M 8 x 1.25	18.1
Bolt fastening brake saddle bracket to bracket plate	M 10 x 1.25	25.3
Bolt fastening brake disc to wheel hub	M 8 x 1.25	10.9
Wheel fastening bolts	M 12 x 1.25	50.6
Nut fastening leaf spring to rear axle	M 8 x 1.25	21.7
Nut fastening leaf spring and strap to shackles	M 12 x 1.25	65.1
Nut fastening the rear spring mount to body	M 8 x 1.25	14.5
Nut for upper shock absorber mount	M 10 x 1.25	26.0
Nut for lower shock absorber mount	M 12 x 1.25	65.1
Nut fastening thrust rods to body & rear axle	M 14 x 1.5	65.1

Brakes

Nut for lower fastening of pedal assembly	M 8 x 1.25	10.1
Nut for pedal assembly strut	M 8 x 1.25	10.1
Nut for brake and clutch pedal	M 12 x 1.5	21.7
Nut for servo brake and mount	M 8 x 1.25	18.1
Bolt for hand lever mount on body	M 6 x 1	5.8
Nut for handbrake intermediate lever	M 10 x 1.25	36.2
Nut for handbrake intermediate lever fulcrum	M 12 x 1.25	57.9

Fig. 125 General circuit diagram

1 Front flasher lamps
2 Front side lamps
3 Headlamps - high & low beam
4 Headlamp with high beam
5 Horn relay
6 Horn
7 Distributor
8 Spark plugs
9 Brush for fan solenoid clutch
10 Alternator
11 Thermoelectric switch for fan
12 Coil
13 Oil pressure warning lamp contactor
14 Probe for remote water thermometer
15 Side flasher lamps
16 Battery monitoring relay for lamp 40
17 Relay for headlamp with high beam
18 Starter
19 Battery
20 Voltage regulator
21 Windscreen wiper motor
22 Foot control for screen washer/wiper
23 Timing control for intermittent wiper operation
24 Reversing lamp pressure switch
25 Pressure switch for handbrake warning lamp
26 Brake lamp pressure switch
27 Engine compartment lamp with integral switch
28 Pressure switch for automatic choke warning lamp
29 Flasher for handbrake warning lamp
30 Flasher for flasher lamps
31 Fuses
32 Instrument cluster lamps
33 Electrical connections
34 Front and rear lamp pilot light (green)
35 Flasher lamp pilot light (green)
36 High beam warning lamp (blue)
37 Fuel gauge
38 Remote water thermometer
39 Electric clock
40 Alternator charging lamp (red)
41 Intermittent red warning lamp for applied handbrake
42 Oil pressure warning lamp (red)
43 Automatic choke warning lamp (yellow)
44 Fuel reserve warning lamp (red)
45 Hand lamp socket
46 Master switch for outside lights
47 Dashboard light switch
48 Electrical cigar lighter (with lamp)
49 3-stage switch for air conditioning fan
50 Fan motor dropping resistor
51 Fan motor with two speeds
52 Glove compartment lamp with integral switch
53 Ignition/starter switch with switch code
54 3-position switch for windscreen wiper
55 Reversing switch for front outside lighting and overtake flasher
56 Reversing switch for flasher lamps
57 Horn pressure switch
58 Pressure switch on front doors for interior side lighting
59 Pressure switch on rear doors for interior side lighting
60 Interior side lights with integral switch
61 Front reading lamp with integral switch
62 Baggage boot lamp
63 Fuel gauge
64 Rear flasher lamps
65 Tail and brake lamps
66 Reversing lamp
67 Registration plate lamps

Colour key for leads

Azzuro	—	blue
Bianco	—	white
Giallo	—	yellow
Grigio	—	grey
Marrone	—	brown
Nero	—	black
INT.	—	switch
Rosa	—	pink
Rosso	—	red
Verde	—	green

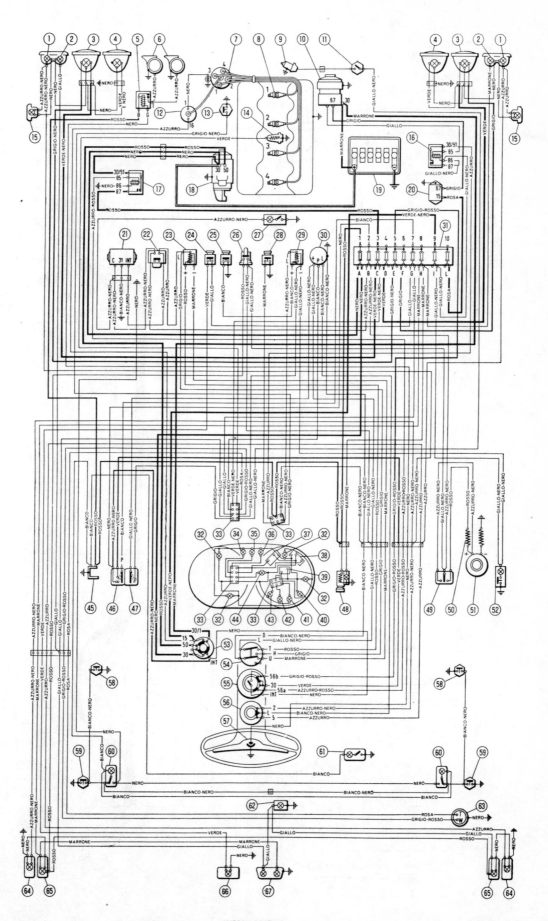

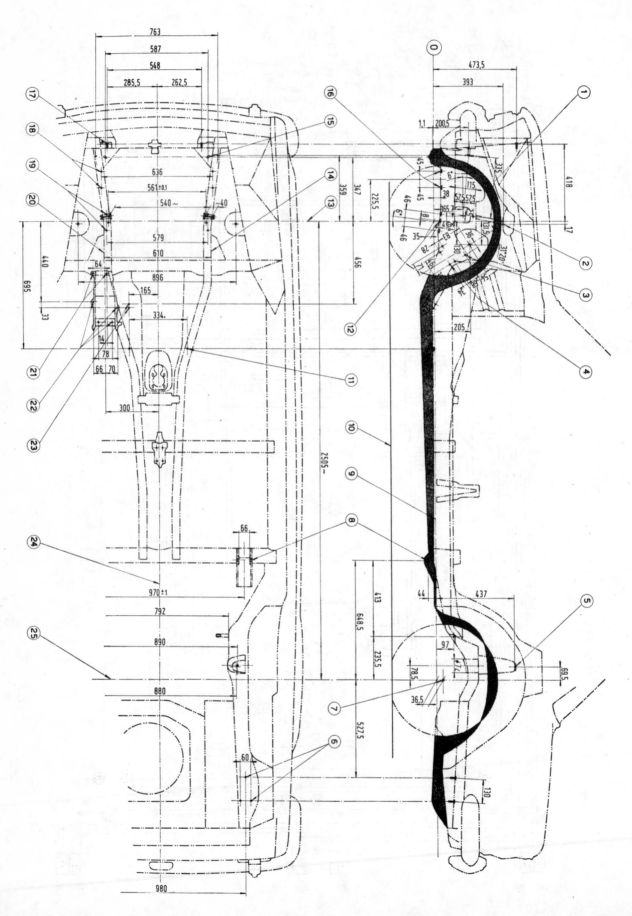

Fig. 126 Overall dimensions for checking the dimensional accuracy of mounting points for mechanical components

1 Measurement to the axis of the bush of the upper wishbone
2 Centre of front upper shock absorber mounting
3 Mounting point of housing and damping unit steering drag link
4 Steering lock
5 Centre of rear upper shock absorber mounting
6 Fastening of rear leaf spring mount
7 Centre of rear wheel
8 Front leaf spring mount
9 Reference line
10 Ground surface line
11 Fastening of final drive mounting
12 Centre of front wheel
13 Centre axis of front wheels
14 Fastening of damper on steering drag link
15 Centre of stabiliser mounting
16 Fastening of stabiliser
17 Upper radiator mounting
18 Mounting of stabiliser pillow block
19 Mounting of wheel suspension cross-member
20 Steering box mounting
21 Servo brake pillow block mounting
22 Pedal assembly and steering column tube pillow block mounting
23 Accelerator pedal mounting
24 Longitudinal axis of vehicle
25 Centre axis of the rear wheels

Fiat 125S Supplement

The following contains the main data on the Fiat S and notes on the distinguishing features by comparison with the Fiat 125.

The five-speed gearbox is similar in construction to the Fiat 125 five-speed gearbox with cone clutch synchronisation, 1st, 2nd, 3rd and 4th gears being synchronised by tapered syncromesh rings. The fifth gear is synchronised by synchro-hub driver springs, a check and thrust block and utilises the same Porsche ring synchromesh system as that on the Fiat 850. Overhaul of the five-speed gearbox is similar to the procedure adopted for the 4-speed version and is based on the 5-speed gearbox illustrations.

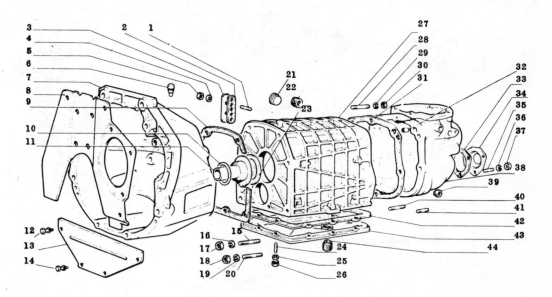

Gearbox, housing and cover - exploded drawing

1.	Stud bolt	23.	Circlip
2.	Gasket	24.	Stud bolt
3.	Cover	25.	Circlip
4.	Circlip	26.	Nut
5.	Nut	27.	Housing
6.	Breather plug	28.	Stud bolt
7.	Housing	29.	Circlip
8.	Cover	30.	Nut
9.	Gasket	31.	Gasket
10.	Gasket	32.	Setpin
11.	Cover	33.	Gasket
12.	Bolt	34.	Cover
13.	Cover	35.	Stud bolt
14.	Bolt	36.	Circlip
15.	Stud bolt	37.	Nut
16.	Circlip	38.	Cover
17.	Nut	39.	Screw cap
18.	Nut	40.	Stud bolt
19.	Circlip	41.	Stud bolt
20.	Stud bolt	42.	Gasket
21.	Screw plug	43.	Cover plate
22.	Screw cover	44.	Screw cap

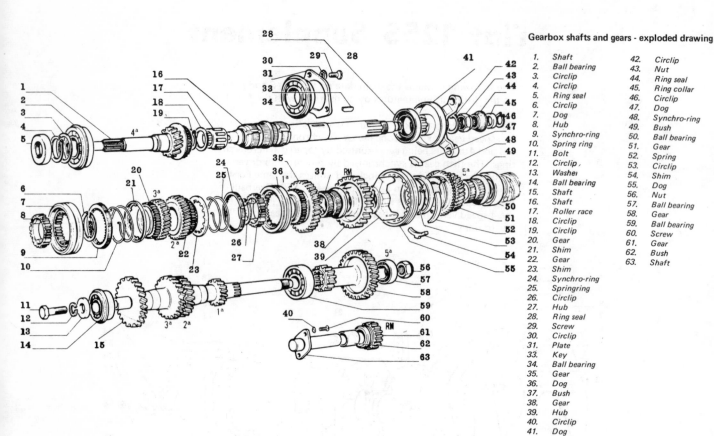

Gearbox shafts and gears - exploded drawing

1.	Shaft	42.	Circlip
2.	Ball bearing	43.	Nut
3.	Circlip	44.	Ring seal
4.	Circlip	45.	Ring collar
5.	Ring seal	46.	Circlip
6.	Circlip	47.	Dog
7.	Dog	48.	Synchro-ring
8.	Hub	49.	Bush
9.	Synchro-ring	50.	Ball bearing
10.	Spring ring	51.	Gear
11.	Bolt	52.	Spring
12.	Circlip	53.	Circlip
13.	Washer	54.	Shim
14.	Ball bearing	55.	Dog
15.	Shaft	56.	Nut
16.	Shaft	57.	Ball bearing
17.	Roller race	58.	Gear
18.	Circlip	59.	Ball bearing
19.	Circlip	60.	Screw
20.	Gear	61.	Gear
21.	Shim	62.	Bush
22.	Gear	63.	Shaft
23.	Shim		
24.	Synchro-ring		
25.	Springring		
26.	Circlip		
27.	Hub		
28.	Ring seal		
29.	Screw		
30.	Circlip		
31.	Plate		
33.	Key		
34.	Ball bearing		
35.	Gear		
36.	Dog		
37.	Bush		
38.	Gear		
39.	Hub		
40.	Circlip		
41.	Dog		

Internal gearshift linkage - exploded view

1.	Bush
2.	Spring
3.	Ball
4.	Fork arm
5.	Fork
6.	Roller
7.	Roller
8.	Fork arm
9.	Fork
10.	Circlip
11.	Bolt
12.	Circlip
13.	Nut
14.	Stud bolt
15.	Cover
16.	Gasket
17.	Spring
18.	Ball
19.	Roller
20.	Shaft
21.	Washer
22.	Spring
23.	Lever
24.	Bush
25.	Spring
26.	Washer
27.	Fork arm
28.	Fork

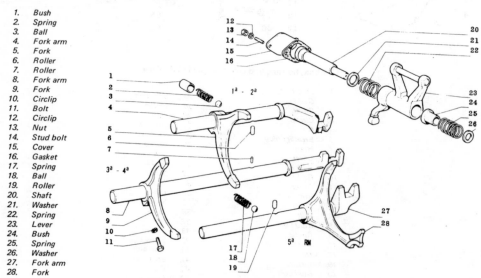

External gearshift linkage - exploded view

1. Nut
2. Circlip
3. Stud bolt
4. Mount
5. Plug
6. Ring seal
7. Arm
8. Limit stop
9. Circlip
10. Bolt
11. Gasket
12. Spring housing
13. Spring
14. Socket
15. Socket
16. Collar
17. Gasket
18. Cover
19. Stud bolt
20. Bolt
21. Circlip
22. Nut
23. Nut
24. Stud bolt
25. Circlip
26. Nut
27. Knob
28. Shift column
29. Gaiter
30. Grommet
31. Bush
32. Spacer
33. Bush
34. Circlip
35. Lever arm

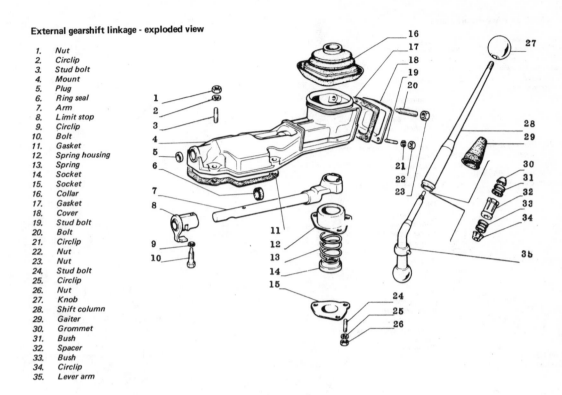

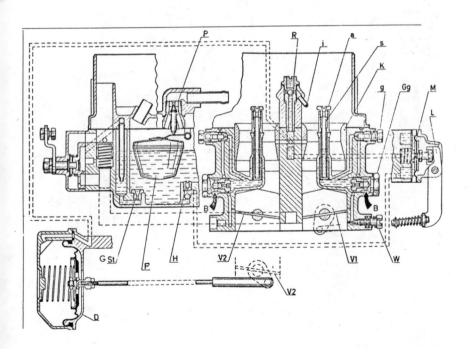

a. Air correction jet
B. Fuel feed
D. Vacuum chamber
F. Float
g. Idler jet
Gg. Main jet
Gst. Choke fuel jet
H. Fuel pump outlet
K. Venturi tube
i. Injection tube
L. Pump arm
M. Diaphragm pump
P. Float needle valve
R. Pump valve
s. Mixer tube
V 1 Throttle flap 1st st.
V 2 Throttle flap 2nd st.
W Idler mix reg. screw

Diagrammatic section (longitudinal) through the carburettor

Exploded view of Solex C 34 PAIA/6 carburettor

1.	Carburettor housing, complete	167.	Gasket
2a.	Throttle flap 7° 1st stage	196.	Recoil spring
2b.	Throttle flap 8° 2nd stage	217.	Filter screen
3a.	Throttle flap spindle 1st stage	218.	Hollow screw
3b.	Throttle flap 2nd stage	258.	Spring ring
4.	Oval head countersunk screw	369.	Linkage
5.	Stop arm		Diaphragm pump
6.	Setscrew	371.	Diaphragm, complete
7.	Locknut	374.	Sub-member
8.	Idler setscrew	376.	Diaphragm spring
9.	Thrust spring	377a.	Pump cover, complete
10a.	Throttle lever, 1st stage, complete	378.	Oval head countersunk screw
10b.	Throttle lever, 2nd stage	386.	Recoil spring
13.	Washer	389.	Lock washer
15.	Idling mixture regulator screw	472.	Stay bolt
23.	Rotary choke plate, complete	491.	Double-arm, complete
32.	Lockscrew	492.	Shaft
33.	Bush	493.	Washer
34.	Nut	512.	Choke plunger
36.	Hex. nut	513.	Thrust spring
39.	Recoil spring	535.	Spacer collar
	Choke, complete	544.	Driver arm
45.	Choke cover	563.	Bush
46.	Oval head countersunk screw	564.	Bellows
47.	Choke lever	565.	Flange
50.	Lockscrew	566.	Gasket
53.	Washer	579.	Washer
62.	Float	583.	Blow-by washer
65.	Cover gasket	591.	Valve, complete
70.	Main jet (Gg)	592a.	Vacuum chamber complete
	Main jet (Gg)	596.	Oval head countersunk screw
71.	Main jet carrier	598.	Gasket
72.	Ring seal		Flange gasket
73.	Air correction jet (a)		
	Air correction jet (a)		
74.	Idler jet (g)		
	Idler jet (g)		
75.	Choke fuel jet (Gst)		
76.	Ring seal		
86.	Venturi tube (s)		
98.	Hexagon nut		
101	Choke tube (K)		
	Choke tube (K)		
102.	Retaining screw		
103.	Carburettor cover, complete		
110.	Float spindle		
115.	Ring seal		
116 .	Float with spring		
126.	Dismantling screw		
127.	Spring ring		
154.	Ball		
157.	Ball valve, complete.		
158.	Eccentric plate		
166.	Oval head countersunk screw		

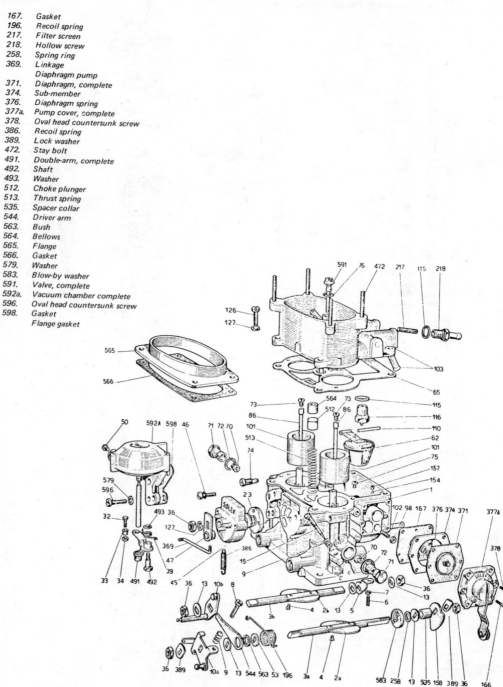

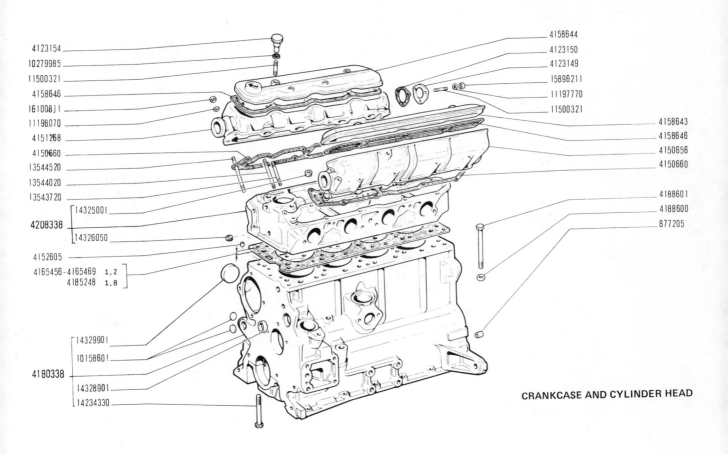

4123154
10279985
11500321
4158646
161008J1
11198070
4151268
4150660
13544520
13544020
13543720
4208338 {
14325001
14326050
}
4152605
4165456-4165469 1,2
4185248 1,8
4180338 {
14329901
10158601
14328901
14234330
}

4158644
4123150
4123149
15896211
11197770
11500321
4158643
4158646
4150656
4150660
4188601
4188600
877205

CRANKCASE AND CYLINDER HEAD

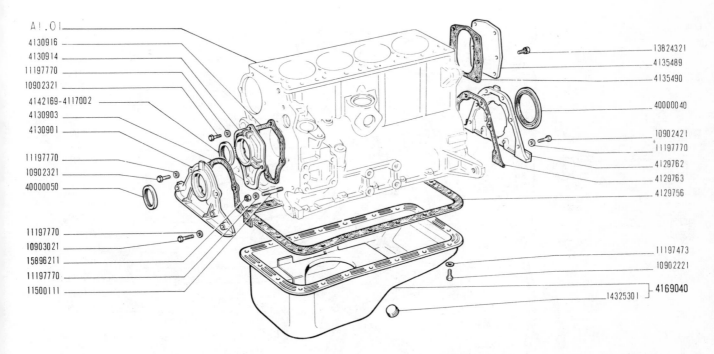

Al.01
4130916
4130914
11197770
10902321
4142169-4117002
4130903
4130901
11197770
10902321
40000050
11197770
10903021
15896211
11197770
11500111

13824321
4135489
4135490
40000040
10902421
11197770
4129762
4129763
4129756
11197473
10902221
14325301 } 4169040

SUMP AND CRANKCASE COVERS

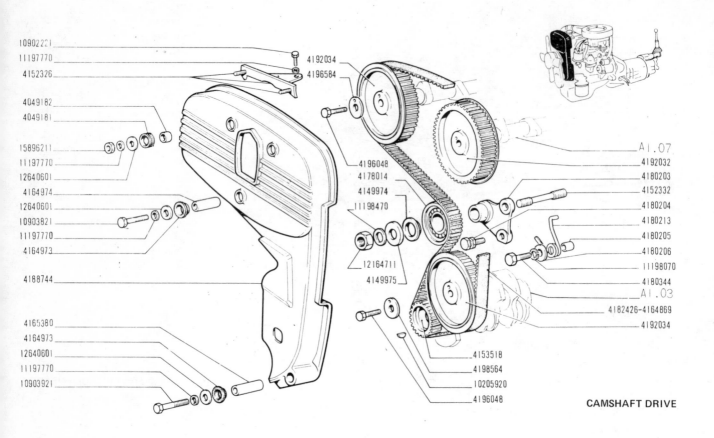

10902221	4192034
11197770	4196584
4152326	
4049182	
4049181	
15896211	4196048
11197770	4178014
12640601	4149974
4164974	11198470
12640601	
10903821	
11197770	
4164973	
4188744	12164711
	4149975
4165380	
4164973	
12640601	4153518
11197770	4198564
10903921	10205920
	4196048

AI.07
4192032
4180203
4152332
4180204
4180213
4180205
4180206
11198070
4180344
AI.03
4182426-4164869
4192034

CAMSHAFT DRIVE

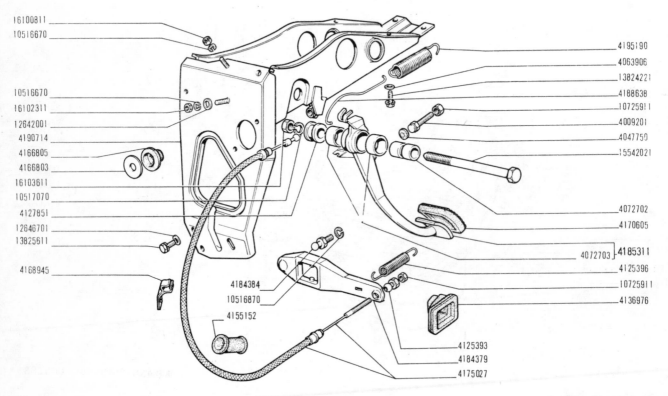

16100811	4195190
10516670	4063906
	13824221
10516670	4188638
16102311	10725911
12642001	4009201
4190714	4047750
4166805	15542021
4166803	
16103611	
10517070	
4127851	4072702
12646701	4170605
13825611	4072703] 4185311
	4125396
4168945	10725911
	4136976
4184384	
10516870	
4155152	4125393
	4184379
	4175027

CLUTCH RELEASE CONTROL

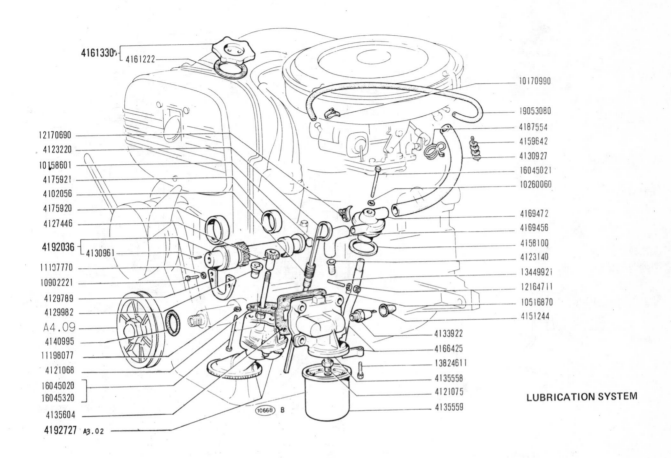

4161330 4161222

10170990
19053060
4187554
4159642
4130927
16045021
10260060

12170690
4123220
10158601
4175921
4102056
4175920
4127446

4192036 4130961

11107770
10902221
4129789
4129982
A4.09
4140995
11198077
4121068
16045020
16045320
4135604
4192727 A3.02

10666 B

4169472
4169456
4158100
4123140
13449921
12164711
10516870
4151244

4133922
4166425
13824611
4135558
4121075
4135559

LUBRICATION SYSTEM

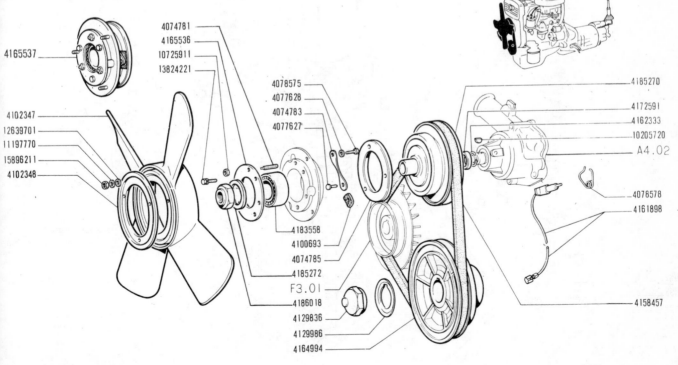

4165537

4102347
12639701
11197770
15896211
4102348

4074781
4165536
10725911
13824221

4078575
4077628
4074783
4077627

4183558
4100693
4074785
4185272
F3.01
4186018
4129836
4129986
4164994

4185270
4172591
4162333
10205720
A4.02

4078578
4161898

4158457

FAN

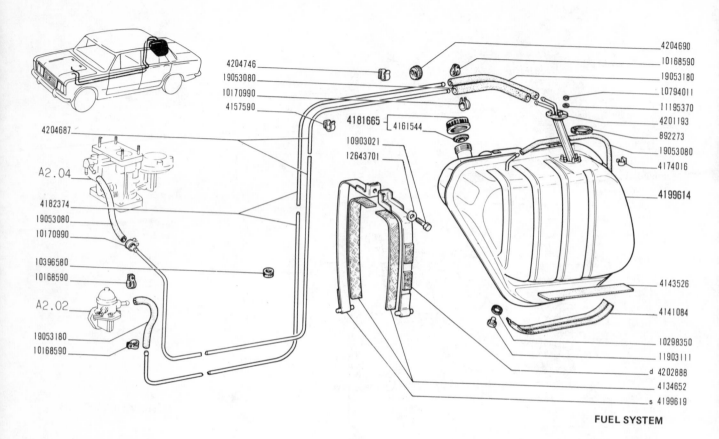

4204746
19053080
10170990
4157590

4204690
10168590
19053180
10794011
11195370
4201193
892273
19053080
4174016

4204687

A2.04

4182374
19053080
10170990

10396580
10168590

A2.02

19053180
10168590

4181665
4161544

10903021
12643701

4199614

4143526

4141084

10298350
11903111

d 4202888
4134652
s 4199619

FUEL SYSTEM

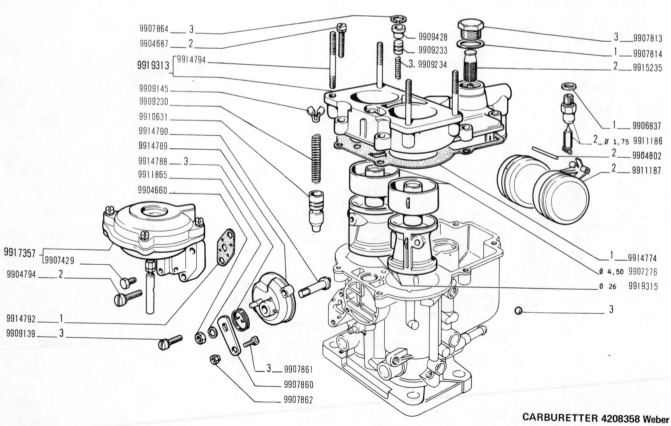

9907864 — 3
9904687 — 2
9919313 9914794

9909145
9909230
9910631
9914790
9914789
9914788 — 3
9911865
9904660

9909428
9909233
3. 9909234

3 — 9907813
1 — 9907814
2 — 9915235

1 — 9906837
2 ø 1,75 9911186
2 — 9904802
2 — 9911187

1 — 9914774
ø 4,50 9907276
ø 26 9919315
— 3

9917357 9907429
9904794 — 2

9914792 — 1
9909139 — 3

3 — 9907861
9907860
9907862

CARBURETTER 4208358 Weber

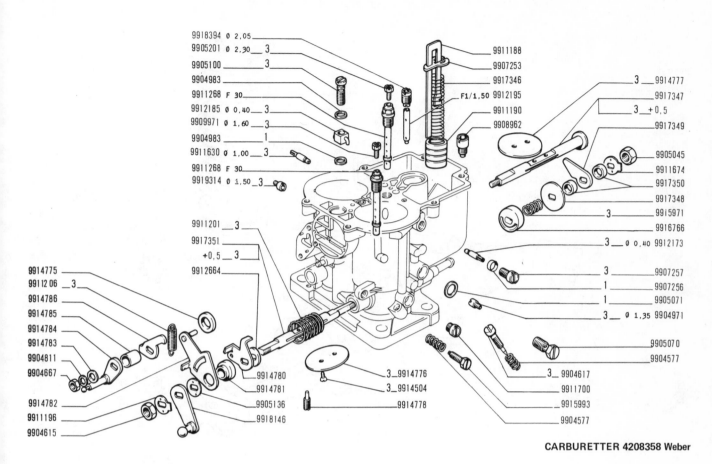

9918394 ∅ 2,05

9905201 ∅ 2,30 ___ 3

9905100 ___ 3

9904983

9911268 F 30

9912185 ∅ 0,40 ___ 3

9909971 ∅ 1,60 ___ 3

9904983 ___ 1

9911630 ∅ 1,00 ___ 3

9911268 F 30

9919314 ∅ 1,50 ___ 3

9911201 ___ 3

9917351

+0,5 ___ 3

9912664

9914775

9911206 ___ 3

9914786

9914785

9914784

9914783

9904811

9904667

9914782

9911196

9904615

9914780

9914781

9905136

9918146

9911188

9907253

9917346

F1/1,50 9912195

9911190

9908962

3 ___ 9914777

9917347

3 ___ +0,5

9917349

9905045

9911674

9917350

9917348

3 ___ 9915971

9916766

3 ___ ∅ 0,40 9912173

3 ___ 9907257

1 ___ 9907256

1 ___ 9905071

3 ___ ∅ 1,35 9904971

9905070

9904577

3 ___ 9914776

3 ___ 9914504

9914778

3 ___ 9904617

9911700

9915993

9904577

CARBURETTER 4208358 Weber

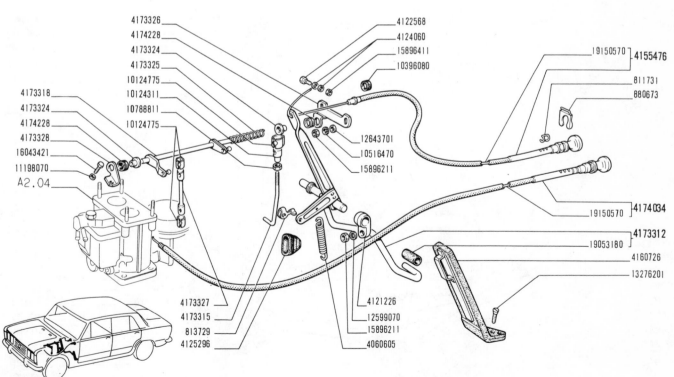

4173326

4174228

4173324

4173325

10124775

10124311

10788811

10124775

4173318

4173324

4174228

4173328

16043421

11198070

A2.04

4122568

4124060

15896411

10396080

12643701

10516470

15896211

19150570

811731

880673

19150570

4155476

4174034

4173312

19053180

4160726

13276201

4173327

4173315

813729

4125296

4121226

12599070

15896211

4060605

CHOKE AND ACCELERATOR CONTROL LINKAGE

125 **Special**

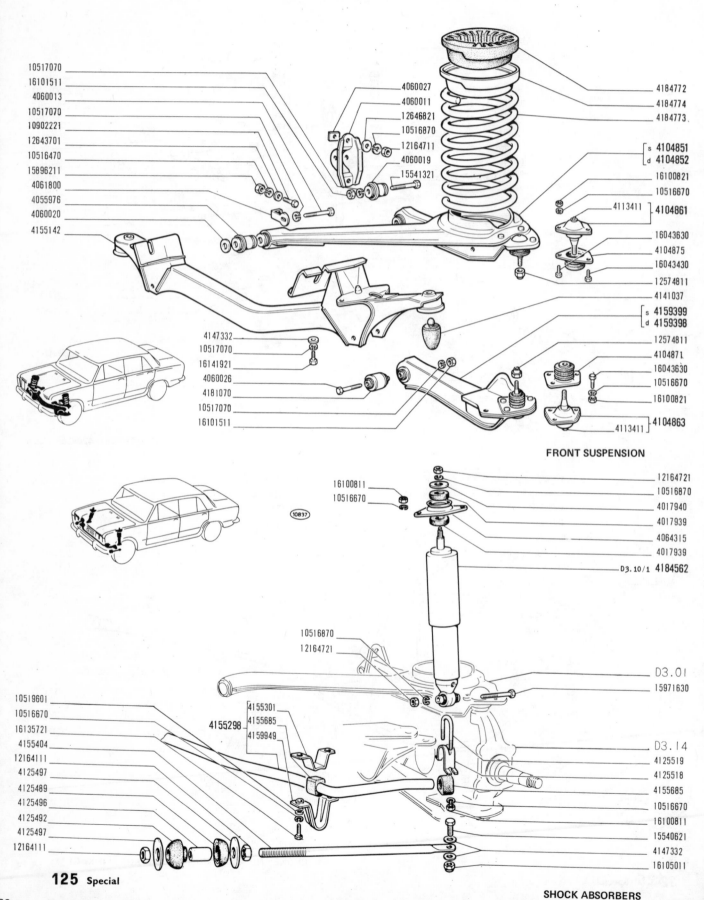

10517070
16101511
4060013
10517070
10902221
12643701
10516470
15896211
4061800
4055976
4060020
4155142

4060027
4060011
12646821
10516870
12164711
4060019
15541321

4184772
4184774
4184773

s 4104851
d 4104852
16100821
10516670
4113411 4104861
16043630
4104875
16043430
12574811
4141037
s 4159399
d 4159398
12574811
4104871
16043630
10516670
16100821
4113411 4104863

4147332
10517070
16141921
4060026
4181070
10517070
16101511

FRONT SUSPENSION

10837

16100811
10516670

12164721
10516870
4017940
4017939
4064315
4017939
D3.10/1 4184562

10516870
12164721

D3.01
15971630

D3.14
4125519
4125518
4155685
10516670
16100811
15540621
4147332
16105011

10519601
10516670
16135721
4155404
12164111
4125497
4125489
4125496
4125492
4125497
12164111

4155298

4155301
4155685
4159949

125 Special

SHOCK ABSORBERS

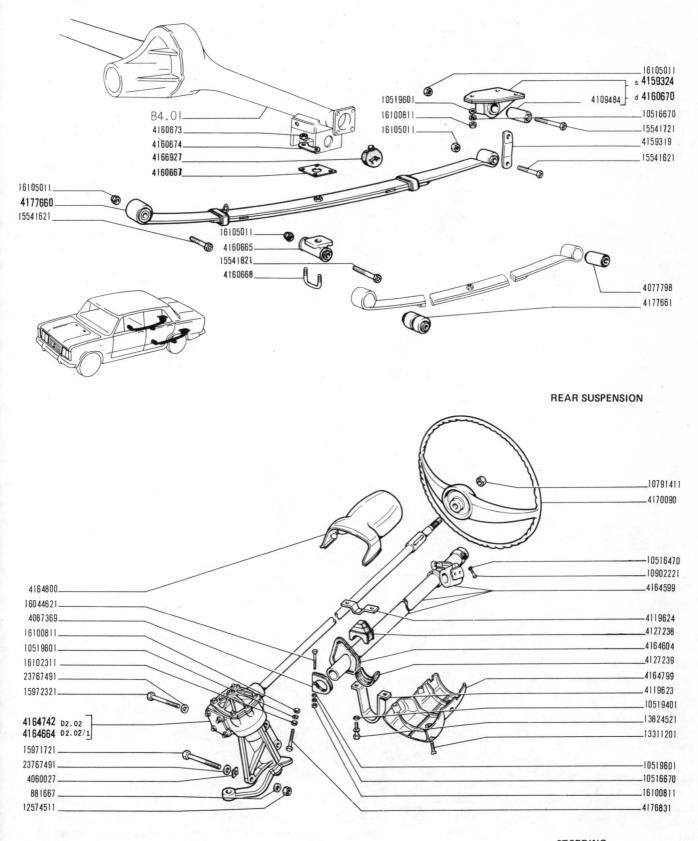

B4.01
4160673
4160674
4166927
4160667

16105011
4177660
15541621

16105011
4160665
15541821
4160668

16105011
10519601
16100811
16105011

16105011
4159324
4109484
4160670
10516670
15541721
4159319
15541621

4077798
4177661

REAR SUSPENSION

10791411
4170090

4164800
16044621
4087369
16100811
10519601
16102311
23767491
15972321

4164742 D2.02
4164664 D2.02/1

15971721
23767491
4060027
881667
12574511

10516470
10902221
4164599
4119624
4127238
4164604
4127239
4164799
4119623
10519401
13824521
13311201

10519601
10516670
16100811
4176831

STEERING

125 Special

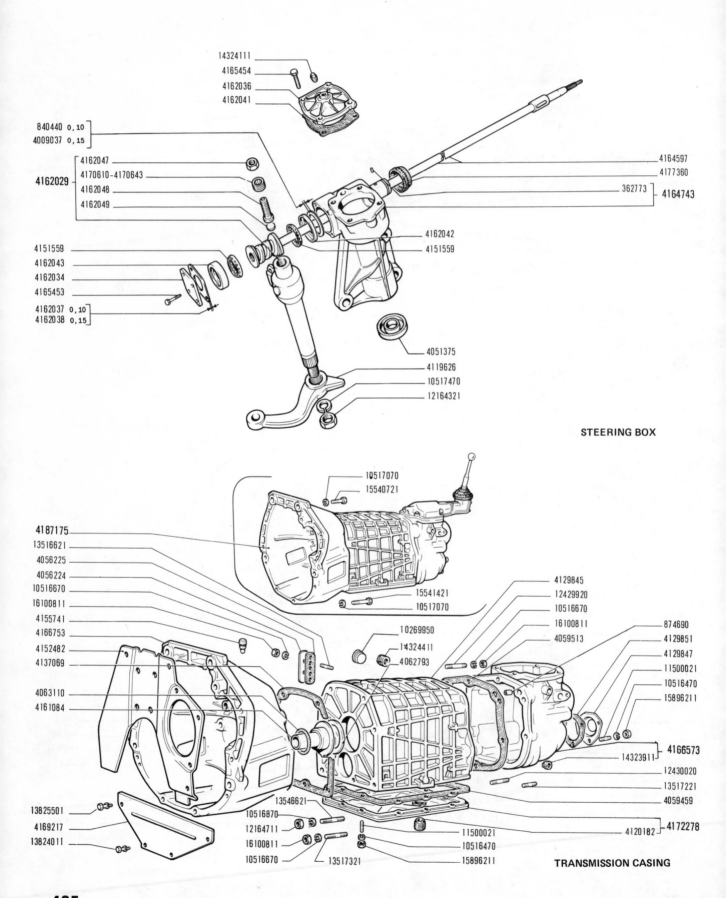

14324111
4165454
4162036
4162041

840440 0,10
4009037 0,15

4162029
4162047
4170610-4170643
4162048
4162049

4151559
4162043
4162034
4165453

4162037 0,10
4162038 0,15

4164597
4177360
362773
4164743

4162042
4151559

4051375
4119626
10517470
12164321

STEERING BOX

10517070
15540721

4187175
13516621
4056225
4056224
10516670
16100811
4155741
4166753
4152482
4137069

4063110
4161084

13825501
4169217
13824011

15541421
10517070

10269950
14324411
4062793

13546621
10516870
12164711
16100811
10516670

13517321

4129845
12429920
10516670
16100811
4059513

874690
4129851
4129847
11500021
10516470
15896211

4166573
14323911
12430020
13517221
4059459

11500021
10516470
15896211

4120182
4172278

TRANSMISSION CASING

125 Special

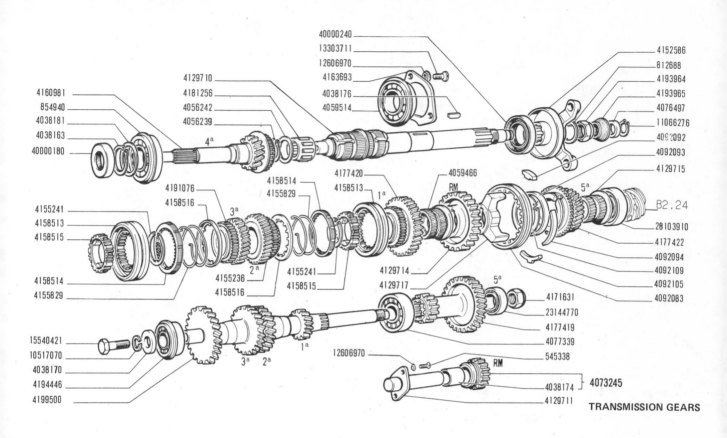

4160981
854940
4038181
4038163
40000180

4129710
4181256
4056242
4056239

40000240
13303711
12606970
4163693
4038176
4059514

4152586
812688
4193964
4193965
4076497
11066276
4092092
4092093
4129715

4^a

4191076
4158516

4155241
4158513
4158515

3^a

4158514513
4155829

4158514
4158513

4158514
4155829

4155236
4158516

2^a

4155241
4158515

4177420
4158513

1^a

4059466

RM

5^a

B2.24

28103910
4177422
4092094
4092109
4092105
4092083

4129714

4129717

5^a

4171631
23144770
4177419
4077339
545338

15540421
10517070
4038170
4194446
4199500

3^a   2^a

1^a

12606970

RM

4038174
4129711

4073245

TRANSMISSION GEARS

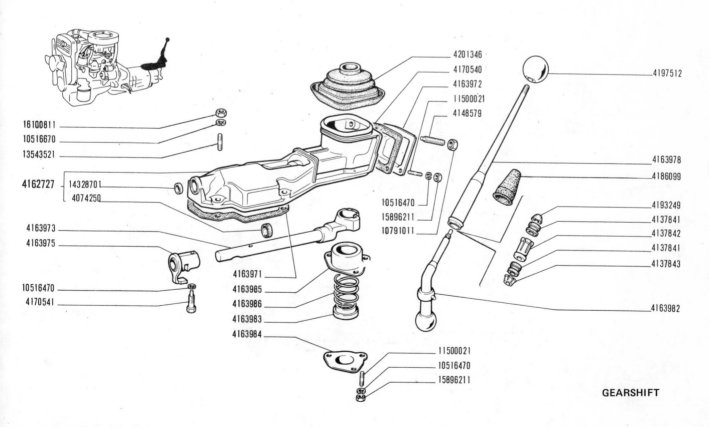

16100811
10516670
13543521

4162727   14328701
            4074250

4163973
4163975

10516470
4170541

4163971
4163985
4163986
4163983
4163984

4201346
4170540
4163972
11500021
4148579

10516470
15896211
10791011

11500021
10516470
15896211

4197512

4163978
4186099
4193249
4137841
4137842
4137841
4137843

4163982

GEARSHIFT

125 Special

WSM 140 Fiat

89

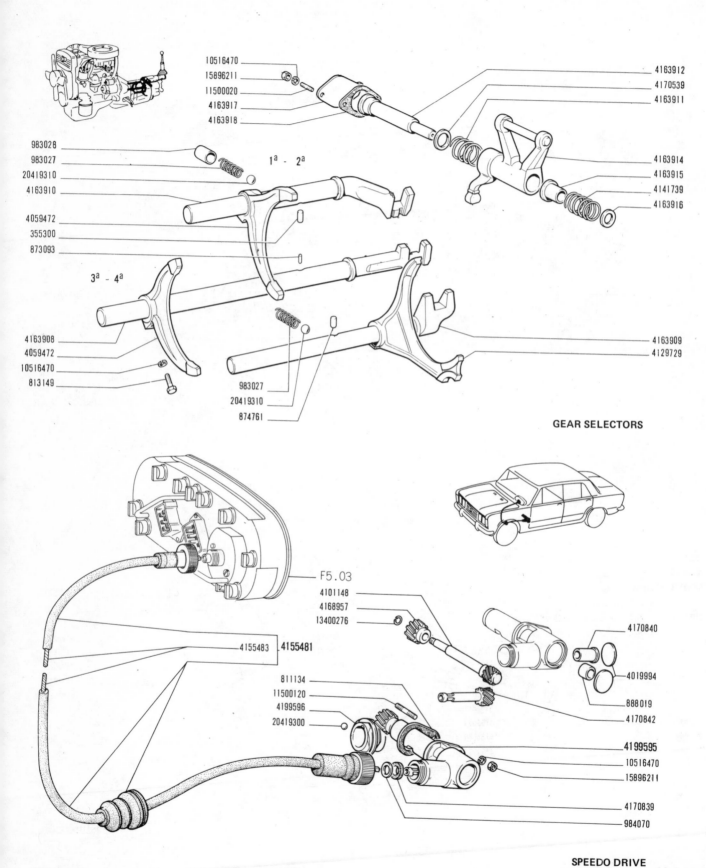

10516470
15896211
11500020
4163917
4163918

4163912
4170539
4163911

983028
983027
20419310
4163910

1ª - 2ª

4163914
4163915
4141739
4163916

4059472
355300
873093

3ª - 4ª

4163908
4059472
10516470
813149

983027
20419310
874761

4163909
4129729

GEAR SELECTORS

F5.03

4101148
4168957
13400276

4170840
4019994

4155483 **4155481**

811134
11500120
4199596
20419300

888019
4170842

4199595
10516470
15896211

4170839
984070

SPEEDO DRIVE

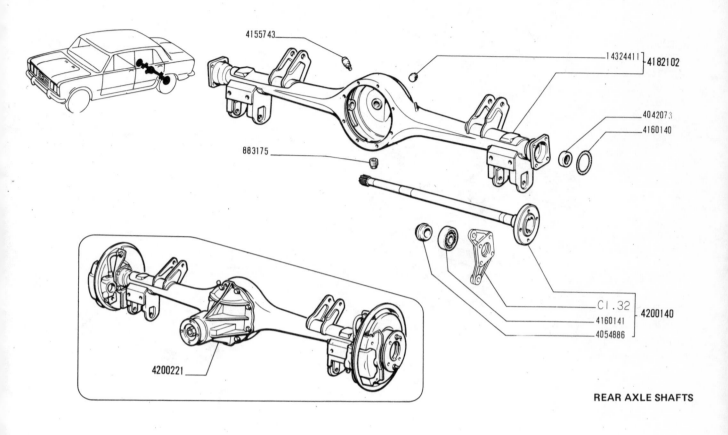

4155743

14324411 · 4182102

4042073
4160140

883175

C1.32
4160141
4200140
4054886

4200221

REAR AXLE SHAFTS

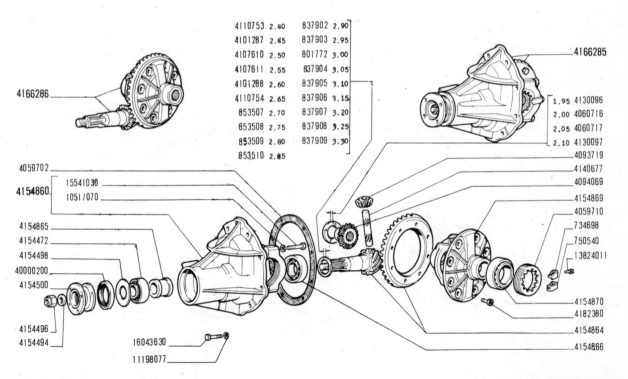

4110753	2,40	837902	2,90
4101287	2,45	837903	2,95
4107610	2,50	801772	3,00
4107611	2,55	837904	3,05
4101288	2,60	837905	3,10
4110754	2,65	837906	3,15
853507	2,70	837907	3,20
853508	2,75	837908	3,25
853509	2,80	837909	3,30
853510	2,85		

4166286

4166285

1,95 4130096
2,00 4060716
2,05 4060717
2,10 4130097

4093719
4140677
4094069
4154869
4059710
734698
750540
13824011

4059702
4154860
15541030
1051/070

4154865
4154472
4154498
40000200
4154500

4154870
4182380
4154864
4154866

4154496
4154494

16043630
11198077

FINAL DRIVE AND DIFFERENTIAL

125 Special

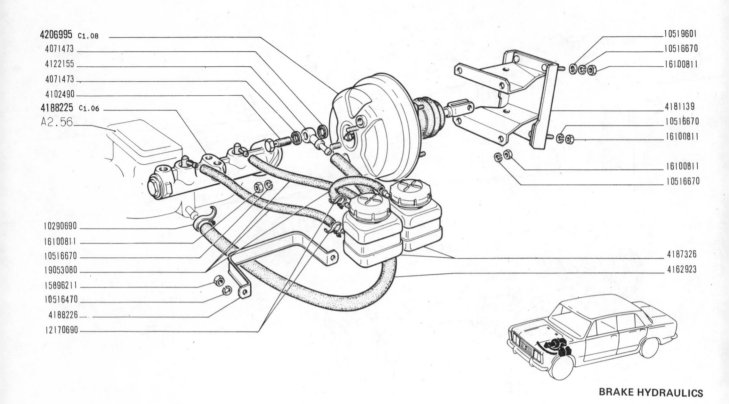

4206995 C1.08
4071473
4122155
4071473
4102490
4188225 C1.06
A2.56

10519601
10516670
16100811

4181139
10516670
16100811

16100811
10516670

10290690
16100811
10516670
19053080
15896211
10516470
4188226
12170690

4187326
4162923

BRAKE HYDRAULICS

4108899
10284460
16043421
10516670
10519601
C1.10 4178745
d 4155749
4182377
15896211
10516470
4108899
C1.32
s 4155751
4077589
4170331
994922

4188233
C1.02
4125949
994922
C1.30
4188229 d
4188231 s
4125949
C1.30

C1.32
d 4177806
s 4177807
4117215
809065
4177805
13824011

BRAKE SYSTEM

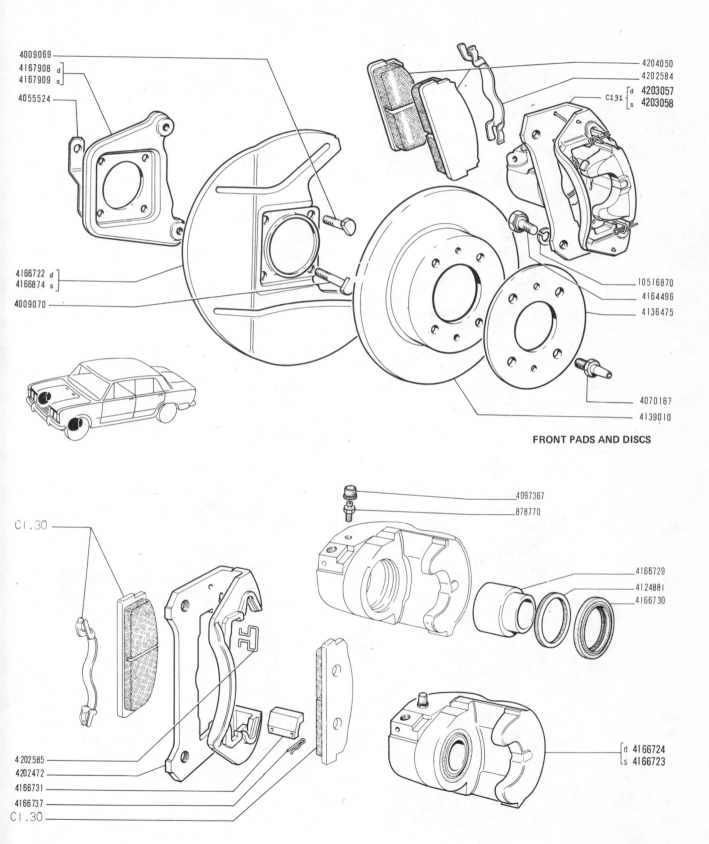

4009069
4167908 d
4167909 s
4055524

4166722 d
4166874 s
4009070

4204050
4202584
C131 { d 4203057
       s 4203058

10516870
4164496
4136475

4070167
4139010

FRONT PADS AND DISCS

Cl.30

4202585
4202472
4166731
4166737
Cl.30

4097367
878770

4166729
4124881
4166730

d 4166724
s 4166723

FRONT CALIPERS

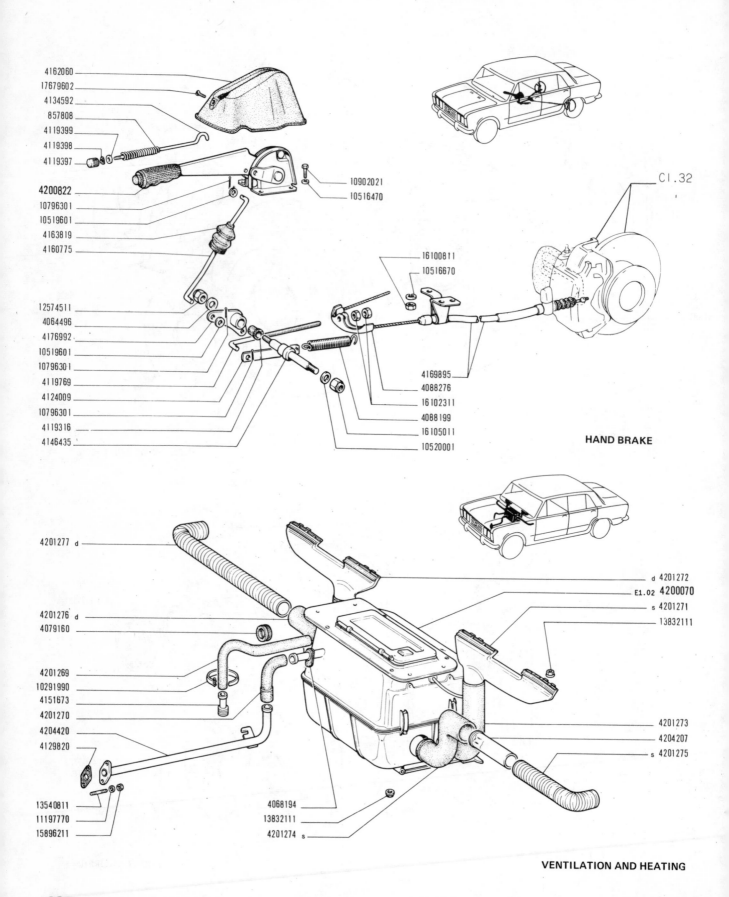

4162060
17679602
4134592
857808
4119399
4119398
4119397

4200822
10796301
10519601
4163819
4160775

10902021
10516470

16100811
10516670

12574511
4064496
4176992
10519601
10796301
4119769
4124009
10796301
4119316
4146435

Cl.32

4169895
4088276
16102311
4088199
16105011
10520001

HAND BRAKE

4201277 d

d 4201272
E1.02 **4200070**
s 4201271
13832111

4201276 d
4079160

4201269
10291990
4151673
4201270
4204420
4129820

4201273
4204207
s 4201275

13540811
11197770
15896211

4068194
13832111
4201274 s

VENTILATION AND HEATING

125 **Special**

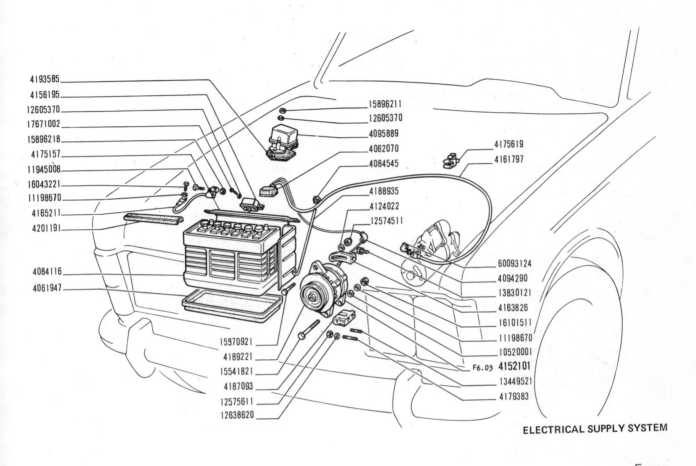

4193585	15896211
4156195	12605370
12605370	4095889
17671002	4062070
15896218	4084545
4175157	
11945008	4175619
16043221	4161797
11198670	
4165211	4188935
4201191	4124022
	12574511
4084116	
4061947	60093124
	4094290
	13830121
	4163826
	16101511
	11198670
	10520001
15970921	F6.03 4152101
4189221	13449521
15541821	4179383
4187093	
12575611	
12638620	

ELECTRICAL SUPPLY SYSTEM

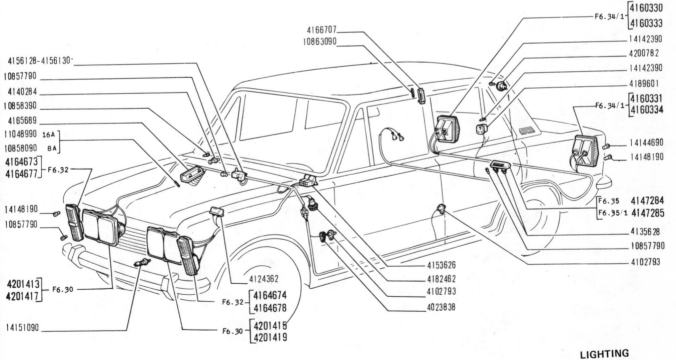

4166707
10863090

F6.34/1 4160330 / 4160333
14142390
4200782
14142390
4189601
F6.34/1 4160331 / 4160334
14144690
14148190

4156128-4156130
10857790
4140284
10858390
4165689
11048990   16A
10858090   8A
4164673 / 4164677   F6.32
14148190
10857790

F6.35 4147284
F6.35/1 4147285
4135628
10857790
4102793

4201413 / 4201417   F6.30

4124362
F6.32 4164674 / 4164678
F6.30 4201418 / 4201419

14151090

4153626
4182462
4102793
4023838

LIGHTING

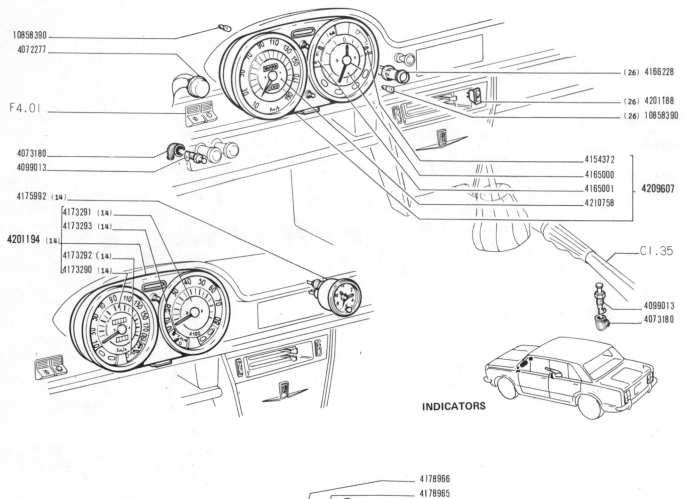

10858390
4072277

F4.01

4073180
4099013

4175992 (14)

4173291 (14)
4173293 (14)

4201194 (14)

4173292 (14)
4173290 (14)

(26) 4166228
(26) 4201188
(26) 10858390

4154372
4165000
4165001
4210758

4209607

C1.35

4099013
4073180

INDICATORS

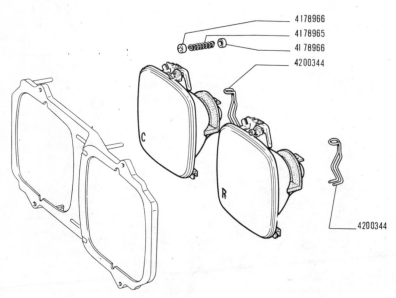

4178966
4178965
4178966

4200344

C

R

4200344

HEADLAMPS - Right Hand Drive

PRECAUTIONS FOR THE WINTER AND HINTS FOR WINTER DRIVING

INTRODUCTION

This section is written for the thoughtful and safety-minded driver, giving recommendations to guide you safely through the hazards of driving during the winter months.

By regular maintenance you will most probably maintain your car in its top performance, however, it might be advisable to follow the instructions in this section to give you added safety insurance during the difficult months of snow, ice and hazardous road conditions.

Battery

As the battery is more called upon during the winter, it must be at all times in good condition to fulfil its function. Shorter days,with consequently more frequent use of the lights,the use of the heater blower and the increased load on the windscreen wipers during periods of snow fall all claim their share from the battery. To maintain the efficiency of the battery, check the electrolyte level and the specific gravity of the electrolyte. The battery performance will be impaired by loose or corroded connections. So in good time, make sure your terminal posts and connectors are thoroughly cleaned and that all connections at the battery, starter motor, starter solenoid switch and in particular the earth connections are absolutely tight. If your car is garaged during the winter, the battery should be re-charged every 4 - 8 weeks to be ready for the spring.

Cooling system

This might be the item every driver immediately connects with frost and winter, as the dangers of serious damage to the engine are well known, if the correct precautions are not observed. The system should be drained, flushed with clear water and then re-filled with a suitable anti-freeze solution. If your cooling system is filled already with a "all-year-round" anti-freeze solution check the specific gravity of the coolant to make sure that the cooling system is protected to the lowest temperature that might prevail in your area. As anti-freeze has a searching effect for leaks check all hoses and clips for tightness.

Brakes

There is little we can tell a driver about braking on ice and snow, but just to remember that the brakes should be in top condition and the braking power to all wheels should be in the correct relation to each other. Brake hoses and connections should be checked to make sure they are not chafed or damaged. All leaks should be rectified. Special attention should be given to the brake pedal rubber. If the rubber is worn smooth, it is easier to slip off with your foot, especially when you just stepped into the car with your shoes covered in snow. A pedal rubber with the proper profile will reduce this danger. When applying your brakes on ice or snow, it should be done firmly and an "apply/release" technique should be used to avoid locking the wheels.If you experience that your car is moving off slowly on a frosty morning, it might be advisable not to apply the handbrake the next night, as the reason for the sluggish behaviour are frozen brake linings. To free a handbrake in this condition, pull and release the lever until the ice is broken. Sudden acceleration or braking and violent movement of the steering wheel should be avoided to prevent skidding.

Tyres

The condition of the tyres is of particular importance during winter driving. Apart of the legal requirements of your country, which will require from you a minimum tread depth whatever the conditions, it will also save you embarrasing situations on ice and snow covered roads. Even if you drive with the minimum tread depth it might be that your journey becomes a nightmare, as confidence in road holding ability can be easily lost after the slightest breakaway.

Special consideration should be given to the use of snow chains or special winter tyres for extremely bad conditions. Even a set of ordinary new tyres will make already a difference when it comes to negotiating a hill or a bend when there is ice or snow on the roads. If the traction of your drive wheels is lost, engage the next highest gear, reduce the engine speed and move away slowly. If your wheels are spinning without showing any grip whatsoever, engage alternatively forward and reverse gears and bring the car to a rocking movement, controlling the accelerator pedal carefully. With patience (and luck!) it might be possible to regain grip on firmer ground. If the described method is not successful, clear away the ice and snow in front of the wheels and place grit, old sacks (or if nothing else is available your floor mats) in front of the driving wheels and try again.

Engine oil

Make sure the oil in your engine sump is suitable for the temperatures to be expected. If your engine is turned over slowly by the starter motor, depress the clutch pedal to disengage the transmission flow between engine and gearbox to remove the additional effort of turning the gears through the cold gearbox oil.

Ignition

The humid and wet conditions of winter can emphasize any weak points in the ignition system. Starting problems on a cold winter's day are not welcome. To avoid them, check all connections, spark plugs, leads and the distributor cap well in advance of the winter. In case that your engine runs normally, but will not accelerate, check your carburettor for icing-up and don't assume immediately that it is an electrical matter. To de-ice the carburettor, stop the car and let the engine run normally for a few minutes.

Lights and lamps

Winter not only brings colder weather but longer nights and day-time fog. This means more driving in the hours of darkness and greater use of lights during daytime. Check your headlamp alignment to avoid dazzling oncoming traffic. Also make sure that all bulbs and lamps are in proper working order. It is advisable to keep a set of bulbs and fuses in your glovebox.

Body

The salt used to thaw up the roads and dissolve ice and snow has its natural usefulness, but shows also a side effect, that is to say is has a detrimental effect on the underbody of a car. It is, however, possible to avoid this disadvantage, if the underside of your car is cleaned immediately after driving over roads with road treatment salts. The investment of having underbody protection sprayed over the vulnerable areas might be well worth considering. Check the paint work of your body and repairs areas that have been scratched with a matching touch-up paint. Winter conditions accelerate the development of rust and subsequent repair of your paint work becomes more expensive than a tin or spray can of touch-up paint.

Never wash or polish your car in direct sunlight or in the open when it is freezing.

Windscreen wipers and washer

Check the condition of your wiper blades well in advance of the winter and replace your rubbers if not in absolute top Wipers have to shift snow during the winter months and they must be able to cope with it, to assure you an uninterrupted vision. Remember that your windscreen washer container will freeze if it only contains water. Yor fill find a proprietary brand of special liquid to be filled into the container, but do not use anti-freeze as used in the cooling system. Do not operate your windscreen washer if the temperatures are below freezing point, if only plain water is filled in your container. A sheet of ice will form immediately on your windscreen. In this connection it should also be remembered that the driving wind will contribute considerably to this danger.

Trouble Shooting ENGINE

SYMPTOMS	PROBABLE CAUSE	ACTION TO BE TAKEN
Lack of power	1. Poor compression	
	Incorrect valve clearance	Adjust valve clearance
	Intake valves leaking	Lap valve seats
	Sticking valves	Replace valve and guides
	Valve springs broken	Replace valve spring
	Piston rings broken	Replace piston rings
	Rings or cylinders worn	Overhaul engine
	2. Ignition improperly set	
	Incorrect ignition timing	Re-set
	Defective spark plugs	Clean, re-set or renew
	Contact breakers defective	Clean or replace, adjust gap
	3. Lack of fuel	
	Clogged carburettor jet	Clean carburettor
	Clogged fuel pipe	Clean fuel pipe
	Dirty fuel tank	Clean fuel tank
	Faulty fuel pump	Check fuel pump
	Fuel filter clogged	Clean or replace element
Overheating	Insufficient coolant	Top-up radiator
	Loose fan belt	Adjust fan belt
	Fan belt worn or damaged	Replace fan belt
	Inoperative thermostat	Replace thermostat
	Defective water pump	Repair or replace
	Clogged cooling system	Clean system
	Incorrect ignition timing	Re-set timing
	Incorrect valve clearance	Adjust clearance
	Incorrect oil used	Refill with correct oil grade
	Radiator fins clogged	Clean radiator fins
Excessive oil consumption	Oil leaks	Find oil leak and rectify
	Defective piston rings	Replace piston rings
	Piston rings worn or sticking in grooves	Replace piston rings
	Piston or cylinder worn	Replace piston or bore cylinder
	Valve stem or guide worn	Replace as necessary
Difficult starting	Improper oil	Change to proper viscosity
	Discharged or defective battery	Charge or replace battery
	Loose connections	Clean and tighten connections
	Defective ignition system	Adjust ignition, check plugs
	Burnt valves	Repair or replace valves
	Pistons, piston rings or cylinders badly worn	Overhaul engine
Engine noisy	Crankshaft bearings or journals worn	Replace bearings and grind crankshaft or replace crankshaft
	Connecting rod bearings worn	Replace bearings and grind crankshaft or replace crankshaft
	Connecting rod bent	Straighten or replace rod
	Piston, piston rings and pins damaged	Check and replace parts as necessary

Trouble Shooting CLUTCH

SYMPTOMS	PROBABLE CAUSE	ACTION TO BE TAKEN
Noises	Damaged or worn release bearing Damaged or worn pilot bearing Loose driven plate hub Driven plate distorted Damaged pressure plate	Replace Replace Replace driven plate Replace driven plate Renew clutch assembly
Chatter or vibration	Gearbox case loose in mountings Uneven contact of pressure plate Loose rivets in clutch driven plate Oil or grease on clutch linings	Tighten mounting bolts Renew clutch assembly Replace linings Replace linings or driven plate
Clutch does not release completely	Excessive pedal free-play Driven plate has run-out Sticky friction linings Clutch friction linings worn Splines on drive shaft or clutch shaft dirty Deformed pressure plate or flywheel Clutch cable defective	Check and rectify Replace driven plate Replace linings or plate Replace linings or plate Clean splines, remove burrs Check and rectify as necessary Check and replace cable if necessary
Clutch slips	No clutch pedal free-play Badly worn friction linings Pressure plate faulty Friction linings oil-soaked Weak clutch pressure springs	Check and rectify Replace linings or friction plate Check and if necessary renew clutch Replace linings or driven plate Replace clutch assembly

Trouble Shooting FUEL SYSTEM

SYMPTOMS	PROBABLE CAUSE	ACTION TO BE TAKEN
CARBURETTOR Flooding	Improper seating or damaged float needle valve or seat Incorrect float level Fuel pump has excessive pressure	Check and replace parts as necessary Adjust float level Check fuel pump
Excessive fuel consumption	Float level too high Loose plug or jet Defective gasket Fuel leaks at pipes or connections Choke valve operates improperly Obstructed air bleed	Adjust float level Tighten Replace gaskets Trace leak and rectify Check choke valve Check and clear
Stalling	Main jet obstructed Incorrect throttle opening Slow-running adjustment incorrect Slow-running fuel jet blocked Incorrect float level	Clean main jet Adjust throttle Adjust slow-running Clean jet Adjust float level
Poor acceleration	Defective accelerator pump Float level too low Incorrect throttle opening Defective accelerator linkage Blocked pump jet	Overhaul pump Adjust float level Adjust throttle Adjust accelerator linkage Clean pump jet
Spitting	Lean mixture Dirty carburettor Clogged fuel pipes Manifold draws secondary air	Clean and adjust carburettor Clean carburettor Clean or replace pipes Tighten or replace gasket
Insufficient fuel supply	Clogged carburettor Clogged fuel pipe Dirty fuel Air in fuel system Defective fuel pump Clogged fuel filter	Dismantle and clean carburettor Clean fuel pipe Clean fuel tank Check connections and tighten Repair or replace fuel pump Clean or replace filter
FUEL PUMP Loss of fuel delivery	Slotted body screws loose Diaphragm cracked Loose fuel pipe connections Defective valves Cracked fuel pipes	Tighten body screws Overhaul fuel pump Tighten fuel pipe connections Replace valves Replace fuel pipes
Noisy pump	Loose pump mounting Worn or defective rocker arm Broken rocker arm spring	Tighten mounting bolts Replace rocker arm Replace spring

Trouble Shooting STEERING

SYMPTOMS	PROBABLE CAUSE	ACTION TO BE TAKEN
Hard steering	Low tyre pressure Incorrect wheel alignment Stiff track rod ends Steering box needs adjustment	Correct pressure Correct alignment Check and replace if necessary Adjust if necessary
Steering wheel shimmy	Tyre pressure incorrect Incorrect wheel alignment Wheels and tyres need balancing Wheel hub nut loose Wheel bearings damaged Front suspension distorted Steering box needs adjustment	Correct Correct alignment Balance as necessary Adjust wheel bearings Replace wheel bearings Check, repair or replace Adjust as necessary
Steering wheel pulls to one side	Uneven tyre pressure Improper wheel alignment Wheel bearings worn or damaged Brakes improperly adjusted Shock absorbers faulty Suspension distorted Steering box worn	Correct Correct Replace and adjust Adjust brakes Check and rectify Check and rectify Adjust or replace
Wheel tramp	Over-inflated tyres Unbalanced tyre and wheel Defective shock absorber Defective tyre	Correct pressure Check and balance if necessary Check and rectify Repair or replace
Abnormal tyre wear	Incorrect tyre pressure Incorrect wheel alignment Excessive wheel bearing play Improper driving	Correct Correct Adjust Avoid sharp turning at high speeds, rapid starting and braking, etc.
Tyre noises	Improper tyre inflation Incorrect wheel alignment	Correct Correct

Trouble Shooting BRAKES

SYMPTOMS	PROBABLE CAUSE	ACTION TO BE TAKEN
Insufficient performance	Leak in hydraulic system Brake pads or linings excessively worn Water or oil on linings	Trace and rectify Replace pads or brake shoes Clean or replace linings
Pedal contacts floor	Pads or linings worn No brake fluid	Replace as necessary Refill and bleed system
Pedal feels spongy	Air in system Insufficient fluid in reservoir	Bleed system Top-up fluid system
Pedal can be depressed without action	Check valve in master cylinder faulty Valve seat dirty	Check and repair Clean valve seat, fit new valve
Brake effort decreases and pedal goes slowly to floor	Brake pipes or hoses leaking Damaged or defective cups in master brake or wheel cylinders	Tighten connections or fit new pipes and hoses Overhaul cylinder in question
Brakes overheat	Compensation port in master cylinder blocked Return spring weak Rubber parts swollen due to use of un-suitable brake fluid	Clean master brake cylinder Fit new springs Drain fluid, remove all rubber parts and flush system. Replace all parts in master brake cylinder
Brakes pull to one side	Loose back plate mounting bolts Oil on linings or pads Loose or damaged wheel bearings Improper operation of wheel cylinder Improper tyre inflation	Tighten Clean or replace Adjust or replace Repair or replace Correct tyre pressure

Trouble Shooting ELECTRICAL SYSTEM

SYMPTOMS	PROBABLE CAUSE	ACTION TO BE TAKEN
Battery in low state of charge, shown by lack of power when starting	Dynamo not charging when running at about 20 mph (30 km/h) with switched on lights:	
	Broken or loose connection in dynamo circuit or regulator not functioning correctly.	Examine charging and field circuit wiring. Tighten loose connections or replace broken lead. Particularly examine battery connections. Examine regulator.
	Commutator greasy or dirty	Clean with soft rag moistened in petrol
	Giving low or intermittent output, when car is running in top gear:	
	Dynamo belt slipping	Adjust belt tension
	Loose or broken connections in dynamo circuit.	Examine charging and field circuit wiring. Tighten loose connection or replace broken lead. Particularly inspect battery connections.
	Brushes greasy or dirty	Clean with soft rag moistened in petrol
	Brushes worn or not fitted correctly	Replace worn brushes. See that the brushes "bed" properly
	Regulator not functioning correctly	Examine regulator
Battery overcharged, shown by burnt-out bulbs and very frequent need for topping-up	Regulator not functioning correctly	Examine regulator
Starter does not operate or operates and does not turn the engine	Poor contact of starter switch contact points	Check switch and replace if necessary
	Poor brush contact	Replace brushes or springs
	Burnt commutator	Overhaul starter motor or clean commutator
	Shorted field coil	Replace coil
	Shorted armature	Replace armature
	Poor contact of battery leads	Clean and tighten leads
	Weak battery	Re-charge battery
	Open circuit between starter switch and solenoid	Check wiring and replace if necessary
	Poor earth connection	Check and rectify
Starter motor operates but does not seem to turn over engine quickly enough	Drive pinion defective	Replace drive pinion
	Flywheel ring gear worn	Replace flywheel or recondition ring gear teeth
Ignition warning lamp goes out only at high rpm.	Generator faulty	Repair generator
	Regulator faulty	Replace regulator
Ignition warning lamp does not light with ignition switched on	Discharged battery	Charge battery
	Defective battery	Replace battery
	Bulb burned out	Replace bulb
	Loose or corroded battery terminals	Tighten or replace terminals
	Loose or broken cables	Tighten or replace cables
	Defective ignition-starter switch	Replace switch
	Poor contact between generator brushes and commutator	Free or replace brushes. If necessary replace brush springs

Ignition warning lamp does not go out or flickers when engine rpm is increased	Loose or broken fan belt Regulator defective Positive lead loose or broken Generator defective Commutator graphited	Adjust tension or replace belt Replace regulator Tighten connection or replace lead Repair generator Clean commutator
Wiper motor does not operate, turns too slowly or comes to a standstill	Brushes worn Brush spring weak or annealed Binding brush levers Dirty commutator Excessive friction in wiper linkages Low operating voltage Burnt out armature	Replace brushes Replace springs Free brush levers Clean commutator Lubricate all moving points; eliminate binding spots Check for voltage drops in connections Replace armature or complete motor
Wiper motor continues to run after switch is turned off or does not re-turn blades to parking position	Contacts in housing damaged Contact spring bent Insulating bracket broken Contacts dirty Wiper motor cannot be switched off Bad connection from wiper switch to earth	Replace contacts Replace contacts Replace contacts Clean contacts Screw switch button back slightly, bend contacts Check connection; replace switch
Motor squeaks, sometimes combined with slow operation	Wiper linkages, bushings running dry. Point of armature spindle (commutator side) against stop of brush holder Incorrect position of motor cover	Grease all moving parts of linkage. Bend stop to clear Reposition cover
Starter motor pinion does not move out of mesh	Pinion or armature shaft dirty or damaged Solenoid switch defective	Overhaul starter motor Replace solenoid switch
Engine misfires	Remove each sparking plug in turn, rest it on the cylinder head, and ob-serve whether a spark occurs at the points when the engine is turned. Ir-regular sparking may be due to dirty plugs or defective high-tension cables. If sparking is regular at all plugs, the trouble is probably due to engine defects.	Clean plugs and adjust the gaps to the figure given in the Engine Tuning Data chart. Renew any lead if the insulation shows signs of deterioration or cracking. Examine the carburettor, petrol supply, etc.

If applicable, read "Dynamo" as "Alternator".

Trouble Shooting IGNITION

SYMPTOMS	PROBABLE CAUSE	ACTION TO BE TAKEN
Starter turns, but engine will not start	Weak battery Excessive moisture on spark plugs or high tension wires Cracked or leaky distributor cap or rotor Broken wire in primary circuit Burned or improperly adjusted points Defective condenser	Recharge battery Remove moisture and dry Replace cap or rotor Repair or replace wire Adjust or replace points Replace condenser
Difficult starting	Defective spark plugs Defective breaker points Loose connection in primary circuit Defective condenser Defective ignition coil Defective rotor or distributor cap	Clean, adjust or replace plugs Replace breaker points Tighten or repair Replace condenser Replace ignition coil Replace cap or rotor
Engine misfires	Dirty or faulty spark plugs Loose ignition wire or faulty insulation Cracked distributor cap Breaker points not correctly adjusted	Clean, adjust or replace plugs Tighten, repair or replace wires Replace cap Adjust breaker points
Ignition circuit interrupted and voltage drop in primary circuit	Burnt or incorrectly adjusted contact breaker gap Defective leads, loose or dirty connections Ignition switch defective Ignition coil defective	Adjust contact breaker gap Check leads, clean connections Check or replace switch Check or replace ignition coil
Secondary circuit interrupted and no current	Spark plugs wet, worn or incorrect gap Defective condenser Defective or broken ignition cable Tracking between coil, distributor cap and rotor Defective ignition coil	Clean and adjust or replace plugs Replace condenser Replace ignition cable Clean and check parts or replace Check or replace coil

Engine Tuning Data

#	Parameter	Unit	#	1967	1968-69-70	1970			L
1	Year		1	1967	1968-69-70	1970			1
2	Model		2	125	125	125 S			2
3	Engine type		3			125B 000			3
3A	EEC	CO %	3A						3A
4	Number of cylinders		4	4	4	4			4
5	Firing order		5	1-3-4-2	1-3-4-2	1-3-4-2			5
6	Capacity	cu.cm	6	1608	1608	1608			6
7	Bore/Stroke	mm	7	80/80	80/80	80/80			7
8	Compression ratio	: 1	8	8,8	8,8	8,8			8
9	Compression pressure	psi/kg/cm^2	9						9
10	Oil pressure	psi/kg/cm^2	10	49-72/3,5-5	49-72/3,5-5				10
11	Rated output	HP/rpm	11	90 BHP/5700	90 BHP/5700	100 DIN/6200			11
11A	Fuel consumption(mpg/Ltr.100 km/DIN)		11A			30,3/9,2			11A
12	Valve clearance - inlet	in/mm	12	0,018/0,45	0,018/0,45	0,017/0,45(c)			12
13	Valve clearance - outlet	in/mm	13	0,020/0,50	0,020/0,50	0,020/0,50 (c)			13
14	Inlet valve opens	°BTDC	14	26	26	26			14
15	Outlet valve closes	°ATDC	15	26	26	26			15
15A	Road horsepower		15A						15A
15B	Km.h/rpm/gear		15B						15B
16	Battery	V/Ah	16	12 V 48 Ah	12 V 48 Ah	12 V 48 Ah			16
17	System polarity	plus/minus	17	–	–	–			17
18	Carburettor make		18	Weber	Solex	Weber *			18
19	Carburettor type		19	34 DCHE	C 34 PAIA	34 DCHE/4			19
20	Idling speed	rpm	20	750	750	800			20
21	Fuel pump pressure	psi/kg/cm^2	21	–	–	0,22 - 0,23			21
22	Distributor make		22	MARELLI	MARELLI	MARELLI			22
23	Distributor type		23	S 125 B	S 125 B	5 136A			23
24	Contact breaker gap	in/mm	24	,017-,019/,41-,48	,017-,019/,42-,48	0,014-0,017/0,37-0,43			24
25	Dwell angle	Degrees	25	57-63	57-63	60 ± 3			25
26	Static timing	°BTDC	26	10	10	10			26
27	Stroboscopic timing	°BTDC/rpm	27						27
28	Timing mark location		28	P	P	P			28
28A	Ignition coil make & type		28A			MARELLI			28A
28B	Primary resistance	Ohms	28B			16,4 - 17,6			28B
29	Centrif. advance - starts	°/rpm E	29	10/1000	10/1000	10/800			29
30	- intermediate	°/rpm E	30	18/2000	18/2000	18-22/1400			30
31	- intermediate	°/rpm E	31	25/3000	25/3000				31
32	- ends	°/rpm E	32	30/3500	30/3500	34-38/3600			32
33	Vacuum advance - starts	°/in- mm Hg	33						33
34	- ends	°/in-mm Hg	34						34
35	Condenser capacity	Mfd	35	0,20-0,24	0,20-0,24	0,20-0,25			35
36	Sparking plug make		36	CHAMPION	CHAMPION	BOSCH			36
37	Sparking plug type		37	N 6 Y	N 6 Y	W230 T30			37
38	Sparking plug gap	in/mm	38	,020-,024/,5-,6	,020-,024/,5-,6	0,020/0,5			38
38A	Starter motor make & type		38A			FIAT			38A
38B	Lockdraw	Amps./Volts	38B			545A/6,9 ±3V			38B
39	Generator make		39	AC	FIAT	FIAT			39
40	Generator type		40	A 12 M	124/12/42M	A12M124/12/42M			40
41	Generator output	A/V/rpmG	41	42/5000	42/5000				41
42	Regulator make		42	FIAT	FIAT	FIAT			42
43	Regulator type		43	RC 1/12 B	RC 1/12 B	RC 1/12 B			43
44	Cut-in closing voltage	V	44			12,5-13,0			44
45	Drop-off voltage	V	45						45
46	Reverse current	A	46						46
47	Open circuit	V	47			13,9 - 14,5			47
48	Closed circuit	A	48						48
49	Current regulator	A	49						49
50	Voltage regulator	V/A/min	50	14,2± 0,3	14,2 ± 0,3				50
51	NOTES:		51			*SOLEX C34 PAJA 16			51
52	from chassis number		52						52
53	from engine number		53						53

Engine Tuning Data

Lubricate and Clean

		No.	6 / 10	12 / 20	18 / 30	24 / 40	36 / 60
CAR UP							
ENGINE	Drain oil	1	●	●	●	●	●
Filter	Change element	2	●	●	●	●	●
	Clean element	3					
GEARBOX/OVERDRIVE	Check oil/top up	4	●	●	●	●	
	Change oil	5			●		●
Filter	Clean element	6					
AUTOMATIC TRANSM.	Drain fluid	7					
Filter	Clean element	8					
DIFFERENTIAL	Check oil/top up	9	●	●	●	●	●
	Change oil	10		●		●	
De Dion Tube	Check oil level	11					
	Clean rubber boots	12					
Limited Slip Differential	Check oil/top up	13					
	Change oil	14					
PROP./DRIVE SHAFT(S)	Lubricate	15		●		●	
SHOCK ABSORBERS	Check oil/top up	16					
CHASSIS	Grease all points	17					
PEDAL SHAFT(S)	Lubricate	18		●	●	●	
HANDBRAKE	Lubricate	19		●	●	●	
GEAR LINKAGE	Lubricate	20					
CAR LOWERED — WHEELS FREE							
WHEEL BEARINGS	Repack	21		●		●	
WHEEL SPLINES/TAPERS	Lubricate	22					
BRAKE FLUID	Renew/bleed syst.	23					
CAR DOWN — BONNET OPEN							
ENGINE	Refill with oil	24	●	●	●	●	●
	Check oil level	25					
Breather Cap	Clean	26	●	●	●	●	●
Air Cleaner	Service element(s)	27	●	●	●	●	●
	Replace element(s)	28	●	●	●	●	●
PCV-System	Clean filter	29	●	●	●	●	●
	Clean valve/hose(s)	30					
	Replace valve	31					
Carburettor(s)	Clean jets/bowl	32	●	●	●	●	●
	Top up pist. damper	33					
	Lubricate linkages	34	●	●	●	●	●
Fuel Bowl/Filter(s)	Clean/replace	35	●	●	●	●	●
Fuel Injection Pump	Check oil level	36					
Filter(s)	Clean/replace	37					
AUTOMATIC TRANSM.	Refill with fluid	38					
	Check fluid level	39					
DISTRIBUTOR	Clean cap & ing. coil	40	●	●	●	●	
Spindle/Cam	Lubricate	41	●	●	●	●	
COOLING SYSTEM	Check/top up	42	●	●	●	●	●
	Flush system	43			●		●
Corrosion Inhibitor	Check solution	44					
Anti-Freeze	Check	45	●				●
Water Pump	Lubricate	46					
SCREENWASHER	Check/top up	47	●	●	●	●	●
BATTERY	Check/top up	48	●	●	●	●	●
	Check spec. gravity	49	●	●	●	●	●
Connections	Clean, grease	50	●	●	●	●	●
STARTER	Lubricate	51					
STEERING	Check/top up	52	●	●	●	●	●
Power Steering	Check/top up fluid	53					
	Grease ram	54					
	Clean filter	55					
CLUTCH/BRAKE	Check/top up fluid	56	●	●	●	●	●
BRAKE SERVO	Clean filter	57	●	●	●	●	●
	Renew filter	58					
HYDR. SUSPENSION	Check/top up fluid	59					
	Renew fluid	60					
	Clean filter	61					
CAR DOWN — EXTERNAL							
LOCKS, HINGES, ETC.	Lubricate	62		●		●	
Door Drain Holes	Clean	63					
WIPER SPINDLES	Lubricate	64					

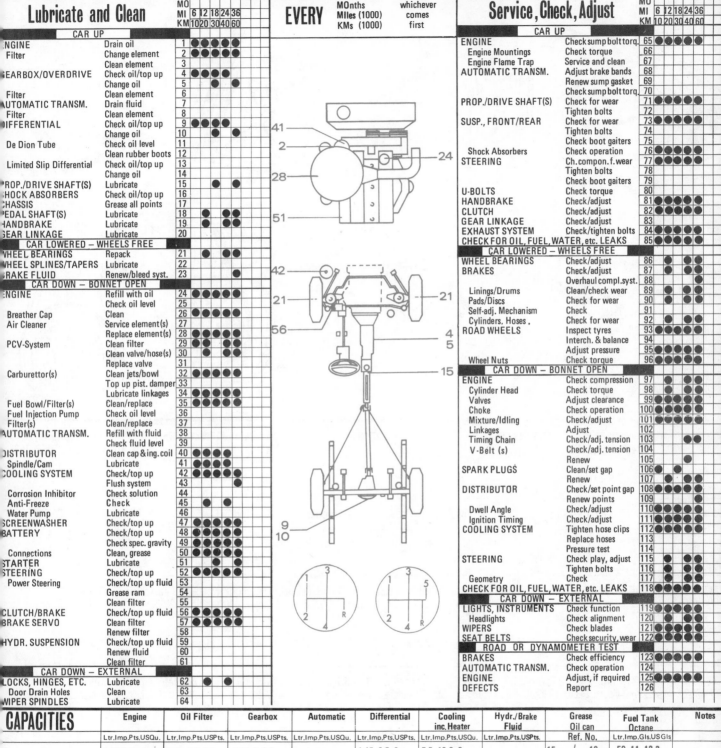

Service, Check, Adjust

		No.	6 / 10	12 / 20	18 / 30	24 / 40	36 / 60
CAR UP							
ENGINE	Check sump bolt torq.	65	●	●	●	●	●
Engine Mountings	Check torque	66					
Engine Flame Trap	Service and clean	67					
AUTOMATIC TRANSM.	Adjust brake bands	68					
	Renew sump gasket	69					
	Check sump bolt torq.	70					
PROP./DRIVE SHAFT(S)	Check for wear	71	●	●	●	●	●
	Tighten bolts	72					
SUSP., FRONT/REAR	Check for wear	73	●	●	●	●	●
	Tighten bolts	74					
	Check boot gaiters	75					
Shock Absorbers	Check operation	76	●	●	●	●	●
STEERING	Ch. compon. f. wear	77	●	●	●	●	●
	Tighten bolts	78					
	Check boot gaiters	79					
U-BOLTS	Check torque	80					
HANDBRAKE	Check/adjust	81	●	●	●	●	●
CLUTCH	Check/adjust	82	●	●	●	●	●
GEAR LINKAGE	Check/adjust	83					
EXHAUST SYSTEM	Check/tighten bolts	84	●	●	●	●	●
CHECK FOR OIL, FUEL, WATER, etc. LEAKS		85	●	●	●	●	●
CAR LOWERED — WHEELS FREE							
WHEEL BEARINGS	Check/adjust	86		●		●	
BRAKES	Check/adjust	87	●	●	●	●	●
	Overhaul compl. syst.	88					
Linings/Drums	Clean/check wear	89		●		●	
Pads/Discs	Check for wear	90					
Self-adj. Mechanism	Check	91					
Cylinders, Hoses.	Check for wear	92					
ROAD WHEELS	Inspect tyres	93	●	●	●	●	●
	Interch. & balance	94					
	Adjust pressure	95	●	●	●	●	●
Wheel Nuts	Check torque	96	●	●	●	●	●
CAR DOWN — BONNET OPEN							
ENGINE	Check compression	97					
Cylinder Head	Check torque	98	●				
Valves	Adjust clearance	99	●	●	●	●	●
Choke	Check operation	100					
Mixture/Idling	Check/adjust	101	●	●	●	●	●
Linkages	Adjust	102					
Timing Chain	Check/adj. tension	103			●		●
V-Belt (s)	Check/adj. tension	104					
	Renew	105					
SPARK PLUGS	Clean/set gap	106	●		●		
	Renew	107		●		●	
DISTRIBUTOR	Check/set point gap	108	●	●	●	●	●
	Renew points	109					
Dwell Angle	Check/adjust	110	●	●	●	●	●
Ignition Timing	Check/adjust	111	●	●	●	●	●
COOLING SYSTEM	Tighten hose clips	112	●	●	●	●	●
	Replace hoses	113					
	Pressure test	114					
STEERING	Check play, adjust	115		●		●	
	Tighten bolts	116					
Geometry	Check	117		●		●	
CHECK FOR OIL, FUEL, WATER, etc. LEAKS		118	●	●	●	●	●
CAR DOWN — EXTERNAL							
LIGHTS, INSTRUMENTS	Check function	119	●	●	●	●	●
Headlights	Check alignment	120					
WIPERS	Check blades	121	●	●	●	●	●
SEAT BELTS	Check security, wear	122	●	●	●	●	●
ROAD OR DYNAMOMETER TEST							
BRAKES	Check efficiency	123	●	●	●	●	●
AUTOMATIC TRANSM.	Check operation	124					
ENGINE	Adjust, if required	125	●	●	●	●	●
DEFECTS	Report	126					

CAPACITIES

	Engine	Oil Filter	Gearbox	Automatic	Differential	Cooling inc. Heater	Hydr./Brake Fluid	Grease Oil can Ref. No.	Fuel Tank Octane	Notes
	Ltr.Imp.Pts.USQu.	Ltr.Imp.Pts.USPts.	Ltr.Imp.Pts.USPts.	Ltr.Imp.Pts.USQu.	Ltr.Imp.Pts.USPts.	Ltr.Imp.Pts.USQu.	Ltr.Imp.Pts.USPts.		Ltr.Imp.Gls.USGls	
	3.75 6.6 4	0,85 1.5 1.7	1.65 3 3.2		1.45 2.5 3	7.5 13.2 8		15 / 18	50 11 13.2	
								21 / 19		
								51 / 34		
								41		
								51		

LUBRICANTS

Engine	Gearbox	Differential	Automatic	Hydr./Brake	Grease
MO 13	EP 3	EP 3	AF	FIAT	GLM / MO

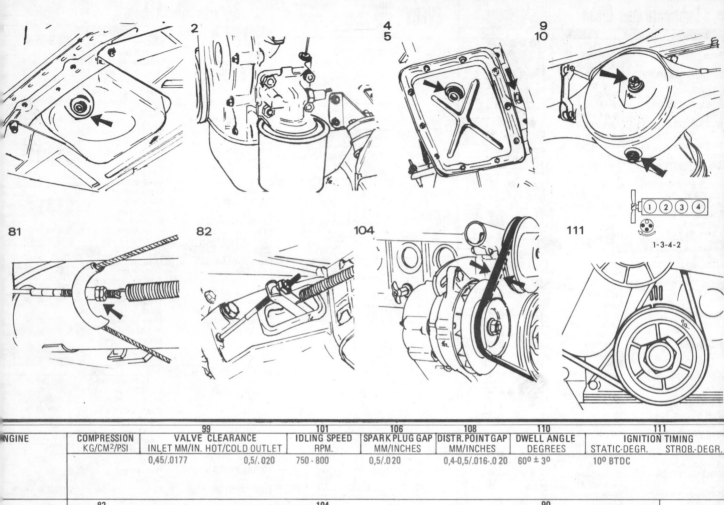

ENGINE	COMPRESSION KG/CM²/PSI	VALVE CLEARANCE INLET MM/IN. HOT/COLD OUTLET		IDLING SPEED RPM.	SPARK PLUG GAP MM/INCHES	DISTR. POINT GAP MM/INCHES	DWELL ANGLE DEGREES	IGNITION TIMING STATIC-DEGR. STROB.-DEGR.	
		99		**101**	**106**	**108**	**110**	**111**	
		0,45/.0177	0,5/.020	750 - 800	0,5/.020	0,4-0,5/.016-.0 20	60º ± 3º	10º BTDC	

MECHANICAL	CLUTCH PLAY MM/INCHES	STEERING PLAY MM/INCHES	RAD. CAP. PRESS. KG/CM²/PSI	V-BELT TENSION MM/INCHES	BLEED SEQUENCE	MIN. LINING THICKN. MM/IN.	PAD THICKN. MM/IN.	HANDBRAKE ADJ. MM/INCHES	NOTES
	82			**104**			**90**		
	25/1			25/1			2/.08		

TYRES/PRESS. KG/CM²/PSI	STANDARD SIZE	FRONT PRESSURE NORMAL/FULL	REAR PRESSURE NORMAL/FULL	OPTIONAL SIZE	FRONT PRESSURE NORMAL/FULL	REAR PRESSURE NORMAL/FULL	WHEEL BEARINGS FRONT-MM/IN.	WHEEL BEARINGS REAR-MM/IN.	
	93	**95**							
	175 S 13	1,7/.24	1,8/.26						

STEERING GEOMETRY	TEST LOAD KG/LBS.	TOE-IN(i)/OUT(o) FRONT-MM/IN.	CAMBER DEGREES	CASTOR DEGREES	KING PIN INCLN. DEGREES	TOE-IN(i)/OUT(o) REAR-MM/IN.	CAMBER DEGREES	TOE-ON TURNS ºat ºlock	
					117				
	4 Persons	(i) 3 ± 1/.12 ±.03	0º30' ± 20'	3º ± 15'	6º ± 20'				

TORQUES									MKG/FT. LBS.
	96	**98**							
	6,9/.50								

TBA	**93**	**48**	**107**	**109**	**2**	**28**	**105**	**121**	**114**
	175S13	12V 48 Ah	Champion N6Y - N9Y		FRAM PH 2807	FRAM CA 660	FERODO V 927		

intereurope   **AUTOSERVICE DATA CHART**   © 1970 – INTEREUROPE